LETTERS TO CHARLOTTE

The Letters from Ellen Nussey
to Charlotte Brontë

CAEIA MARCH

IndePenPress

First published in Great Britain by Indepenpress

All paper used in the printing of this book has been made from wood
grown in managed, sustainable forests.

ISBN13: 978-1-907499-43-2

Printed and bound in the UK
Indepenpress is an imprint of Indepenpress Publishing Limited
25 Eastern Place
Brighton
BN2 1GJ

A catalogue record of this book is available from
the British Library

Cover design by Jacqueline Abromeit

Introduction

Jane Eyre was our standard text at secondary school in industrial South Yorkshire, in the 1950s, but despite its compelling gothic drama and alluring romantic themes, we didn't connect it with a wild, moor-land village located 'somewhere in the Pennines'. The author's home remained distant in time and space from Dinnington near Sheffield.

However, in the 1970s, I took my two small sons to the Isle of Man, where my father was incumbent of an isolated moor-land parish, 'Jurby and Andreas'. My parents had fallen in love with their new home [the island being my mother's birth-place] and commenting on the old stone residence with its lovely proportions, mullioned windows, courtyard and out-buildings, my mother named it 'our very own Brontë Parsonage'. So, ironically, that's when my journey to Haworth really began.

By the late eighties, I was a published novelist, a locally based performance poet and writer of non-fiction articles. I worked for London University, Goldsmiths College, teaching women's creative writing, women's international history, and women's studies-through-everyday-English. My working life was focussed upon women's lost history, so I was completely fascinated when Elaine Miller's essay on Charlotte and Ellen, in *Not A Passing Phase*, was published in 1989. Ellen? Ellen *who*? I had so many questions, some of which were answered in 1993, when Barbara Whitehead published the biography entitled: *Charlotte Brontë and her Dearest Nell*. By then, I was completely hooked.

I began by reading C.B.'s letters on inter-library loan in early collections including those by Clement Shorter [Charlotte Brontë and her Circle, 1908]; T. J. Wise and J.A. Symington [The Shakespeare Head collection, 1932]; and a reliable and informative biography, *The Brontës*, by Juliet Barker, 1994. Subsequently I really enjoyed *The Brontës – A Life in Letters*, also by Juliet Barker, 1997.

The letters of Charlotte Brontë [C.B.] revealed two women, Charlotte and Ellen, life-long friends, who lived, loved and wrote to each other. Some of Charlotte's letters were extremely passionate.

But why was I so drawn to Ellen?

The entire Brontë family loved this intelligent, confident girl who became a welcome guest in their parsonage for twenty-two years. She was calm, kind and generous. She was asked by Emily Brontë, in May 1843, to travel to Brussels, where Charlotte was lonely; and asked *for* by Anne Brontë in May 1849, during her terminal illness in Scarborough. Moreover, an important piece of lost history is that Ellen brought a rare but essential gift to the Brontë sisters, because as a young girl she had attended the Moravian Ladies Academy, with Mary Taylor.

The Moravian community has a concept of love that is the complete antithesis to Calvin's concept of retribution. Ellen knew that, and she brought her ideas to Charlotte, Emily and Anne. Ellen never lost this philosophy – of redemption, love and optimism – which sustained her throughout her adult life. To what extent did the sisters desire this gift? And did this make Ellen different? Was it part of why they loved her?

I continued my reading and research and meanwhile I moved to Land's End – my escape to the country! In Cornwall I discovered the history of the Branwells of Penzance, and became entranced by Barbara Hepworth's studio and garden in St. Ives. The Tate of the West displayed diaries charting her migration from the West Riding and observed similarities between the moors of West Cornwall and those around Haworth.

Everywhere I went I seemed to meet Brontë references.

So, in 1996, I planned a research vacation in Haworth. Sunshine steamed the night's rain from churchyard slabs as I walked to the parsonage museum. I spent hours in the library, surrounded by dark wooden bookcases, and dimly lit original manuscripts, which were protected from sunlight by heavy cream blinds on tall windows. I was aware of ghosts and voices, and, as I lingered in the museum's carefully designed, tastefully decorated rooms, I was transported through a holograph of images from my Yorkshire childhood. We had inhabited a complex household of multiple contradictions around class and ethnicity, in a social environment where rich and poor were juxtaposed. We were a highly politicised family, my Dad being an ardent socialist, and the Yorkshire folk were the salt of the earth. Dad's clergy stipend being insufficient to sustain a growing family, he took a second job teaching night-school English. Indoors, my mother pined for her island and the sea. It wasn't easy, smooth, or always happy, but we laughed, cried, argued and muddled along. My sister and I were exposed to uneven shifting shadows around visible and invisible lives; and the boundaries between public lives and private interactions were uncertain, unreliable, and open to criticism. What saw us through was Dad's unshakeable optimism and infectious sense of humour, and Mum's pure Celtic voice, filling our world with songs.

During that same Haworth vacation in 1996, I read Ellen's letters to Arthur Bell Nicholls [A.B.N.], in the Brotherton Collection, Leeds University. I asked: But why only these remaining letters? Why haven't we got Ellen's letters to Charlotte as well?

Because someone destroyed them – but why would anyone want to? What was their content that made them 'as dangerous as lucifer matches?' What did Ellen really mean to Charlotte? Why was she asked to burn Charlotte's letters? Why didn't she? How did C.B.'s letters become dispersed? And what was Ellen's role? How did she feel about that? My attempts to answer these questions became the driving force for this book.

So, I was living in Cornwall and in 1996, on return from my study period in Haworth, I began to write Ellen's replies. However, in September 1998, I left the West Country alone, following Maria Branwell's route north, with my partly written manuscript in my luggage. I started my life over again, with new hopes and dreams.

But what were Ellen's hopes and dreams?

Hopes of a long and happy life, filled with love, creative work, loving friends and a fast-easy-end were not fulfilled for Ellen's good friends, Emily and Anne Brontë, who each suffered dreadfully through a painful, degenerative demise. This intensified my empathy for Charlotte and Ellen because my friends and I were also familiar with the realities of terminal illness and debilitating disease among our friends and families. I realised that our human emotions of anger, fear, joy and sorrow link all of us across time and space. I found that C.B.'s letters revealed *her* fears and hopes, desires and dreams. But without Ellen's letters I wondered, what were *Ellen's* experiences? What did *she* write about and *how* did she express her longings and her fears?

As I continued to write Ellen's replies a wonderful resource became available, and it is with the deepest respect and gratitude for this magnificent work of rigorous scholarship that I acknowledge: *The Letters of Charlotte Brontë*, in 3 Vols., edited by Margaret Smith, for the Clarendon Press, Oxford University.

Volume One 1829-1847 published, 1995, with corrections 1996

Volume Two 1848-1851 published, 2000

Volume Three 1852-1855 published, 2004

I lived in Bradford for almost two years, with many opportunities for expansion of my Brontë research and my previous studies of nineteenth century social history. Several years of editing, reading aloud, listening and re-editing led to my jettisoning Ellen's narrative, in first person past tense, which had been the main component of my first draft. The book became entirely composed of letters – almost all written by Ellen, almost all written to Charlotte. However, not all could be sent: some were really private outpourings in Ellen's journal; others were composed by the bereaved Ellen craving continuity and communication with Charlotte.

During that same time span I re-met an old friend, Cynth Morris, whom I met originally through my first novel, *Three Ply Yarn*. In the year 2000, I re-located to Devon, to live with her there. Cynth Morris and I have made many journeys together – and had some adventures too. All have been processes of transformation, including travelling for poetry readings from *moonseanight*, in 2007, visiting our baby grand-daughters in London, and re-locating to West Yorkshire in September 2009. To Cynth Morris I owe years and years of interest and support for all my novels, and with her I found a loving relationship within which to complete Ellen's replies.

Caeia March

West Yorkshire, Spring 2010

Collections of Ellen's Letters

Five bundles of letters are created by the fictional Ellen from her interpretation of Emily Brontë's passion for the natural world.

Font Times New Roman and *Font Italics*

Charlotte's Letters: The non-fictional letters – the real ones – are printed in italics – be they whole, in extract, or as short phrases in quotations. All are sourced from *The Letters of Charlotte Brontë* ed. Margaret Smith, Vols. 1,2,3. The only exception is from Charlotte to Ellen 22 December 1837 – although it is set in italics to keep the flow, this letter is fiction.

Dates: Charlotte did not always date her letters. They might just say, for example, Haworth, Tuesday. Dating and sequencing Charlotte's extant letters took Margaret Smith many years and she describes the history of Charlotte's letters in Volume One. For this novel I have written dates in full – e.g. 14 February 1854 – adhering to given, suggested or probable dates in Vols. 1, 2 or 3.

Punctuation: I have adhered to the punctuation used by Charlotte – it is somewhat quirky, for which she was famous – even though it gives the appearance of bad proof-reading. I have used the convention ... ... to indicate omitted content.

Formatting: In contemporary publishing, inconsistent paragraph indents and underline as emphasis, are usually avoided, but are reproduced here because they arise in Charlotte's letters. However, signatures for both C.B. and E.N. are formatted consistently at the left hand margin.

Spellings: I have made only minor changes to Charlotte's spellings. These include taking off the extra 'l' that Charlotte puts on Gomersal, and the 'e' from Ellen's sister, Ann, to avoid confusion for readers. Charlotte's sister Anne is always spelled with an 'e'.

Ellen's Letters and Journal Entries

Fiction: Ellen's fictional letters are set in standard print Times New Roman.

Real letters: These are set in italics and sourced as follows:
From Margaret Smith Vols. 1,2,3: *21 May 1844 Ellen to Mary Gorham; 21 February 1854 Mary Hewitt née Gorham to Ellen; November 1854 Ellen to A.B. N. ; Spring 1855 from A.B.N. to Ellen. 30 March 1855 Revd. Patrick Bronte to Ellen* **From Barbara Whitehead page 193**: *Summer 1855 from Ellen to A.B.N. [the same letter is referred to in Margaret Smith Vol. 1 page 27.]*

Other real people and addresses : Ellen's solicitor was H.F. Killick; her friend T. Wemyss Reid was the editor of the Leeds Mercury; and later in life she met Lady Sophia Anne Morrison. Their addresses are real.

Dates: Ellen's letters and journal entries have been standardised in cardinal numbers with a day, month and year for every item e.g. 27 January 1831. This somewhat formal approach is chosen because it allows story-lines to free-flow instead of halting at every year heading and, more importantly, it allows cross-referencing with Charlotte's letters.

Conventions in nineteenth century names: It was common for anyone called Mary to have the nickname Polly, and those named Martha were often known as Patty. I have sometimes used formal names to avoid confusion unless it is absolutely clear about whom Ellen is writing. Family members were often referred to as 'friends'. If Charlotte wrote, 'I hope your friends are well' or 'your friends will not release you', she meant Ellen's family, her closest relatives. Likewise, Charlotte's phrase, 'I consider myself one of them', should be read in this context. Sometimes girls had boys' nicknames – eg. Joe Taylor's daughter, Emily Martha, born September 1851, was nicknamed Tim.

Biographical Details

Charlotte Brontë	21 April 1816 – 31 March 1855
Ellen Nussey	20 April 1817 – 26 November 1897
Patrick Branwell Brontë	26 June 1817 – 24 September 1848
Emily Brontë	30 July 1818 – 19 December 1848
Anne Brontë	17 January 1820 – 28 May 1849
Mary Taylor	26 February 1817 – 1 March 1893
Martha Taylor	1819 – 12 October 1842
Mary Gorham	1826 – 1917
Arthur Bell Nicholls	6 January 1819 – 2 December 1906
Revd. Patrick Brontë	17 March 1777 – 7 June 1861

Note: Anne died age 29 but C.B. and E.N. erroneously stated her age as 28. Her gravestone, in Scarborough, still reads age 28

Ellen's Siblings

John	1793 – 1861	Apothecary, London
Ann	1794 – 1868	Housekeeper
Joseph	1797 – 1846	Wool manufacturer
Joshua	1798 – 1871	Clergyman
Mercy	1801 – 1886	Teacher/housekeeper
Richard	1803 – 1872	Wool manufacturer
William	1807 – 1838	Apothecary with John
Sarah	1809 – 1843	Invalid?/Disabled at home
Henry	1812 – 1867	Clergyman
George	1814 – 1885	Wool manufacturer
Ellen	1817 – 1897	Housekeeper

Ellen's Sisters-in law

Mary Walker (second cousin) m John

Anne Elizabeth Alexander m Joshua
Elizabeth Charnock of Leeds m Richard
Emily Prescott, Everton, Lancs. m Henry

Ellen's Brother-in-law

Robert Clapham m Ann

Ellen's Life-long Correspondent

Mary Hewitt née Gorham born 1826, Ruckinge, Kent

Census information from 1871 Census

Thomas Swinton Hewitt incumbent Leysters, Herefordshire
Recorded erroneously as Thomas Saintort
Their children, births registered
Edward 1854
Mary Sara? 1857 recorded erroneously as Warysara
Katherine Elizabeth 1860
Frances Garcia 1863
James Bradley 1864

Births, Marriages, Deaths Index for 1837 – 1915

Thomas Swinton Hewitt 1817 – 1886

Minor Characters

All the minor characters mentioned in Charlotte's letters can be found in the index for Margaret Smith ed. Vols. 1,2,3, then referenced to an appropriate foot-note. For example, John Gorham, Mary's brother, can be traced via the index, Vol. I, to footnote 7 for 6 August 1845 re horse riding with Ellen. There are no additional/fictional characters in *Letters To Charlotte*.

FIRE

Ellen's Journal and Letters
January 1831 to September 1836

It's your eyes that draw me, from this moment. Brown eyes, deep as pools. You know how it seems, this colour, the very same – when sunlight slants on the surface of the peat pools, high in the hills?

Oh if I could but speak this.

Your eyes – they are large, wide set and deep. Deep not dark. They call to me of wild pain, like a broken bird upon the moors. Calling of wind, tempest and rain. In your eyes I witness sorrow – such as I have not seen in anyone until this day, and the more unexpected in the eyes of one so young.

If only I may enter behind this grief, I may perchance find in you some hidden fire, from a warm, beating heart.

You crouch in the window seat of our schoolroom, at the front of this large gracious house, overlooking the grounds. You are a stranger to me, for it's my first day here.

My brother Henry has just brought me from home, in this bitterly cold January. My friend Mary Taylor will come soon. We've known each other since early childhood – we attended the Moravian Ladies' Academy together. So, Charlotte Brontë, here am I, looking forward to my studies with which I shall endeavour to make good progress – thereby fulfilling my mother's wishes for me to complete my education with honour.

There is a tradition of letters in my family and I have always penned lines like this in my notebooks, which I keep in my wooden box, with an inner drawer, under my bed. Oh I simply adore to write letters. Shall these be secrets? Is it not true that all young girls love secrets? But never before have I felt *this* way.

Although I'm from a comfortable family in Birstall, it is imperative that I waste not a penny of my family's income in idleness. I am truly grateful for this chance of education, and I promise my mother, before God, that I shall be diligent and trustworthy here.

I walk around the bookshelves, contemplating the many bound volumes with awe and some trepidation, then I turn to look out of the window. To my astonishment I discover you.

My first glimpse of you. A warm glow has begun, deep in my body. Perhaps I may love you from this moment. Who shall say? Am I too young to answer the question, 'what is love'? How shall I describe this elusive gift, which, I am told, burns beyond pity, compassion, gentleness or elation?

You are in the shadows by the tall bookcases. Between us – also – there is a long table covered in a crimson cloth, which hides us more or less from each other.

You are in despair. Weeping silently. You're very small, brown-haired, old-looking and weary. Your appearance is of someone bowed down under a burden. Your clothes are sombre and terribly plain.

But you are not at all plain. Not to me. Your eyes, full brimmed with tears, are the most beautiful eyes I have seen in all of my thirteen years.

Journal
Roe Head School, 2 a.m. 30 January 1831

My new friend,

We have our own bed, which is usual in girls' schools. I am curled around you, listening to your breathing, aware of other sleeping strangers in the high-ceilinged, heavily-curtained room. You are familiar with the warmth of sleep of your sisters, and I, of mine, but here beside you, I cannot sleep. Trembling with heat, I rise from my bed, creeping silently to our schoolroom, whence I begin my second letter, writing in this notebook. These are my words from fire, rising. I place my hands on my belly, feel my interior warmth.

In my body, deep inside my hips, there is a bright flame, which resembles molten heat merged with a quality of sunlight. Embers of a fire are thus kindled, deep, inside my organs.

On our first meeting, when your distress seems so intense and personal, I feel I should not intrude, should turn away quietly, leaving the schoolroom softly, with respect. But in this moment my heart goes out to you, whilst you make a valiant attempt to recover your dignity, unwilling that I might inspect your feelings. I can neither simply walk away nor abandon you.

Instead I gently speak, telling you my name and that I have just arrived here. You reply that you have been three weeks, suffering the while from homesickness.

'I have had no time to be homesick,' I respond. 'But perhaps one day you shall comfort me for the same reason, for I'm the youngest of a large family and shall sorely miss them all.'

Your birthday on twenty-first April will be your fifteenth, and mine, one day prior, will be my fourteenth.

'My great-aunt said that a year less a day was a magic number, revered by people long ago,' I tell you.

'Do you still have her, and your parents?'

'No only my mother, for my father died when I was nine. I miss him most dreadfully for I was the baby, on whom he doted.'

'At home we are cared for by Aunt Branwell, my mother's sister. She came from Cornwall when my mother died. I was very young.'

'I am so sorry for that. Your aunt is a long way from home is she not?'

'Yes, she is. She yearns for the cliffs and the great roaring seas in a storm. She is a storyteller, most awesome. She recounts the old legends par excellence. You shall sometime come and visit Haworth, then you may make your request – though it's not in my aunt's nature always to submit.'

We laugh, you and I, conspirators in wheedling our ways through a family maze.

Are you my fate, my destiny, Charlotte Brontë? With what kind of magic do you hold me in your spell?

I write to you in my un-scrutinised moments of night: I take cognisance of you during numerous supervised activities by day.

If I could make of my belly a secret chamber, I could en-treasure therein this kindling, these testaments of fire, more safely than I carry them, whilst walking newly ignited, beside you. My new fire implies impulse. I unfold my instincts cautiously. Touch, taste, smell, sight and sound. My fingertips measure pulse-beats, previously unknown. I am conscious of my hands on fire. Barely do I comprehend the unknown territory of desire, this melting and burning, nor do I yet know how love yearns, between you and me, like this candle, incandescent, its blue-yellow flickering flame.

Journal
Roe Head School, 2 a.m. 24 April 1831

Dearest Charlotte,

Will ever there come a time when I reveal to you these letters?

I write in the dim schoolroom, my pen driven by pure joy. How shall I find lexicon sufficient for my happiness here? You fill my world with interest and ideas, my days with company, my nights with your arms across my sleeping body.

You and I reside here as singletons, for which great good fortune I thank God, who has brought us together in one shared bed. I bring you the gift of sleep, yet do I wake often, after midnight's chime, and make stealthily along dark corridors to my desk. It is a lie to sneak from my bed. It's forbidden, but I care not for that because I ask God to forgive me every Sunday. He is my friend. He knows how I love you, and I would defend you and care for you always. He knows and it's all right. He always forgives me. Love and kindness are not mistaken, even for someone like me.

Do all young women write letters in secret? No one must know, rather do I suffer resolutely my discretion. Yet do I shine for all to see, if they but knew how to regard me.

I am being raised to be a gentlewoman but I do not feel gentle. I'm obliged to be everyone's pretty child, smiling daintily, usually agreeable. I am a fine actress, am I not? Inside I'm alive, on fire, obsessed by my infatuation. I shall train myself to hide the private person, the one who loves passionately and will be fiercely loyal.

My womanhood has woken, this month. The older girls here understand. We wash our rags, about which we never speak. Some get cramps. Myself I bleed most easily. Clean, bright. It's my fire, flowing freely because I love you. I tell no one how I feel.

Never have I met anyone who sets me alight, as you do. My bosoms are growing; I press against your back as you sleep, a great surge of fire moves down through my belly to my womb, then blood flows with ease.

I watched my cat have kittens and saw my foal being born, of course I know these things. I am a country girl, a young woman. The war in Europe is over – and I was born in peace-time. It's wonderful to be alive. Spring arrives here at Roe Head. Everything is waking up.

My new friend, you're so unusual – so different from anyone else I shall meet throughout my life. Your imagination is at variance with all of us, every other girl in the school. It's more vivid, more dramatic, more lyrical, more sustained than ours could ever be. It's a highly trained, polished imagination. You say it's hell-and-high-water, trouble and joy, threatening to sweep you away with its intensity, like a flood.

Nevertheless, we benefit from the fruits of your mind – how eagerly we wait for your ghost stories. You 'make them out', forming your ideas and events from somewhere behind the pain. You draw upon a rich heritage of words and characters, an inner encyclopaedia, from reading your papa's books since an infant; you know the poets and their ways of words far beyond the mere morsels which schoolgirls recite by rote.

How evenly and fluidly flow your words, bringing detailed pictures of people and places as your tales unfold. Then always – a twist and turn of events and characters, until we gasp, gulp and squeal. But also we laugh for you are singularly funny, and funnier still from the fact that you realise it not. Such merriment we have with your stories.

One day I shall meet Branwell, with whom you've shared your childhood worlds of fantasy, and Emily, your bed companion. How glad I am not to be your sister. This warmth I feel, it's how sweethearts are supposed to feel, not sisters. I stroke myself along my belly, over my mound. Shall I reveal, one day, how I feel?

When I curl myself around you, the word for my feelings is foreveralways. One word, which says all. You sleep a calm and peaceful sleep. It is our gift to one another from now, forwards.

I am no storyteller, nor composer with words, though I am trying to tell you who I am, as best I can. Much time shall pass. These are my early days. We are still so young. How shall it be, when I am very old, searching back through all my memories? Shall you be in my bed, Charlotte, foreveralways?

Journal
Roe Head School, 3.30a.m. 15 May 1831

For you, Charlotte,

Miss Wooler says this afternoon that I am clever. That you, myself and Mary are her young lions. It is my great delight to be so respected. I enjoy my studies, which come to me easily, especially the French language, but never shall I attempt to replace in your life the words and tales you share at the parsonage with Branwell, Emily and Anne, whom I am yet to meet.

Here we are a triangle – Mary, you and me. Mary and I recognise your passion for literature, so we acknowledge your gift and cherish it. Mary and I made a pact: we shall show you that we are delighted with your lively mind, inspired by your unusual turns of phrase, and thus shall we nurture as best we can your power of writing. We want this for you because we are your true friends.

For myself, there's more. I want to be near to you. I realise – even though I am young – that you, Charlotte, you're a candle inside a lantern, shining. If this very special light is always to shine so brightly, someone must hold the lantern steady. I desire to be your lantern bearer. From the first time that you told us one of your stories, I have known that being a storyteller brings life to you. If ever you cannot find expression through writing, then your life could fade away. That is what I have learned about you, my Charlotte Brontë. My Charlotte, you are a storyteller – a writer from the centre of your soul. It is your true self. Anyone who really loves you, must honour your need to write.

These are our wonderful days in school. These are good nights also. You and I curl around one another under the blankets. You grow plumper from happiness. Your confidence blossoms all around, like summer flowers in our school gardens. Our food is well prepared and there is plenty of it. As time passes, and you're changing how you eat – a little meat gravy with vegetables, and now a small amount of meat itself – we regard your strength and health returning, to our satisfaction. Gone is that bowed down, burdened grief-stricken lonely girl who was weeping in the window seat. Allelujah. May God and all his angels rejoice to watch you coming alive again!

However, as to exercise, our school is no substitute for the vigour and verve of walks with your sisters at Haworth. You are one of the wild children of the moors and will not easily adapt to less stimulating natural worlds. Nothing matches the impact of the moors upon you!

You describe for us the wide skies; the piling of the great white clouds; the movement of shadows and light; the many varied shades of green of the heathland grasses; the tiniest of the perfect purple bells of autumn heather; the sound of rushing waters; and the surprise of bright green patches of sward. These and the changing flowers and migrating birds through the seasons, these have been a natural habitat from when you arrived in Haworth from Thornton, at the innocent age of four.

Beautiful as our schoolgirl walks are – down narrow lanes, where fragrant honeysuckle adorns the hedgerows and we pass under canopies of old green trees – all walks hereabouts are tame – pertaining to places where people cultivate and alter the land.

I suppose that is why I am so happy here – for I am not a wild child like you, with your brother and sisters. My early childhood was more conventional. I have simply not known the pain of the wild as you have – nor its variety, nor its richness, nor its loss.

I love you, Charlotte Brontë, with every secret part of my body and soul.

One day, I shall read this to you.

For you, Charlotte,

I miss you my sweet friend, Charlie, my treasure, my special girl, someone to curl around every night. This past term at school has served to affirm my feelings, that I have found you and desire never to lose you. I feel keenly my loss when separation from you is necessitated upon me. I miss you especially amid the festivities, without your voice and your laughter.

Every night, I hold tenderly to my spare pillow, curled around with my arm across. I stroke its thick cotton covering, which resembles your night-clothes. I imagine myself sleeping around you again, yet is my pillow but poor substitute for your sleeping form. It feels not at all the same – even though my sleeping body keeps it warm. It has not your smell. It has not your thick brown hair, tumbled and shining against my face. When I wake in the dark and reach out a foot to touch your leg, there is but an absence.

I trust my heart, and when time and my household duties allow, I shall pen you some lines, in friendship.

Rydings, 4 January 1832

Dear Charlotte,

How are you, at home in Haworth? I hope that you and your sisters and all your 'friends' are well. I have been to visit with Mary and Martha Taylor at the Red House, but the family is suffering with colds. Do you recall that Mary's father knows much about art and that he collects paintings? He is indeed very pleased with Mary's drawings from our last lessons at Roe Head – and he desires that he shall have two of them displayed with fine frames. Is that not exciting?

I have news about the strange electro-magnetic machine that Mr. John Murray demonstrated at the Mechanics Institute. My older brother, Richard, has now seen it – he was most enthusiastic – but there is also further news about the 'galvanic' therapy, which fills me with distaste.

I do not like it –it seems fearsome to me. Would it not be a most awesome experience to have electrodes attached to our bodies and then a current passed through? I hope, most sincerely, that I am never inflicted with a disease from which it would be thought wise to pursue such a course of treatment. What do you think?

Christmas here at Rydings has been a generous and enjoyable season, notwithstanding that my mother and my brother George were later stricken with colds over the New Year. I enjoy all the festivities – but especially the music and carol singing. The tunes and words stay with me, lingering in my memory for days afterwards. I sing them for my sister Sarah, who is in chronic poor health. I myself am very lucky in having a stronger constitution than she does, although I am not as active as you and your sisters, striding out upon the moors. I would rather ride my pony – I have called him Lord Nelson!

This old house, which is owned by my Uncle Richard, is very dear to me. It is a large spacious dwelling, which suits us very well indeed. Most fervently do I hope that you will see it – perhaps next summer after we leave Roe Head, I shall persuade my mother and my older sisters to invite you to stay with us. We have a beautiful home, with stables, hot houses, a park, woodlands and plantations. One of the mares expects her foal sometime during the summer holidays.

There is no more news this time – soon we will be together at Roe Head – with again all our pleasure in our friendship. Please give my kindest regards to your sisters, your brother and your aunt and your dear papa.

Always your affectionate school friend,

Nell

Journal
Roe Head School, 2 a.m. 17 February 1832

For you, Charlotte.

These are my fire-nights.

Sometimes at night Miss Wooler invites us into her sitting room, reading to us or talking to the three of us by her fireside. Then am I happy, sometimes silent, perhaps listening to her lovely voice, or linking arms and walking with you round and round Miss Wooler's table. You and Mary are debating the national and foreign news, with the firelight flickering and the globes of the oil lamps shedding softly their lamplight upon your animated faces.

Tonight you change the subject, begin talking about poetry and literature, and I am linking arms, walking, listening. I want to spend my life with people like you and Mary for we have all fine, quick minds, clever language, warm hearts and easy laughter. My hopes and dreams are being forged in the red, hot coals and yellow, shining, walled caves into which we gaze and imagine our future lives. Together, we rehearse the discussions and arguments that rage in Mary

Taylor's family about girls' education and the role of women in the wider world of finance and commerce. But I know that my family has sent me to school only to make me more marriageable. Shall I not be consulted in plans for my future? I think not, because my relatives regard my life as their theatre – they intend to write my part for me. Yet do I desire to be my own playwright, to script for myself my own speeches – and I wish you to be my leading lady because you have become the centre of my world.

How may I lead my own life independent of my family? There are no easy answers. In secret I scrutinise my almanac – as if therein I may find magical solutions. Oh Charlotte, you and I are both Fire signs, born under the sign of Aries, the ram. What may that mean? I shall not disclose my magical quests. It is contradictory to the rules of my Church and my household to harbour any silly ideas beyond my calling: to find a good husband, be married and raise my own family.

Mary, on the other hand, is from a family of Dissenters and is personally outspoken both at home and in school, where she eschews all ideas of marriage. From the earliest age she has wanted to leave home and be independent – she longs to follow her brothers' interests in commerce and finance.

You, Charlotte, you want your independence also, to earn your own living. In truth, this derives from the weight of responsibility, which lies heavy upon you, the eldest daughter, so that you may help your papa with the household finances. The only way forward for you is to become a governess but now you tell me that you dream of running your own school and I burn with the fire of hope – could I not be the housekeeper for such a school? If we study hard here, could not you and your sisters be as successful in your own right as Miss Wooler is now?

In the firelight, in Miss Wooler's study, I forge my plans – I am determined to concentrate on attaining my highest marks, performing my neatest tasks, staying open-minded to all my education. I know who I am and what I want, because my dreams are rising like living flames.

On the outside I'm a simple Yorkshire lass, fourteen years old, calm and loyal, yet is there unseen fire inside. No one shall take it away without my per-mission. No one should try, for it is my own fire, God-given, my birthright. It is there to keep me warm, because I was born under the sign of Aries. My secret fire is built from dreams, with images of red and gold, and its origin is you – Charlotte Brontë – another girl, older than me by a year less a day.

Dear Charlotte,

In my favourite secluded bower, with my sewing in my hands, my fingers busy and occupied, I am free to think what I like. What I like is to think about our recent schooldays. Charlotte, we have made a promise, you and I, to write regularly to one another. Although I am still young – what my brothers call 'a mere slip of a girl' – I know that my friendship with you is authentic and unchanging. I write to remind you of the steady but passionate vow to one another, that evening in the gardens at Roe Head – I shall remain your loving friend, loyal to the bond between us.

Whenever the days are sunny and dry I am allowed to do my 'work' without having to remain indoors. There is plenty to be done because my brothers require new shirts, and the household sheets must be turned.

Sometimes I feel imprisoned hemming yards and yards of bed linen – a most tedious task, which is almost unendurable, but my mother is a kind woman, whom I do love most dearly, and she does not insist that I do this work indoors.

As often I say to you, I have no illusions about my relatives – if ever I shall challenge their attitude towards my 'work', it shall but leave me disturbed and unhappy, because insurmountable obstacles shall be laid across my path. It's best I recognise the constraints and try to accept them because in truth there is little opportunity else.

It's my great good fortune to live with a loving and kind family, where I am fed, cared for and treated with some consideration. However I am not allowed to possess strong views of my own. I am not encouraged to be outspoken like Mary Taylor, and besides, I'm the youngest – not worth regarding as to my own perspectives on family life, nor my own wishes, nor my own dreams. Nevertheless, my education brings you to me – I take courage always from you and Mary who are inspired to speak out for yourselves. Perhaps I shall yet rebel against the inactivity of needlework, which I am being trained to accept without complaint.

I love my home here and, now that my mother has re-designed these gardens, she has created private spaces by separating the herbaceous borders into smaller and smaller plots with windbreaks, as a protection against our fierce winters. Some areas so enclosed are so small that we nickname them our 'broom cupboards' and in these are set wooden seats, very warm and soft to the touch. I love to be in one of them in particular, with the smell of summer flowers, where, having completed my sewing tasks for the day, I am permitted to read. I carry with me the latest novel, which you have advised, and my favourite book of the stories of the saints.

My current novelist is Sir Walter Scott. I read and read, absorbing myself in his language, and involving myself in the plots and characters of his thrilling books. All around me the sunshine is a warm cloak, carrying the memory of you reading to me at Roe Head. My favourite legendary saint is St. Bridget. She is patron saint of fire and of sunlight. The stories portray her tending the sick, and visiting the houses of the poor, wherein she brings daily comfort, and where, with no hook upon the door, she hangs her cloak upon a sunbeam. Is that not beautiful? In my sunlit bower, with a copy of your letter as a bookmark, it is neither my needlework nor my book of Saints, nor even the great Scottish novelist himself, who sparks my imagination. It is my school-friend, my correspondent, whom I now miss most dreadfully, whose image falls like a sunbeam across my mind.

I write to extend to you and your brother my mother's invitation to visit Rydings. Please say that you will come, in early October, for the autumn season is so beautiful hereabouts.

Your affectionate school friend,
Nell

Rydings, 26 October 1832

Dear Charlotte,

The great mature trees, which you so admire on your visit here, are tossing in the east wind, scattering their amber, golden and russet leaves as I write.

I look down the driveway, listening for the wheels of the gig, which brought you and Branwell for your visit.

Oh how glad am I to have met your brother, albeit briefly. He is an amusement to everyone, including my mother whose gay laughter echoes through our house as if he is still here. I miss his infectious enthusiasm, entertaining Mama with exaggerated descriptive stories, taking pleasure in his new surroundings.

Now you've met my mother, you know she's a warm generous woman who imparts her delight in her home and gardens: it is to her that I owe my obsession with flowers and shrubs. It was a witness to her liking for you both that she decided to personally guide my visitors all around our home. Today I am repeating that journey – looking for your ghosts, re-living your and Branwell's pleasure in the wide stairways, the wooden panels, the old paintings, and the flowers with which every nook is adorned. I hear you and your brother laughing, responding to the way Mama receives you, welcoming you into our home. So doing, I appreciate my good fortune that she is still alive; and feel a strong yearning to hold you, Charlie. The strong bond between you and Branwell is evident – you finish one another's sentences – you dwell inside one another's minds.

I love my older brothers yet there is no single brother to whom I cleave in quite that same way. You were so very young when you shared early adversity and bereavement – you are as close as twins but also you're Branwell's little mother as well as older sister. I pray for your mother, Maria, with deep compassion for you, my beloved friend. I want to spread my family's love around you, like one of my mother's old cloaks in which we would be enveloped on outings. I have treasured memories of myself and my brother George, the two youngest of my mother's chicks, snuggled to her on night-time journeys in the gig, reassured by my mother's body, enclosed in her soft thick cloak, under her warm feathery wings.

Come, Charlotte, come again with me – my tour begins at the top of the house, by unlocking the attic door to the roof, from whose battlements and parapet we take a bird's eye view, over Rydings in its own grounds, beyond which are the mills and working people's houses. I rejoice that Birstall is still very wooded, with fertile agricultural land between small pockets of industry. Yorkshire's tumbling streams provide the force for our wheels – overshot where the valleys are steep, undershot where they widen and the water drop is less significant. Our larger mill at Brookroyd employs forty-two people, and is now powered by steam, and there we stand, you and I, listening again to the noise of the weaving sheds carried on the east wind, blowing across Birstall beck.

Now I descend again to the first floor, where our curtained windows overlook our gardens, stables, woods and plantations. Many of the trees are still in autumn foliage, offset by hawthorns in abundance, their berries so dark they appear deep maroon. Here are blue-black mulberries and shining Sorbus berries, bearing bright scarlet clusters in the autumn light.

It is almost dusk as I return to the ground floor via Rydings' central stairway. I enter our huge kitchen, in which are installed all conceivable modern conveniences. Mama likes gadgets, which she procures by scanning the small adverts in the pictorial newspapers for the latest addition to her culinary collection. While your papa scrutinises the local and national news, passing to his children a flair for religious controversy and questions of a philosophical nature, my mama scours the small classifieds for lotions, potions, and utensils for the modern home.

The kitchen currently smells very good – there's a pan of thick soup on the black-leaded fireplace. On your visit, we are very hungry young friends, are we not? But first my mother leads us to a low-lintel beside the range and, warning us to hold tight to the hand-rail, she opens the narrow door, and bids us descend stone steps to the basement.

Come, Charlie, see again my favourite room at Rydings. It's the keeping of her still-room that is my mama's singular talent. Here I am again – a stone-lined chamber, with high windows, always very cool due to its deliberate location on the north side of the house. Never have I felt cold here, because my mother customarily lights many candles. In these flames leap and dance Titania and her entire retinue, playing fairy games as they jump from convex to concave glass, from stopper to bottle base, from green to brown mirrored surface, flames floating, wafting like fairy smoke in the fire-dancing eyes of myself as a young child.

I cannot speak to you and Branwell of this silliness, can I, standing there in front of Mama, who is now holding an oil lamp, but I fancy that in your and Branwell's smiles I catch glimpse of my erstwhile childish delight in this place.

'When I was small,' I say, 'before my head could barely reach this first stone shelf, one of my brothers would lift me, standing me on these wide slabs so that I could count the jars with Mama.'

Branwell is rotating, turning on his right heel, in the spacious stone room. My mother explains to the eager boy that we bottle the fruit in our large kitchen and store the bottles of all shapes and sizes here on stone shelves. It's autumn, so the room's full to capacity. It's quiet and peaceful, presently dancing with light and shade – and you understand now that every container is part of my mother, part of her knowledge, how she takes good care of all of us. She ensures, through her work and her gardens, we shall have an ample harvest of delicious fruit.

With this letter I send a hamper, bottles packed in straw, for your family, with love from Mama.

Mama chuckles at Branwell's open face and wide-eyed interest, joking with him, 'There is an elegant sufficiency of enoughness, is there not?' For once your brother is lost for words. All he can do is gawp.

But you laugh quietly, your brown eyes filled with warmth, and reply, 'Oh, indeed, Mrs. Nussey, ma'am, any more would be a superfluity!'

You move along the rows reading the labels: summer fruits laid down in syrup, wine and plum colours, crimson and ruby red; crab apple jelly, dozens of jars of it, their tops sealed with wax; gooseberry jam, rhubarb as well; bottles of mead beside jars of honey comb; apples and pears in golden syrup; and my favourites, quince, in jams and jellies, in gleaming rows; all with my mother's curled handwriting giving the contents and the date.

I say, 'I used to beg to accompany Mama here in the dark when I was little. We would light some candles and then I'd laugh at all the reflections shining and winking from every surface – it's magic, really it is.'

So, Branwell thinks Rydings is paradise. He stays but a few days, at the commencement of your visit, before returning to Haworth, leaving you here. Now you also are gone, and today is warm and sunny, despite the wind, so I roam the grounds, as did we three, swishing through the fallen leaves and watching the acrobatic squirrels hoarding their store cupboards. Our winters are bitter indeed but, to Branwell, nothing compares to the howling gales and snow-laden clouds that habitually obliterate his 'mountain', for he derides our softer forthcoming winter 'down here in the valleys'. Thence, from this valley, to your mountain, I miss you!

We hope that you enjoy the contents of our hamper.

Your loving and affectionate friend,

Nell

To Mrs. John Nussey,
4 Cleveland Row, St James's Park, London
3 July 1833

Dear Mary,

It is but seventeen miles from my friend Charlotte's house to Rydings, yet it is a difficult journey across country. I am at present residing with the Brontë family in the parsonage, where at last I may begin my friendship with Emily and Anne. Everyone is most kind and I shall endeavour to describe for you this household wherein I have been made so welcome.

Emily is the bread-maker for her family, which art I have learned from her rather than from Mama. In London, this everyday task is performed of course by your kitchen servants but here in Haworth, the kneading of dough, setting it to rise above the hearth, shaping it and baking, provides a silent companionship between Emily and myself. She is not one for speech, except to Anne, with whom she is to be found often in quiet conversation, but Emily and I have a simple understanding through work with our hands. Do you recall that I was most weary with the tedium of sewing before I left Rydings? There is none here for me – therefore am I indeed content with my new-found freedom from the needle! Do not tell Mama – for I shall be satisfied to return to my sewing when my temporary sojourn is here completed.

The moors hereabouts are wild and peaceful, with lapwings and large birds of prey. Here is fresh air, scented with hazel, birch and lime. The heather is not yet in flower, but we have walked to the meeting of the waters – where two streams conjoin in a tiny valley, like a fictional, fairytale place. Charlotte tells me that the waterfall is a torrent in winter – in summer we must use imagination for it dries to a thin windblown scatter. Yet there is sparkle where the water trips and falls, and I have seen rainbows therein, when a strong breeze lifts and blows the droplets. The sward is very lovely, strewn about with tiny white and yellow flowers. Therefore am I out walking frequently, with my new friends, accompanied by Tabby the servant, of whom I am most fond. When you come next to Rydings you shall find me with not a little bloom in my cheeks, for I am grown plump with happiness during this holiday.

Mama asks me to convey her love to all the family. Please remember me to the children – Affectionate greetings from your sister-by-marriage,

Nellie

Journal
Brontë Parsonage Dining Room,
Midnight, 4 July 1833

For Charlotte,

I take some small risk on the stairs, which creak most audibly, yet I had need of the privy, unusual for me at night. Then by the still warm embers in this room, I come to this table to write.

You tell me that never do you wish to marry, that our loving is the easy outcome of our sharing a bed together, a natural expression of our happiness in one another. I reply that you are my beloved, with whom I am satisfied, in the Biblical sense. I had missed you so much at nights since our school leaving, therefore am I delighted to re-kindle our bodies' source of true, abiding joy.

We shall speak of this nowhere. I comprehend that whenever in your letters to me you call me your very own dear dear Ellen, I am to recognise our code for the kind of loving between us. Afterwards, you slip into deep sustained and un-tormented sleep. Curled away from me on your side you rest as if seated on my knees, my legs folded warmly beneath you. Your repose is peaceful in my embrace.

Between these papers do I lay my heart, as between your sheets I lay my soul. Speak silence else, though I should like the world to know.

My wooden box holds my secret hopes, upon the wooden stairs my secret tread, accompanied only by the night owl's cry, to your side, Charlie, to our secret bed.

4 Cleveland Row, London, 15 February 1834

Dearest Charlotte,

I am writing to you, in answer to yours of 11 February.

I am heart-warmed to read that you think of me, your *'only un-related friend,'* daily, nay, almost hourly. Do you imagine me surrounded by friends and companions, so that soon I may forget such an *'insignificant being'* as yourself in the *'solitude of your wild little hill village?'* If you but knew how I miss you, you would have no such anxieties. How can such a friend as you ever be insignificant or forgotten? It is pure folly to think so. I shall have none of it. Now then, that is a right hard talking to, is it not?

Here in London, John and Mary are well positioned now that he's an apothecary to the royal household. Their friends abide in spacious houses with gracious architecture. The women have beautiful clothes and the men have money and influence. Here, I ride in the parks and walk beneath the great trees, yet I long for home. If I were on the moors, with you and your sisters, you would be talking gaily – I would be reading the expressions on your face, enjoying your laughter. Then, without tilting my head, I would glance beyond you and there would be the sky, in all its changes, all its moods, meeting the road on all our journeys.

Mary says, 'You're confused, Ellen, what troubles you?' and I reply, 'I cannot find the sky.' Then she comments, 'What a singular child you are. It's above the houses, where would you expect it to be?' I look up, until I have a crick in my neck, and I respond, 'I'm used to fields and woods and in Haworth, where Charlotte lives, the sky comes all the way down – down to touch the earth.'

I shall write to you often, my sweet friend, because I miss you.

Your affectionate friend,

Nell

Dearest Charlie,

You write that you're overwhelmed with my visit to the great metropolis, astonished that it does not entrance me. You fear that its allure might pull me away from the north to stay in London's high society. It seems that I have the capacity always to surprise you – I have no need or want to linger here. I am won over neither by the fashionable costumes, nor the glories of the metropolis. In short, I am not bedazzled. Interesting and friendly as my sojourn here continues to be, I shall be glad to return – where the sky and the earth are stitched together, with no rent in their hemlines, no fraying of their seams. I will write again soon.

Your loving, affectionate friend,

Nell

4 Cleveland Row, 18 April 1834

Dearest Charlie,

I write to wish you a happy birthday, also to say again that I miss you. I shall be home some time in June, so says my brother John. Meanwhile, I have something rather serious to talk about. It is this – during my visit I have become aware of the meaning of entrapment for unmarried daughters in families like mine. Of course, with a fortune of my own at my disposal, I could lead a free and creative life, doing what I liked, going whither I chose, with constraint neither of duty nor protocol. But my family is not landed gentry – and I am not an heiress. London society illuminates the barriers of wealth and inheritance.

In truth, some members of my family own property – my Uncle Richard bought Rydings where my widowed mother and my sisters Mercy, Ann, Sarah and myself make our home. Nevertheless, family money comes primarily through trade; my brothers Joseph, Richard and George all earn a living therein; and friendship is primarily with other wool manufacturers such as the Taylors of Red House. Perhaps the distance between London and Birstall brings clarity of perspective?

At night I lie alone, missing you, my dear Charlie. I would like to speak face to face, not in these letters. I have a confession – forgive me – in my newly found awareness I'm a little jealous of you, my sweet friend, because your dear, loveable, eccentric papa believes in his daughters' rights to earn their own living. Of course, there is no joy in becoming a governess – I am without illusions. In any case, that option is closed to me – I cannot take employment as teacher or governess. My mother would be horrified at the suggestion and my older brothers would expressly forbid such an audacious request. I love all my brothers – they are kind and considerate of my welfare, but control me they do, most certainly, because I have none other money than they deign to give. As a small girl I learned, like so many others, to wheedle and smile for pennies and presents. As a grown woman, I do not enjoy it. My London visit confirms all my erstwhile suspicions – I am expected either to marry or remain at their disposal to help with their children in their various houses all over England. This is my first taste of entrapment – do you wonder that I wish to return home? It is late, and I must finish this now and continue in my next letter...

Your loving and affectionate friend,

Nell

4 Cleveland Row, 5 June 1834

My dear Charlotte,

Do not be afraid that I will stay in London. I am not a city dweller, you know. You surely know me so well, by now? My home is in Birstall, and I am a Yorkshire lass at heart. Although our valleys are filled with mills and noise, are not our hills nevertheless beautiful? I love the moors around your home and I long to walk again with you there. I want to linger with you and your sisters by your waterfall, on a sunny day in the height of summer. I want to be there when the dazzling sunlight is pouring down from the sky; and witness its fire transforming those very droplets into magical rainbows, when the spray rises into the sunlit air. I long to hear your delighted laughter – and its echo in wild birdsong. I yearn to see a flock of lapwings scudding like wind-driven clouds over the high heather.

Do not fear that I have changed in any fundamental way by being with my southern relations! Never will I become distant to you. I long to hold you. I am still your Ellen and I love you still above all else.

Write to me soon.

Your devoted,

Nell.

My <u>own</u> dear Ellen,

I may rightfully and truly call you so now. You <u>have</u> returned or <u>are</u> return-
ing from London, from the great City, which is to me almost as apocryphal as
Babylon, or Ninevah, or ancient Rome. You are withdrawing from the world (as
it is called,) and bringing with you, – if your letters enable me to form a correct
judgement – a heart as unsophisticated, as natural, as true, as that you car-
ried there. I am slow <u>very</u> slow to believe the protestations of another; I know
my own sentiments, because I can read my own mind, but the minds of the rest
of man and woman-kind are to me as sealed volumes, hieroglyphical scrolls,
which I can not easily either unseal or decipher. Yet time, careful study, long
acquaintance overcome most difficulties; and in your case, I think they have
succeeded well in bringing to light, and construing that hidden language, whose
turnings,windings inconsistencies and obscurities so frequently baffle the re-
searches of the honest observer of human nature.

... ...

I say no more: remember me kindly to your excellent sisters, accept the good
wishes of my Papa, Aunt, Sisters and Brother, and continue to spare a corner of
your warm affectionate heart for
Your <u>true</u> and <u>grateful</u> friend
Charlotte Brontë.

Dearest Charlotte,

Since my return to Yorkshire I have occupied my time with letters – reading
your replies over and over. From our earliest school-days, I have loved you, my
cherished friend. It was ever thus from my point of view. The hidden language,
of which you write, so eloquently, is understood now, openly between us. It is
the language of the heart, of warmth, of embers, and of fire.

At my bedside before I sleep each night, I watch my candle burning. In its
flame is once again our hidden language. The colours of that language are so
beautiful, are they not – the blue and yellow blend one into the other? I miss
you, always, and especially as I fall asleep.

Meanwhile I have returned both to pleasant news and some that is yet un-
settling. My brother Richard is to be married. That's the good news. He seems

very happy. The engagement is to Elizabeth Charnock whose father also owns a woollen mill. The wedding date has yet to be decided. Our bad news is that we may have to leave Rydings as my brother's namesake, Uncle Richard, is unwell and, according to Mama, we shall not stay here after his decease. We have not yet another place to dwell. However, Mama says the likely scenario is that John will purchase Rydings in order to provide a home for his mother-in-law, Mrs. Mary Walker, and her unmarried daughters Elizabeth and Catherine.

There is another property called Brookroyd, which will be inspected to see if it is suitable for a new home for us. I trust my brother – John is a good man, a kind son to my mother – he will not give cause for undue anxiety. Having just returned from John's home, I feel this a realistic appraisal. John is now forty-one, and he will have all the family's interests at heart.

We are fortunate indeed to have resided at Rydings but I shall miss the gardens. As indeed do I miss you.

Good night.

Ever your devoted friend,

Nell

Journal

Rydings, Midnight, 24 June 1834

For you, Charlotte

I cannot sleep after completing my epistle. It's a beautiful soft night, shortly after the summer solstice, a dark and starry night. The day has been the festival of St. John the Baptist. I think of the young John, striding off into the desert, proclaiming his faith, following his vocation; then of my brothers, all of whom have the freedom to follow theirs.

This night it's not jealousy of wealthy heiresses which obsesses me, nor of you, my poor Charlotte – a jealousy of which I'm now ashamed. I am jealous of my brothers with their freedoms to marry, to earn money, to buy and sell houses. I want the same for me. I want to write and propose marriage to you, the same as my brother Richard has done to his Elizabeth.

If we were man and woman we would have been betrothed and married, but I cannot offer marriage to you.

I myself have not until tonight desired to be a man. But to have the freedom to live and love, in such a way that others might say we are married, would give security and companionship – our dream come true.

If you, my Charlie, were a man I would be thrilled and honoured to be your wife, keeping house and home so that you could work daily on your writing. I want to be with you each and every day, but we have control neither of our own lives nor our family fortunes.

We might lose Rydings – so, I cannot sleep. With a very warm shawl wrapped around me, I steal out of my chamber and upstairs to the parapets. Overlooking the great trees, the peaceful gardens, I watch the shooting stars until my eyes ache. I regret being the youngest daughter, with no independent means. Had I been a son born to the Nusseys I could propose marriage to you. Hypothetically, had you been your papa's son, Charles not Charlotte, my family would encourage me to be flirtatious, to allow myself to be wooed, to become affianced to you. You say to me, '*I am no bird and no net ensnares me. I am a free human being with an independent will.*' That is true. But the will of our brothers and the will of us daughters is a very different matter. Do we not regret that we lack the power ascribed to our brothers – the right to define our own dreams; the equality with them to choose how to live and whom to love; the freedom to say that we want to be married; the possibility of security, love and companionship with each other, to last us all our days?

Journal

Rydings, 27 February 1835

For you, Charlotte.

We curl together in my bed, murmuring quietly in love voices. The silent house and the dark night absorb our thoughts, as if to acknowledge them and keep them safe within these walls.

'What are your wishes for the future, Nell? Say five years hence?'

I'm silent, gathering my courage, while you pursue me with further questions. 'Do you not know what your hopes and dreams might be?'

'My silence signifies my lack of courage, not an absence of dreams.'

'You can trust me, Nell.'

'Then I shall.' I pause, searching your face. 'You're the only person to whom I dare reveal my wishes. If I had money, I should like to buy you a cottage and should like to be your housekeeper. My dearest wish would be to reside with you and sleep every night in the same bed. I would hope that you would write, and make paintings and drawings.'

'You would wish that for me? How generous you are, Nell.'

'I think that art and literature belong in your soul, Charlie. We don't speak of this and I shall never ask you. I consider you a very private person, upon whose imaginative art I should not intrude. You have my word upon it. You may completely trust me never to ask you.'

'Thank you. I do. I trust you, Nell, absolument, ma chérie. It's a wonderful dream – for you to keep house would be my wish also. It would be our perfect solution.'

'Good. That makes me happier than anything else. I need that dream, therefore do I hold onto it. So to that end, I learn all there is both from Mama and from Mercy. But as to reality, my intuition informs me of a burden currently upon you – to go out, to be a tutor hereabouts, is that not so?'

'Your intuition never fails, Nell. You may depend upon it. Oh Nell, I desire to be a tutor neither here nor anywhere. I'd rather be a grave-digger.'

We laugh, and you hug me, snuggling closer.

'That's the honest truth, Nell.' Your seriousness returns: 'But I must bring some money to our household. Papa has to pay for Branwell's art education. It's Papa's wish for him to study at the Royal Academy.'

'What about your art education? You are equally as good as he is. I know you love him – so do I – and he makes me laugh. But much as I love him, I don't want your life spent supporting him. It isn't fair.'

'We are daughters, not sons. Branwell has been raised with the expectation of becoming a great and famous artist. Papa has done very well by all of us, employing a drawing tutor for us girls, encouraging Emily in her pianoforte, far more than most parents hereabouts. I am not ungrateful. I have always known that my art education could be never as significant as that of Branwell. Besides, I'm the eldest child now. It's my duty to support the family in any way that I can.'

'Yes I know. I respect your sense of duty – we both have a strong sense of duty, rightly so – but it saddens me to watch its intersection with your own wishes.'

'I must continue to search for a situation, Nell.'

I fall silent, thinking that you were made to write, not work long hours for someone else's children. I ask, 'Did you hear a rumour that Miss Wooler shall seek a new governess, because Marianne may marry ere-long?'

'No. How came it to *your* ears?'

'From the Red House. I wondered if Miss Wooler might approach you? Has she not?'

'No, not a whisper, not yet.'

'What would you do, if she did?'

24

'I don't know. The hours would be exhausting.'

'In truth, Charlie, that's what concerns me. Those tutors work half the night as well as all day. They do all the mending for the girls – we were young at Roe Head – we gave such things no consideration. But now we work hours with the needle ourselves, and tedious it is sometimes. I just finished turning all George's collars. My fingers are like pin cushions and my eyes – I thought they were going to roll to the back of my skull.'

'There's no end to it is there, Nell? But think on – there would be a positive aspect – Miss Wooler would welcome you, wouldn't she? If I were offered such a position, you would be so much nearer, compared with Haworth.'

'Yes that's true. So your return to Roe Head would at once delight and worry me. I would be delighted because you'd be nearer to Birstall, so that I might anticipate much happiness, visiting with you. But I'd also worry – you would work long hours tutoring dull girls, correcting their tasks, trying to stimulate their silly untrained minds. It's inevitable that you would suffer exhaustion.'

'How accurate you are, Nell. How well you know me. I see that I can't delude you for a moment. You're aware, my darling, that my only reason for tutoring is to remove the burden of my keep from my father's purse.'

You lean over me and kiss me, full on the lips, until conversation is halted, and our night leads to loving warmth, which satisfies all our longings for intimacy, until at last, contented, we fall asleep.

Rydings, 1 April 1835

Dearest Charlotte,

You left here your umbrella, which I have asked Kelly to deliver to the Bulls Head Inn at Bradford. Therefore shall I take this chance to write and shall tuck my letter safely into the fabric. After you left I, too, was melancholy, and thought many hours about our brothers, and in particular your love for Branwell, which is intense, rightly so. When first you came here, I saw how it was between you. I recall your first arrival at Rydings – when he accompanied you in the gig. When he returned home, leaving you with us, we all missed him. Rydings seemed much quieter without his infectious laughter. With your brother, I am friendly – he's very interesting – and there is something so wild about him, which is part of his charm. I wonder whether anyone could succeed ever in taming him. For the things he enjoys, he exhibits such enthusiasm as to be contagious, so that everyone wants to be near him.

Now I'm thinking about *my* brothers. I am close in age to George – when Papa died he was so kind to me – and for a while afterwards, George and I rode miles – nay, tens of miles. Our shared grief for my father was fusion by fire. My grief was white hot. Hot as Nebuchadnezzar's 'fiery firey furnace'. To this day the trust between myself and George is of steel, welded by fire. I am older now, and George is a man. This being a man's world, we are no longer daily companions and rarely do we ride together.

In truth I am anxious now on your behalf. Some grief is mine, when I consider your talent, on account of the discrepancy between you and Branwell. I take pleasure in your excellence – at line drawing, making miniatures and copies of engravings. I desire for you the chances that exist for Branwell. If I had money, my dearest, you would want for nothing. I would pay for ink and paper, materials for your literature and art. All that I have would be yours, to free you from servitude.

Now then – from such unworldly economies I must return to my reality, to Rydings, from whence there is not much news.

Mr. Harrison continues to show interest in Mercy, who reveals not her dreams to me – I am too young and she'd close her door if I showed curiosity – so may you understand how I'm trained not to inquire about sensitive matters. As to politics, please write and tell me any news. I desire to receive the same kinds of letters as Mary Taylor.

I must finish this because Kelly is waiting, with your umbrella.

Au revoir, ma chérie,

Your loving affectionate friend,

Nell

Rydings, 15 May 1835

Dearest Charlotte,

Thank you for your latest, and now at last I comprehend the long gap in our correspondence. Upon completing my last letter I walked in the orchards, admiring the blossoms, and searching for eggs. Many of our hens prefer to lay in warm grass by the south facing wall. Thereafter, I spent my days happily awaiting a reply – but there was none. There ensued this strange gap, for over a month. Now I discover that your carrier did not remember the umbrella and it seems my letter lay, in its secret hideaway, until after our May Day festivities. So, my dearest, I am joyful at hearing from you at last. Now to answer your queries – Mercy is going to write to you, but why do you desire a letter from her? I think I know the reason – [pertaining to her work as a Sunday school teacher?] – but I am confused. Mr. Harrison has left the area, but Mercy suffers only from relief. She had made her decision – he was not the one for her.

We heard that Rev. Allbut is vicar-designate for Dewsbury, and presume, therefore, an increase in stipend. Thus we anticipate no further delay in his marriage to Marianne Wooler. It is rumoured for the beginning of July. I wonder whether you shall receive ere-long an invitation to a situation at Roe Head.

There was much discussion in my family at the change of heart of Lord Morpeth. That he, who had always been Tory, should default to the Whig administration caused quite a stir in Birstall. To a man my brothers vote Tory, of course. However, there were not enough of like mind to favour Stuart Wortley against Lord Morpeth, about which my family, like yours, suffered bitter disappointment. My mother caused a furore at our dinner table by asserting that if she had voted, she being 'trustworthy blue', Stuart Wortley might have stood a chance. This led to a heated debate with my brothers about voting and enfranchisement. Mama invoked Mary Wollstonecraft. The like has never been known in my home – indeed, you may recoil. You may imagine the voices – with Mama and Mercy on opposing sides. Mercy holds not with women's equality to men. My mother took us by storm, declared that she had taken on responsibilities since my father died, and felt frothed up like strong beer. Polly Taylor would have enjoyed the debacle. You and I would have talked all night thereafter. I miss you most acutely, lonely at night, in need of your warmth. I shall anticipate with pleasure my next visit to Haworth – how I love the moors in summer. I pray every night for you, and your sisters.

Give them my love.

Your loving and affectionate friend,

Nell.

Rydings, 27 July 1835

Dearest Charlotte,

I write to welcome you and Emily. When you receive this letter you will already have arrived at your new teaching post at Roe Head, for the commencement of the new term. Your note informing me of these changes arrived at the beginning of this month. As you rightly acknowledge, '*Duty – Necessity – these are stern Mistresses who will not be disobeyed*', but I understand that you love and respect Miss Wooler, so your lines have "*fallen in pleasant places*".

Your letter leaves me in no doubt that your main reason for accepting the change is financial, and Miss Wooler has offered, as an encouragement and inducement, a free place to Emily as a pupil, which relieves your papa of school fees. It's true that all human affairs are mutable, and I am accommodated already to the speed of change, which brings you away from hearth and home, out into the world of work.

It seems that our precious three-year interlude is over, during which we have grown to appreciate and love one another, being welcomed into one another's homes. In all truth I was very disappointed to be unable to reside with you in Haworth this summer. Yet have I been already aware that you contemplated becoming a governess. Your return to Roe Head at once delights and worries me. I'm delighted because you are now only four miles from Rydings but I'm sad for you that your family's situation places you in this necessity.

However myself and Polly Taylor are your trusted friends in the vicinity – and shall we not have wonderful walks this autumn under the fine old trees around the school? Therefore take good heart, my dearest, and I shall come to see you on the second Sunday in August. I had also a kind note from Miss Wooler informing me of your proximity and welcoming me to Roe Head whenever time allows me to visit.

Please give my love to Emily – your mutual presence will be of great comfort in your new situation.

Your ever affectionate, loving friend,

Nell

Journal

Rydings, 24 August 1835

For you, Charlotte.

I write at midnight, my chamber lit by moonlight and candles. Their reflections are winking, shining, twixt mirrors and window glass.

I write, while memory is fresh and bright. Linking arms, we walk together for a private hour, through the countryside where the harvest is being gathered in, exchanging news, enjoying being side-by-side again.

'They're bribing me, you know. If I stay here, Emily gets a free education. What do you think?'

'I think it depends on your own hopes and dreams. You don't wish to be a governess here, do you?'

'No, not at all. I have no wish to be a teacher either here or anywhere else, but I simply must bring money to the household – because Papa has to pay for Branwell's art education. It's Branwell's wish to study at the Royal Academy.'

'What about you? You've already exhibited in Leeds. You're equally as good. You were made to write and run your own school, not drudge long hours for Miss Wooler.'

'Yes, but you are here, aren't you? Oh Ellen, it's so wonderful to be walking with you, talking with you again.'

'I long for the means to provide an escape for you. I cannot. If tutoring it must be – in this circumstance or a million miles away in some remote and private household – then I must thank my stars that you've chosen Roe Head.'

'Bless you, my dear dear Ellen. What would I do without you?'

'Don't ask such a question. I forbid it.'

'Masterful? Well, my dear Nell. When you're in such a mood, no-one is more alluring.'

'So be it. Foreveralways.'

Rydings, Tuesday, 15 September 1835

Dearest Charlotte,

A quick note – you may expect me Sunday, as promised. I will bring St. John's Wort for Emily. The herb will lift her spirits and she shall take the tea of it, lukewarm if possible. Not too hot. We shall speak on every visit and shall take cognisance of her wellbeing. That she pines already for the parsonage is the effect you and I both feared. I shall bring also wild Valerian, Mama's remedy for restless nights. You shall try also some camomile tea. You're right not to wake her even though she mutters incomprehensible phrases in her sleep – for she would be the more pale and listless in the morning.

When last I saw her, she was so pale, as if her vitality were transmuted to the wild environment – rose-hips in the hedgerows drawing oval droplets from her life blood. On each visit I see that Emily is unhappy – in the years of my friendship, never have I seen such a diminishing of her countenance – her hair is dull and lustreless, and she, who erstwhile loved words and music, shows no interest or motivation in her studies.

You acknowledge rightly, dearest, that you're in no mind to witness the decline of another beloved sister, after the disaster at Cowan Bridge. You *are* right to challenge this circumstance. *Yes*, of course you should inform your papa. Now then, my dearest, please give Emily my love, for we have this in common – she and I – that we are in unison through commitment to hearth and home. That's all. That's what I know.

I shall be with you very soon,

Your loving and affectionate friend,

Nell

Rydings, 11 October 1835

Dearest Charlotte,

As the year turns and the earth settles down for its annual rest, I am deeply troubled that there's no rest for you. I am witness to your duty and self-sacrifice. With your pupils you're generous hearted and patient – Miss Wooler speaks so highly of you. What would I not give to remove the burden of your responsibilities – your early mornings, your long tedious days, your evenings taken with sewing, mending, preparations for the morrow.

However the good news is that your papa agrees to remove Emily – I am not a little relieved – and I feel that Anne will truly benefit from an education at Roe Head, when she takes Emily's place. Take heart, my dearest C.B. – I shall be with you very soon.

Your loving and affectionate friend,

Nell

Journal
Rydings, Midnight, 3 November 1835

For you, Charlotte,

Before going to bed, I open my casement and watch the moon over the trees around Rydings. I am wrapped in a sense of foreboding with which I dare not burden you, and cannot explain. Not a small part is that Uncle Richard's health is now failing – we shall all miss him, and there are serious consequences of hearth and home. But the larger part is my concern for you – the cause of your troubles lies with Branwell. Without you, Branwell has no one with whom to share his thoughts or who understands, as only you do, his eccentric creative nature.

I kneel and pray:

Dear God, in Heaven,

Please give Branwell strength of purpose and direction. Guide him in his studies so he will waste not his sister's generosity. Look most kindly upon Charlotte at Roe Head – From ill health, protect her; from exhaustion, sustain her; from all morbid thoughts, defend her. In Your kindness and mercy bring her on life's pathway to that place where artistic talent and writing can be encouraged. Heavenly Father, she is your child and it is from you she receives her need to write. Please, in your wisdom, divine Father, show us how to make a life together. Amen.

Rydings, 2 December 1835

Dearest Charlotte,

There are changed circumstances for us at Rydings. I write with apologies, because I cannot come to Roe Head on Saturday as planned – we are now in mourning for Uncle Richard, who died on 30th last month.

When the period of mourning is completed I shall return to you as soon as possible. I will write and inform you, when I know Mama's plans. Forgive the haste, dearest, but there is much to do here in the house. I love this home, which will no longer be ours – I had mentioned before that my brother John intends to purchase Rydings – we shall find elsewhere in the neighbourhood, the most likely residence being Brookroyd House. It seems that we shall be here for another half year, possibly longer.

Please give my love to Anne and Miss Wooler, likewise to Emily when next you write.

Remember always, C.B., that I love you very dearly.

Your loving and affectionate friend,

Nell

P.S. If you are in Birstall church on Sunday, I may see you, briefly, after the service. E.N.

My journal, I write to you, for in whom-so-else shall I confide? I have no one upon whom to vent my feelings.

Branwell is the source of my disquiet. He embarks upon new strategies with much enthusiasm, vowing his entire commitment and a promise of future progress. Yet without Charlotte he is able neither to complete his projects nor maintain the momentum with which he initiates them. His London adventure to the Royal Academy is one such example. Whether he did arrive there – I'm not really certain to this day. His entire intercourse therein seems a brief, unmitigated disaster. I shall never witness the full story, which is probably known only to Charlotte herself.

She is usually disposed to forgive him, at least outwardly. Yet as she endures long hours at Roe Head, bitterness creeps into her tone when there's mention of her brother, revealing an underlying sadness at the reality of inequality. She cares about supporting him more than he about respecting her. Branwell himself becomes in turn melancholy, obstreperous or morose. The family's response is to call this behaviour Branwell's 'illness'. No one refers to his drinking. Branwell continues to confide in Charlotte and to confess his misdemeanours in anguished letters begging her forgiveness. She can be won over so easily by his pleas, which makes me wild with frustration.

Rydings, 12 February 1836

Dearest Charlotte,

I desire to continue our conversation when last I saw you at Roe Head. I love you dearly, my sweetest friend, therefore my sense of justice is outraged, because I witness that you wear yourself out for a brother who disregards your best efforts and dissipates your labours. He appears to have little regard for the welfare of those around him, with an accompanying inability to be reliable in his art, his paid work, or his leisure. I cannot bear to see your work at Roe Head wasted in such a manner. Yet of course I understand your desires – and from you I learn about duty, honesty, and trustworthiness. No one could work harder for your family than you, my dearest. As to Branwell's part – my Christian compassion is challenged; and the values of my religion are sorely tested.

Therefore, donning my riding habit, I ride for hours in the hills around my home. Only the wind in my riding bonnet and the fast canter upon deserted bridleways can satisfy me. It is a risk, but to date I remain undiscovered in my subterfuge – providing that my unladylike equestrian accomplishments remain unseen by other human beings. I lie to my family about my whereabouts, fabricating 'visits to an erstwhile school friend' for afternoon tea. Then I kneel by my bed to confess – so my nightly prayers are a round of transgressions and requests for absolution in extreme circumstances. The Good Shepherd is kind – surely he will understand? I feel His comfort and turn more fervently to prayer to the Almighty to calm me down. But when I fall asleep, I dream vivid, disturbing dreams.

I dream of fire, although the images take many forms. Occasionally, I'm at the parsonage, reading to you by candlelight, or walking arm in arm around the dining room table with the sisters, talking quietly by fire-light. Sometimes I'm collecting firewood, or gardening in an abandoned cottage where you and I have found shelter.

In my most recurring dream, I wander the moors around Haworth, in search of home. I am solitary at sunset with red rays on distant hills ablaze with bracken, turned deep russet in the slanting light, the colour of red fox-fur, or searching among winter's silver birch trees whose purple tipped branches exaggerate the sense of fire. I am burning with longing for my friend, my companion, someone to curl asleep with, someone to have and to hold – a sweet friend whose brother drinks firewater, which drives him to misdeeds and enrages those around until their fire must surely turn to despair.

Then I search moors at night, alone in the moonlight, solitary and cold, while the moon's silver casts a chill stillness upon the hills and valleys. I'm feared of shadows, which turn my limbs cold with frost burn. I burn with the ice-cold heat of slicing anger. Cold knives isolate me from my companion. Why must I be so separated? Why must there be endless sacrifice of women of every generation? Church bells chime in the distance.

Write soon to me, lest bad weather prevent my visiting on Sunday.

I long to hear from you,

Your loving and devoted friend

Nell

Rydings, 12 March 1836

Dearest Charlotte,

Strange that when we met you told me of broken nights – yours are broken if one of the girls seeks your kindly attention. Perhaps I hear you, awake, unable to sleep – perhaps we are listening the one for the other? Another disturbed night has trembled me awake with dreams of fire and ice. On waking, I heard church bells across the valley and can only assume that their sound entered my mind during sleep. I have already told you of my moonlit sojourns, my desire for a safe and peaceful life with you, my hope of companionship. Perhaps my dreams include church bells through my familiarity with their everyday sounds. If, in each of my dreams, I may find my way to these bells, perhaps I may safely reach 'home'.

You tell me that my letters always remain in your mind. I wonder if somehow, some day, you shall write a poem or a tale for me, wherein a woman searches for the chimes to bring her home? Meanwhile, I have heard from Emily, who asks that I walk the four miles to Roe Head 'as often as shall possibly be convenient'. She is well again and assures me that you and Anne derive the utmost comfort from my visits. Of Branwell's illness she says little, except that your papa suffers sadness and disappointment – thus it is that from my perception of Branwell as a charming boy in whose company I laughed gaily, I sadly revise my viewpoint and reinterpret my feelings. Put quite starkly, I am angry with him on your behalf. He is self-absorbed, and his behaviour renders him effectively cruel towards those beings he purports to love, yet it is not in his nature to be cruel deliberately either to people or to animals. I would take all these troubles and woes from you, if I could – So I shall be with you on Sunday. Take good heart, dearest, until then.

Your loving and affectionate friend,

Nell

Rydings, Palm Sunday, 27 March 1836

Dear Charlotte,

I write with an invitation to come to Rydings. My mother sends her warmest greetings to you and all your family. Come as soon as possible and stay as long as possible. I long to see you again.

Your loving and affectionate friend,

Nell

Rydings, 13 April 1836

Dear C.B.,

So you could not come here, and now you are returned to Roe Head, and I am desolate not to have been yours, during this time. Yet my frustration and disappointment does dissipate whenever I think of your drudgery at Roe Head. I understand that you must accommodate to your role, having little choice but to earn your living. I sent my gentlest love for your health and welfare during the summer term. I trust you will find that the sunshine and good weather will allow of less fatigue. The girls will perambulate the lanes around Roe Head as we did, thus shall you take respite from weary work indoors. Did we not become joyful during the summer terms at our lovely school? The countryside is still beautiful there, is it not? So my dearest, I am missing you so – but shall see you here before long, if Miss Wooler will allow you leave to visit one of her (not-so-young) lions. Please let me know, soon.

Mama sends her greetings and a new umbrella with which I enclose
birthday greetings –
Your devoted friend,
E.N.

Rydings, 12 May 1836

Dear C.B.,

We have just received your letter of 10th May and I hasten to reply immediately. I cannot come to Roe Head at present. We are busy packing and I am needed here. Please can you come to visit here at home? Surely Miss Wooler will allow?

Your friend,
E.N.

Rydings, 30 May 1836

Dear C.B.,

I refer to your letter written on 28th May after a tantalising gap, in consequence of which I have little choice but to accept your suggestion to visit for only one night here. This may be our last opportunity for time together before my family moves to Brookroyd House. Do you feel yourself so immersed in attention to your pupils that you must refuse yourself adequate rest from work? It is my feeling that Miss Wooler would be not at all offended were you to ask for a short visit. Do you consider that allowing yourself more than one night would be dereliction of duty? Are you to have eternal fatigue and neither respite nor recuperation? This is pure folly. Even a most devoted employee shall have the right to a small amount of pleasure and restful sleep. Ne'er did I expect to be jealous of Mary Taylor – though she shall have a visit from you at Gomersal on Friday *and* Saturday – oh, well, I am resigned to one night only! Of course, I shall meet with you at church on Sunday, 5th June, and you shall return here to Rydings, as you propose.

Your friend,

E.N.

P.S. Oh but I cannot stay angry with you for long. I ought to but I cannot.

Rydings, 1 June 1836

Dearest C.B.,

Rarely do I write angry words to you, my sweet friend – I was ashamed the instant my last letter was despatched. I am wrong ever to have employed terse or formal lines. I have amplified our pendulum-swing by penning my anger. My actions sit in contradiction to my hopes. I try usually in my letters to achieve serenity, because your position at Roe Head is so demanding that weariness shall oft-times threaten to engulf you. Was I not already aware that words on paper shall linger long after their author has regretted them? You will read my foolish outburst and be hurt by it, whilst already I am apologetic and dismayed. I did not add my true regrets to the post script – an over-sight for which, later, I berated myself quite forcefully.

E.N.

Rydings, 14 June 1836

Dearest C.B.,

I understand now that Miss Wooler has fixed the end of term for this Friday, 17th June, after which you will return to Haworth for the commencement of the vacation. Thank you for your invitation to Haworth – but I cannot leave Rydings whilst we are midst of the chaos of packing. All is hustle and bustle here. Every night, before I sleep, I pray to overcome my frustrations at our separations. I wish to sleep peacefully without my heart disconnected from you. I imagine that during this time – the high summer – there is a tussle for both of us between intellect and emotions. We desire to pour out our hearts in letters, then reason intrudes with warnings not to permit such flow of feelings. I am truly sorry that I cannot come to Haworth – do not forsake me, I am desolate, else.

Your devoted friend,

Nell

Brookroyd, Tuesday morning, 23 August 1836

Dear Charlie,

I was glad to receive your latest epistle and to know that we are friends again. I am looking forward with pleasure to the arrival of Miss Wooler and her visitors Elizabeth and Harriet Upton, but I scribble this quick note because my mother has other arrangements and we cannot meet this afternoon. Please ask them to come tomorrow instead. They will – I am certain of it – bring a letter from you. I shall send this by our messenger boy. I eagerly await your reply.

Always, your friend, Nell.

Roe Head, 23 August 1836

Dear Ellen when your note arrived, Miss Wooler and les desmoiselles, were just setting out accoutred in grand style. my ladies in gay green dresses – fit for a ball-room rather than for walking four miles on a dusty road; they looked most terribly blank at the recall – what was to be done   they could not lose all their trouble in dressing and preparing, they must go out somewhere so off they trotted to Mr Kitson's, leaving orders that your messenger should wait for about an hour and that if they did not return in that time I should send him off with the tidings that they would do themselves the pleasure of waiting upon you to-morrow.

Ellen you are far too kind what right have either Anne or I to receive presents from you ... ... you leave nothing for us to do but to iterate and reiterate "thank you." I had written a foolish note to you before the boy came but it is in Miss E Upton's custody. she will deliver it to you if they should go tomorrow. I shall be sorry if the delay of the messenger should occasion you any inconvenience but it is not my fault   Miss Wooler's dictum must be obeyed, at least by me

Is your Sister returned? Remember me affectionately to her if she is, Give love also to Miss Mercy and to your Mother and believe me my <u>own</u> darling, my <u>kind</u>, <u>sincere</u> Ellen Scribble

Your affectionate Coz

Charlotte Scrawl

Tuesday afternoon

I am now at liberty to announce that to-morrow my Superior and their Serene Highnesses, the ladies E & H. will shower the light of their glorious green apparel upon you, id est that they will come to Brook-royd.

I am thine

Charles Thunder

I've sent one note within the other, write me just a scrap and send it by the Uptons to-morrow do – do it will cheer me. any-thing

Brookroyd, Wednesday, 24 August 1836

Dearest Charlie,

I was warmed to receive your notes – and that we can be again unto one another the way we were. I vow that never again shall I commit to paper any angry feelings towards you – my lesson has been fire upon my skin. I walked in the gardens here in the cooling rain, so anxious until you became once again my Charlie, my Charles Thunder. Fire signs we are, and shall be. But let not me again send fire arrows to you, my dearest. They mis-fire, as indeed I have learned most painfully!

Brookroyd is a beautiful new home for us and we are busy with linen and hangings. When you visit you shall feel the loving care we have bestowed upon every room. It is tangible.

Our gardens are wonderful and I have here a bower, towards the south side of the garden in dappled shade from three mature Rowan trees, which are coming now into soft red and orange berries. There is a hedgerow behind them – of hazel with lime trees and hawthorns, whose berries are just forming small and tight. This is a quiet part of the garden, where an arched frame of old polished wood is 'wound-a-round' with honeysuckle and rambler roses. Assiduous, yeah ruthless, dead-heading, shall encourage new flowers until first frost. It is here that I sit to read your letters.

38

Write soon, for the days are warm and sunny – I take my sewing outdoors and betwixt hems and headings shall write to you and read your replies. Your hand-writing brings you into my bower. I see again your hands, holding the pen as they keep me informed of your days, until there follows the image of your hands holding me, making me truly thine.

I am always your affectionate friend, and will send this letter, sealed, of course, by the Uptons,

Your very own,

Nell.

Brookroyd, Sunday, 18 September 1836

Dearest Charlotte,

I searched for you in church this morning – could not find you – are you ill? Have you taken a chill?

It is beautiful here this happy-sad day, when my heart should be full of colours and scents of harvest but is yet empty from missing you.

Let me paint a picture for you – blackberries grow fat and full in the hedgerows; grasses flower and fluff themselves in the waysides; late herbs – marigolds, borage, fennel – transform the borders orange, blue and gold; rose-hips swell red and round with sunlight; old English apples ripen in Brookroyd's orchards and early heather wraps the hills in purple cloaks.

Birstall church is a spectacle to behold, its countenance adorned with flowers in every window, and the sun through stained glass slants pools of coloured light upon the polished pews.

At home, we have the Taylors from Red House, for which in preparation, myself and the kitchen lasses troop indoors, our arms filled with Michaelmas daisies, golden birch, crimson Cherry leaves and Chinese lanterns, until the interior shines with colour. This tableau of a bounteous Brookroyd decorated for harvest I offer to you, for I miss you most keenly, when my home rejoices with friends at such times.

I shall ride over to see you on Saturday,

Your loving and devoted friend,

Nell

Brookroyd, 22 September 1836

Dearest C.B.,

How glad I am to receive your note telling me you are well – yet sad that Anne is in poor health. You are right not to leave her. I shall arrive with the gig on Saturday – rather than by horseback – for I shall carry baskets of jellies, fruits and conserves with me.

Until then I send my finest greetings for her recovery – and my love and warm friendship for the both of you. Expect me around eleven o'clock,

Your loving and devoted friend,

E. N.

P.S. Decipher, if you will, my *coda* – for I am both 'Ellen' and 'Nell' also, by desire and design, E.N., wherein E is for 'ever' and N is *your* Nell. Till Saturday, my love, and always.

Roe Head, 26 September 1836

... ...

Ellen I wish I could live with you always, I begin to cling to you more fondly than ever I did. If we had but a cottage and a competency of our own I do think we might live and love on till <u>*Death*</u> *without being dependent on any third person for happiness*

Farewell my own dear Ellen

Brookroyd, 30 September 1836

Dearest Charlie,

Witness my happiness, seated on my wooden bench, reading your letter under a canopy of fire-bright honeysuckle berries and autumn roses. Sunshine illuminates them red within. My clever, affectionate friend, you fill me with wonder – your declaration does match exactly my feelings for you. I do cherish your words to which I respond without hesitation. It would be my finest dream to love you, share a cottage with you and make a life together. I, Ellen, being certain that we should need no other person to complete our happiness, give you, Charlotte, my reply: Yes, to you. Yes, a thousand times.

Your very own affectionate Nell

WATER

Ellen's Journal and Letters
October 1836 to early June 1838

Wet and windy weather tosses the great branches of the trees around my home. The storm rages all evening, following a day of brooding skies, during which the rain clouds have been gathering, building layer upon layer like grey roof tiles over the world. I think of Charlotte and her pupils, trapped indoors while grey sheets of sleet slash at Roe Head's windows, and the girls become fractious, forgetful and uncooperative. At such times, she finishes her day's work with a sense of absolute fatigue.

Roe Head, 6 October 1836

… … …

It is a Stormy evening and the wind is uttering a continual moaning sound that makes me feel very melancholy – At such times, in such moods as these Ellen it is my nature to seek repose in some calm, tranquil idea and I have now summoned up your image to give me rest   There you sit, upright and still in your black dress and white scarf – your pale, marble-like face – looking so serene and kind – just like reality – I wish you would speak to me–.

Journal
Brookroyd, 10 October 1836.

Charlotte writes that if it is our lot to be separated and to live at some great distance and never see one another again… in old age she will call up the memory of our youthful days and – '*what a melancholy pleasure I should feel at drawing on the recollection of my Early Friend Ellen Nussey!*' Her letter makes me cry.

I long to be near enough to comfort her. We love one another but the complexity of our lives prevents us fulfilling our wish to be together. She feels that very few people in the world could understand those qualities in her that made her miserable – and that her peculiarities will burst out sometimes, and that she will hate herself for the explosion of them. Perhaps she refers to her hot temper which she works hard to control, but rather, also, she is frustrated because the time she craves for her writing is now withheld from her.

Surely she misses Branwell and their shared world of fiction, a world I cannot enter? I imagine their words are bright jewels in a dark cave, the entrance guarded by a raging waterfall, with a narrow ledge behind, along which only they could pass. I understand the metaphor.

This takes me to Miss Wooler, through whom we all – Miss Wooler's young lions – went back in time to the first meanings, often from Greek or Latin. We had no formal study of those languages, but through our beloved Miss Wooler, we travelled sometimes to those forgotten worlds, and comprehended their influence upon us. In Greek the word *metaphor* means transport or transfer – the transfer of meaning.

Where the deep waters in Bolton Abbey flow between huge boulders, there is a rock formation known as The Strid. It is dangerous to approach, even when the river is calm. In winter's flood or autumn's storms, the river becomes a furious torrent such that any fool who dared leap over would be swept away. In such a manner do I not only understand Charlotte's need to write, but also the danger of approaching uninvited into that strong current which carries private dreams and deep emotions.

On stormy nights, I know that Charlotte longs for the flow of words, time to allow them their full force, their powerful propulsion towards freedom, and their underlying transforming emotions.

Anyone who loves Charlotte as I do must understand that her words are always there, gathering potential, waiting in urgent rain clouds. Gentle or dramatic, from an infinite source, her words feed the streams down the hillsides, pour into the rivers in the woodlands, meander through wide valleys, and shimmer upon estuaries, to emerge in wide-mouthed freedom at the open, welcoming sea.

The free flow of Charlotte's writing is as necessary to her as breathing, eating and laughing. For Charlotte, writing is as essential as loving, as intimate as desire.

Brookroyd, 16 Oct 1836

My dearest C.B.,

Your lovely words have touched me very deeply – and I truly hope that my image, which you conjured up, has brought you peace and calm again.

44

I keep your letters tied in lavender ribbons in a carved wooden box given to me last birthday by my brother George. Usually before I sleep, I untie them and read one or two, especially your *honeysuckle cottage* letter – as it is named – and sometimes I close my eyes and hold the box as if your genie might manifest therewith in the room in front of me. But I know it cannot for I am no longer a child, to believe in fairy tales.

Our juvenile days are over. We are no longer young schoolgirls. That fact seems to evade the consciousness of my family. You are twenty and I, nineteen, and you are in the outside world – working as a low-paid teacher to support your family.

My poor C.B. I am so sorry that you are melancholy – how hard it must be with no time for yourself, no time for shared words with Branwell, no time for poetry, nor visionary flights of fancy, no time for the expression of your astonishing imagination. I long to have the means to alleviate your necessity of this working life. I am most anxious for you, because your writing has to find its route from your heart and mind onto paper. Therefore I trust that you shall find time for your writing once again when you return to Haworth for Christmas.

However, I do not intend to pry. I do not mean it in that way. Your words are your private sphere, and I have no intention to intrude. I mean you only to understand that I know your writing to be essential to you – and that is why we have intense discussions about how educated women like ourselves can survive in a world where we are not allowed to use our education to the full.

Now then, my dearest, I am so sorry for what I have to write in this next – You will be agitated by it and so am I, for I yearn to be of comfort to you. Household events make it difficult for me to come to Roe Head at the present time. My mother and Mercy are making it impossible for me to suspend my household duties. My sister Sarah is most unwell at present – Mercy does not always show to Sarah the sympathy and kindness one would hope, nor as her name would suggest! I have no wish to spend all my days at Sarah's bedside, yet do I recognise that she must not be left alone mournful and afraid for hours on end. Meanwhile the house is very busy because many of our furnishings brought from Rydings must be altered for these beds and windows. There are yards of sewing to complete!

Forgive me, my dearest, for I long to be with you. You know you have all my heart, and I shall fix my hopes on Christmas.

Each night when I pray for you, for us, I ask the almighty to make our *honeysuckle cottage* possible.

Believe me, your very affectionate friend,
Nell.

All my notes to you Ellen are written in a hurry – I am now snatching an oppor-
tunity – Mr J Wooler is here, by his means it will be transmitted to Miss EW – by
her means to Henry by his means to you – I do not blame you for not coming to
see me   I am sure you have been prevented by sufficient reasons but I do long
to see you and I hope I shall be gratified momentarily at least e'er long – Next
Friday if all be well I shall go to Gomersal – On Sunday I hope I shall at least
catch a glimpse of you   Week after week I have lived on the expectation of your
coming, Week after week I have been disappointed–
*   ... ... don't desert me – don't be horrified at me, you know what I am — I*
wish I could see you   My darling, I have lavished the warmest affections of a
very hot, tenacious heart upon you – if you grow cold – it's over – love, to your
Mother and Sisters.
  C Brontë

Brookroyd, 2 November 1836

Dearest Charlie,

I thank you for your wonderful epistle, via Miss Wooler's sister Eliza, at
Rouse Mill. How clever you are to scheme such a delivery, Rouse Mill being in
the parish where Henry is now a curate. Thus did Henry deliver your epistle by
hand. Do not fear that I shall grow cold. There is no chill in the heat of thunder.

I hold your words to my face and I kiss them. You have whispered to me
long ago that Brontë is the Greek word for thunder – we have spoken, often,
have we not, of the great passion of thunder storms, the force of light and beauty
in the over-arching skies. Brontë, used in such a manner, signifies thee and me
– searching for home as does lightning seek its point of earth. Brontë indicates
thee and me – waking in the aftermath of thunder storms, curled around one another in our cottage, warm in the shared morning, listening to the wind beyond
the glass panes, and the falling of refreshing, cooling rain. Soft it is upon our
passionate limbs, this being not likened unto 'cold'.

Have we not spoken so often of metaphor?

Speak to me therefore of thunder, and so shall I comprehend your meaning,

Beyond alphabet, beyond metaphor.

I love you, C. Brontë, more than three words can convey.

E.N.

These are dull days, as the sun drops further behind the afternoon's horizon, and the twilight closes in, silent herald of winter's long nights. Meanwhile there prevails a dank, cold mist around the edges of our lives, resembling a white shroud of fog over a cruel and unfriendly lake. Henry has now begun to voice the abominable doctrines of Calvinism and I stand up to him best I can:

'If I had been a man, maybe I should have studied Theology as you have done, then I would be able to mass my arguments and my counter-arguments and make my points emphatically.'

'Perhaps, little sister, if you had been a man you might have taken Holy Orders as I have done.'

'Don't mock me, Henry. In the first place I've never in my life wished to be other than I am; and secondly, I would not have wished to take Holy Orders. It would not suit me at all, as well you know,' I respond, barely resisting the temptation to chide him that public appearances do not suit him, either. He is not always confident in his curacy, which makes him nervous sometimes, too ill to speak in public. It's a trial to him.

'I do not hold with your focus upon Calvin, because Calvin was a mere mortal. He was not God, nor even a prophet – you are forgetting that God sent us his Son, Our redeemer, Our Shepherd who is *merciful*. I do not believe it right or true that some of us are predestined to go to Hell. We are all sinners and we can all be saved. Not one sincere soul who truly repents will be abandoned by God.'

'You hold to the Lord our Shepherd most strongly then, Nellie.'

'Yes I do. I witness there is enough goodness in this world that I can believe in harmony and love between people. I have received so much kindness and love in my own life even though I am but nineteen years old, enough already to convince me that giving and receiving kindness is the most important thing. Is there not enough fear, despair and sickness in this world already, Henry, without such ideas invoking terror in the hearts and minds of good people?'

Thus leaving him, I storm off, and spend the afternoon reading to Sarah until she falls asleep.

I am sure Ellen you will conclude that I have taken a final leave of my senses, to forget to send your bag— when I had it hanging before my eyes in the dressing-room for a whole week. I stood for ten minutes considering before I sent the boy off   I felt sure I had something else to entrust to him besides the books, but I could not recollect what it was – These aberrations of Memory, warn me pretty intelligibly that I am getting past my prime.

... ...

I wish exceedingly that I could come to see you before Christmas, but it is impossible – however I trust ere another three weeks elapse I shall again have my Comforter beside me, under the roof of my own dear quiet home– If I could always live with you, and daily read the bible with you, if your lips and mine could at the same time, drink the same draught from the same pure fountain of Mercy – I hope, I trust, I might one day become better, far better, than my evil wandering thoughts, my corrupt heart, cold to the spirit, and warm to the flesh will now permit me to be. I often plan the pleasant life which we might lead together, strengthening each other in that power of self-denial, that hallowed and glowing devotion, which the first Saints of God often attained to – My eyes fill with tears when I contrast the bliss of such a state brightened by hopes of the future with the melancholy state I now live in, uncertain that I have ever felt true contrition, wandering in thought and deed, longing for holiness which I shall <u>never</u>, <u>never</u> obtain — smitten at times to the heart with the conviction that your Ghastly Calvinistic doctrines are true— darkened in short by the very shadows of Spiritual Death! If Christian perfection be necessary to Salvation I shall never be saved, my heart is a real hot-bed for sinful thoughts and as to practice   when I decide on an action I scarcely remember to look to my Redeemer for direction.

I know not how to pray – I cannot bend my life to the grand end of doing good   I go on constantly seeking my own pleasure   pursuing the Gratification of my own desires, I forget God and will not God forget me? And meantime I know the Greatness of Jehovah   I acknowledge the truth   the perfection of his word, I adore the purity of the Christian faith, my theory is right, my Practice – horribly wrong.

Good-bye Ellen

C Brontë

Write to me again if you can   your notes are meat and drink to me.
Remember me to the Family I hope Mercy is better

... ...

I wish I could come to Brookroyd for a single night but I don't like to ask Miss Wooler She is at Dewsbury and I'm alone at this moment   eleven o'clock on Tuesday night   I wish you were here   all the house in bed but myself   I'm thinking of you my dearest

Return me a scrap by the Bearer if it be only a single line to satisfy me that you have got your bag safely. I met your brother George on the road this afternoon I did not know it was he until after he was past and then Anne told me – he would think me amazingly stupid in not moving – can't help it

To Mary Taylor, The Red House
Brookroyd, Wednesday, 7 December 1836

Dear Polly,

I am writing because I must meet with you soon and talk – as we used to. I refer to the doctrines of Calvinism, which urge people to prepare for hell in the life to come if they are disobedient or unrighteous in the life being lived.

Charlotte and I are both trying to face our family responsibilities and be good Christians: Charlotte is under pressure to be a faithful, dutiful daughter, by teaching very long hours for the sake of family finance; and I am persuaded that my responsibilities lie in tending the sick at home. The fears generated by the prevalence of Calvinistic ideas prey on Charlotte's mind to such an extent that, in these cloud-ridden mid-winter days, I am sincerely worried about her through all hours of day and night.

The theories themselves seem nowadays to swirl around us, unexpectedly voiced by members of our own churches, and re-appearing via the printed pages in journals, which are being read by my brother, Henry. I am very fortunate, being insulated by my belief in the Gospels as the giving and receiving of love. This belief, to which I now cling with profound gratitude, originated from our early schooling, Polly, shared with your dear self, under the tuition of the Moravians, for whom salvation is a kindly, welcoming event, available to all sinners. I feel under no obligation to believe the premise that we are born either 'one of the elect to be saved' or 'one of the reprobates forthwith to be damned'. I think of Mary Magdalene at the foot of the cross, and of all the sinners saved by our Lord, and I pray for strength to resist the Calvinists, and openly to disagree with them and their vengeance on the world.

I can – usually – take my mind off Calvinism – because I have much to distract me – I enjoy the daily round of housekeeping and gardening, with its reliability and stability. Brookroyd is a busy, sociable household – my days are filled with people, despite the tedium of too many hours at Sarah's bedside. Meanwhile, Charlotte is not so fortunate – these ideas are, in her present circumstances, most troublesome to her – so, my dear and reliable friend, I must discuss further these appalling doctrines – you may remind me of all we ever learned, and more, please, Polly!

Write to me soon, very soon, to make an arrangement for a visit.

Remember me to Martha and all the family.

Your affectionate friend,

Ellen.

Brookroyd, 9 December 1836

My dearest Charlotte,

This was to be a short note to inform you that the bag arrived safely. However your letter gave witness to deep distress, and, unable to hold you, touch you, I hasten to provide comfort by the power of my pen.

We all like to talk in my family, which is also what I love about your household when we are together in Haworth: the fire in the great range in the kitchen, steam issuing from the spout of a huge copper kettle suspended above the grate; linen airing and dough rising; Tabby fussing about and the scullery girls popping and out from the back. By late evening, we're in your dining room, walking – round and round as taught by Miss Wooler. There can we discuss – anything – everything – and push easily away the awful doctrines of punishment and retribution – but it is so much harder for you when isolated, worn down by tutoring. Then the ghastly dank damp spectre of Calvinism hovers in the shadows, attacking your weary self, thus angering me on your behalf.

When in your letter, I read the phrase 'your' Calvinistic Doctrines, I take it that you mean 'people generally' not 'mine' – you already know they are not 'mine'. Polly and I learned about the love of God from the Moravian missionaries in our first school. You shall be reassured when next we meet, that I continue to reject all Calvin's doctrines, and I shall continue so for the rest of my life.

Remember dearest, you are one of the flock, and the Good Shepherd will never desert you. If you wander away from Him, your spirit anguished, thus embarking upon a lonely road, or entering a desolate valley, he will find you, reach with His crook and rescue you, return you to His fold. Charlotte, I should remind you, in these cold dark winter days, when you toil long hours for little remuneration, to think again of our warmth, our friendship, and the loving fireside to which, in only one week's time, you shall return. Take good comfort that you are loved by many people and always by our merciful Father.

In my letters to you, and in your writing, my beloved friend, we adhere, both of us, to the old maxim that *the pen is mightier than the sword.* Thus, wielding the only weapon at my disposal, I shall always write to you, I shall never forsake you, I shall always be your genteel Amazon who wages war upon the isolation and hopeless tedium of the employment that you so valiantly endure. When you are sad, lonely, exhausted or unwell, you need glimpses of beauty, peace, love and warmth. Here are my glimpses of such love, for you, because I am and shall be always,

Your devoted and affectionate friend,
Ellen

Roe Head, January 1837

My dear, dear Ellen,

I am at this moment trembling all over with excitement after reading your note, it is what I never received before – it is the unrestrained pouring out of a warm, gentle, generous heart, it contains sentiments unstained by human motives, prompted by the pure God himself, it expresses a noble sympathy which I do not, cannot deserve. Ellen, Religion has indeed elevated your character. I thank you with energy for this kindness. I will no longer shrink from answering your questions. I do wish to be better than I am. I pray fervently sometimes to be made so.

... ... I may be in utter midnight, but I implore a Merciful Redeemer that if this be the real dawn of the Gospel it may still brighten to perfect day. ... ...

... ... This very night I will pray as you wish me. May the Almighty, hear me compassionately! and I humbly trust he will – for you will strengthen my polluted petitions with your own pure requests. All is bustle and confusion round me, the ladies pressing with their sums and their lessons.

... ... If you love me do do do come on Friday, I shall watch and wait for you, and if you disappoint me I shall weep. I wish you could know the thrill of delight which I experienced, when as I stood at the dining-room window I saw your brother (George) as he whirled past, (on the way to Huddersfield market*) toss your little packet over the wall. I dare write no more, I am neglecting my duty. Love to your mother and both your sisters. Thank you again a thousand times for your kindness – farewell my blessed Ellen.*

Charlotte.

My dearest Charlotte,

I treasure every word of your letters, as if they're fragments of conversations, glimpses of the ways in which we love and speak when we're together. I keep each one carefully wrapped in its own envelope in a wooden box. I went with Richard once to the papermaker in Leeds – one of the most fascinating visits of childhood. The man was tall, robust, hearty of complexion, with a white beard like Père Noël. He took a liking to me, led me by hand, showing his recipe and his own integral mark, the 'water' mark, with which same mark is made each matching envelope. Now my brothers come from journeys with gifts of paper, tease me, la petite écrivaine.

When we are separated I yearn for safety, nay protection. In lonely moments, just before bedtime, I open my box and take out a letter. Hold it, turning the envelope over, reading again *Miss Ellen Nussey*, in your hand. Trace it, with fingertips, the shapes and shadings on the watermarks. Stroke it, soft against my lips, the texture and quality of the paper. I unfold the letter paper, again read your words therein, very slowly. You may think me a romantic fool but those are precious, private moments – like unto meditation – bringing my beloved to me. At ten o'clock I commence my prayers, again to experience connection beyond miles, through our mutual promise of simultaneous communication with God. Then on reflection, I affirm that Religion is the mainstay of our lives, giving shape, purpose and meaning. Religion makes sense of the world around us. Without God we are nothing, mere specks of dust in the history of the earth.

I desire my whole life to be about Religion. In my house and yours, do not we live and breathe it? Do not we imbibe it for breakfast, lunch and dinner; stir it into our jam pots, spoon it with our porridge, knead it into bread dough, cleanse it with each gallon of water used? Is not Religion our moisture? For it gives life, flows within us, without us, all around us, above and below us. To understand our love for one another must we not comprehend the significance of Religion?

You are a gift from God. I believe that God planned my conception and birth to manifest a year less a day later. It is my destiny therefore to be yours. I cannot imagine my life either without God or without you.

As to our letters, habitually do I now make drafts of mine, keeping copies to help develop my ideas. Very much enjoyment do I derive from committing my thoughts and my feelings to paper. Meanwhile, I have composed little names for our letters so that I remain clear as to their order, number and sequence. I read them, at night, as if they're a book – which they are, in a way. Therefore do I name your latest as my *trembling* letter! So beautiful are your words therein.

Tremble do I also, with thought of you,

Your loving, affectionate friend,

Nell

Brookroyd, 10 February 1837

My Dearest C. B., my dear one,

On all the farms around us the first lambs of the year can be heard bleating across the valleys. According to your papa, the Irish call this time of year Imbolc – the feast of Saint Bridget – which coincides with the commencement of the lactating of the ewes. My family attended church as usual to celebrate Candlemas, and although the weather's bitterly cold there can be heard, at last, the familiar drip, drip of melting snow. The sound is music to my ears because it is herald of the end of winter. Slowly the dark forms of our trees emerge from the frosty shapes and ghostly outlines to which we have become accustomed. I am working a new lace collar as a gift for you – and anticipate with pleasure my imminent visit to Roe Head – I will write with details as soon as the gig can be arranged.

Your loving and affectionate friend,

Nell

Brookroyd, 16 February 1837

I have just this morning received a letter from my brother John in Cleveland Row. Dearest, I do not want to make you unhappy – which I fear will be the outcome of this letter – but my presence is requested urgently to help with the older children, because John's wife is expecting their next baby. I am, of course, very fond of my brother and I love looking after the children, but the timing is more than a little inconvenient because you and I so need to be near to one another this spring.

It is ironic, is it not, that if I were openly wearing your diamond ring and if we were publicly planning our futures – searching for our cottage – then my reluctance to leave would be fully understood at Brookroyd. Indeed I doubt that anyone might dare to stand in our way. However, my wishes are not to be taken seriously by my family; and indeed are so unspoken that no one has the slightest notion why I might be put out by this familial request. My dearest one, write to me as soon as you can. I am, as always, your very own dear Ellen. My feelings for you are true and equal in all ways to yours for me.

Yours sadly, and very affectionately,

Nell

Journal

Brookroyd , 21 February 1837

Charlotte's reply, written in distress on 20th February, arrives with barely any time to spare before my departure. I run with it upstairs to my room, for I cannot go outside because the winter's day is bright and cold, so I sit by my window letting the wintry sunshine fall on me as I open the seal. As I read her words, I weep. I feel her dismay at our separation and in my heart I experience once again a keen sensation of the loss of her.

Roe Head, 20 February 1837

I read your letter with dismay, Ellen, what shall I do without you? How long are we likely to be separated? why are we so to be denied each other's society. It is an inscrutable fatality. I long to be with you because it seems as if two or three days or weeks spent in your company would beyond measure strengthen me in the enjoyment of those feelings which I have so lately begun to cherish. You first pointed out to me that way in which I am so feebly endeavouring to travel, and now I cannot keep you by my side, I must proceed sorrowfully alone.

Why are we to be divided? Surely, Ellen, it must be because we are in danger of loving each other too well; of losing sight of the <u>Creator</u> in idolatry of the <u>creature.</u>

... ... I must see you before you go, Ellen; if you cannot come to Roe Head I will contrive to walk over to Brookroyd, provided you will let me know the time of your departure. Should you not be at home at Easter I dare not promise to accept your mother's and sisters' kind invitation. I should be miserable at Brookroyd without you, yet I would contrive to visit them for a few hours if I could not for a few days. I love them for your sake. I have written this note at a venture. When it will reach you I know not, but I was determined not to let slip

an opportunity for want of being prepared to embrace it. Farewell, may God bestow on you all His blessings. My darling–Farewell. Perhaps you may return before midsummer, do you think you possibly can. I wish your brother John knew how unhappy I am; he would almost pity me.

    C. Brontë.

4 Cleveland Row, 4 March 1837

Dearest C.B.,

My brother John, and his wife Mary, tried several times for another boy so that the name of John Nussey might be yet more fruitful down the generations – great celebrations pervade their London home. I love my small nieces and the new baby boy, John Thomas Hartley, is a delight.

Nevertheless, I had not wanted to leave Brookroyd, only four miles from your work place, and somewhere in dim recesses of my brain there abides a niggling enquiry, a cobweb in a dusty attic's cornice. It persists, fragile, flimsy, floating beyond reach, being tantalisingly tenacious. However hard I attempt to brush it away, it refuses to depart: have Mama and my sister Mercy begun to recognise what you and I truly mean to one another? – and have they conspired to separate us, in the hope that several months without our seeing one another might dull the spark between us?

Time passes – I witness the changing foliage in the great parks around Cleveland Row. There are times when I long for the wide-open moors and huge skies around the parsonage. I dream of days out with 'the Quartette' – you, Emily, Anne and myself. What would I not give for a prolonged visit to Haworth, with the sight of you, my dearest Charlotte, and the sound of your voice.

Write to me soon,

Your devoted and affectionate friend,

E.N.

Journal
4 Cleveland Row, 12 March 1837

John is a good man, whom I have always trusted, and I approach him early in my London sojourn: 'I have a small favour to ask of you,' I say, smiling, aware that I have always been his baby sister, his favourite. 'I am worried about my friend, Charlotte. She is not contented at Roe Head school where she tutors dull girls for Miss Wooler. I desire to provide some comfort, especially as we were unable to meet at Christmas – we were so very disappointed. You know that their servant Tabby fell on the ice, do you remember?'

'Yes, of course I remember, Nellie. I was glad to hear that the Reverend Brontë could call upon the services of a local apothecary. I trust that Tabitha's leg is mending very well?'

'Yes, it is, thank you, John. Would it be reasonable for me to write often to Charlotte – by the post, I mean?' (I then smile warmly at him, because paper and ink are expensive and I have no money of my own. He shall also have to pay postage on receipt of Charlotte's replies.) 'I would like to write some of my long letters full of the news of London.'

'Of course you may write by the post, my dear Nellie. Charlotte is most fortunate to have a good friend and correspondent such as you. Yes, Nellie, you shall write to her as often as you wish. It is the least I can do after all your kindness to Mary and the children. What would they do without you? Little Georgiana seems to think you make the sun shine *every* day *especially* for her.'

We're laughing now: 'You're very generous. I shall write this evening, after supper.' I fling my arms around him – as always I have done.

4 Cleveland Row, 12 March 1837

Dearest C.B., my dear one,

It is truly springtime and the trees in the park are in early bud. The narcissi are nodding star-like, white with joyful yellow centres. We stroll with the perambulators and take the children to feed the ducks and admire the swathes of crocuses. This is a beautiful city – one cannot deny it – I have been to St Paul's Cathedral to hear the choirs and even to Westminster Abbey. The latter is very grand but I long for home. It does not impress me here because the society here is false. I would give all these trees in new leaf if I could see the laughing faces in your kitchen in Haworth.

At first I was disturbed, truly unsettled, homesick for Yorkshire, but I am calmer now, although I miss the wide-open moors and huge skies. I recall your descriptive powers and your eyes filling with tears when you speak of the moors clad with bright gorse and all the spring flowers. I miss the bleat of lambs on the hillsides, and the sound of horses galloping over the hard tracks. These tame London riders trot sedately, all airs and graces – I do not respect them.

I have spent so many cheerful visits at Haworth, where we may walk from the back door directly into the countryside! Here my lungs are filled with city dust. You must not think me unaware of the mills nor palls of smoke that hang in our industrial hollows. I don't forget such things – our countryside is a hard-working place, upon which is built the wealth of our nation. But even the poorest mill-hand may oft-times marvel at sunsets over the Pennines.

I believe there is no greater beauty on earth than the paths from your home – imbued with the laughter of my friends, your sisters, and the delight with which we witness sunshine on the falling waters when the snow melts and the streams are tumbling down the cliffs. I miss you and I miss my home. My dreams of our 'honeysuckle cottage' fade onto some distant horizon and I despair they mayn't manifest for us. No one here knows of this. How could it be otherwise?

My friends in Cleveland Row are generous, kind and warm-hearted. My brother married wisely and I am fond of my sister-in-law. Their children are lively – I love to watch them grow. John asks, 'Would you like to marry and raise a family of your own, Nellie?' I reply, 'I'm not ready, John. I haven't given it much thought.' That's a lie, for of course I have done nothing for years but talk with you and Mary about our futures. Are there not enough children in my family? I do not want endless confinements like all the married women around me. I want to live with you, peacefully, harmoniously. I do not need a child to complete me. I need you. I ask, 'How long am I needed here to help with the children? Could I perhaps return home by midsummer?'

Oh Charlie, what are we to do? How are we to be? I treasure your letters with the greatest of care but I wonder, would it not perhaps be wisest not to keep these new ones, for are they not more revealing than we had intended? But I could not destroy a single word in your handwriting. So there you have it.

Every night, at ten o'clock, I open my Bible at random, in search of guidance. I cherish the Biblical women who travelled far from home, and encouraged by you, I try to imagine how they endured separations from their nearest and dearest.

I am not changed by London. I am changed by loving you. I try to stay calm for your sake. I try to imagine heather-clad moors, windswept hills, not too high, rounded in the sunshine, with calm, cool shadows made by passing wisps of cloud, or peaceful places by quiet streams.

We cannot return to our schooldays. They are long gone. We must proceed to our roles as adult women. You have instilled into me the sense of duty for which I so admire you, nevertheless, your question accompanies me into the lonely hours after midnight: *'Why are we to be divided?'* I do not think I love you more than my Creator. Truly I do not elevate you nor commit sacrilege in such a thought – but the truth is I love God *and* I love you. I desire to be the housekeeper at the heart of my household, with you at its centre, by its hearth. I shall end this now because it is very late. May God hold you in His care this night, my dear one.

Your loving and intimate friend,

E.N.

4 Cleveland Row, 17 May 1837

Dearest Charlie,

I shall try to describe for you our most most spectacular day out – into the green woods of Epping Forest. Come with me – the blue light bedazzles us – leaping and dancing upwards from thousands of Bluebells. There is such light loveliness – never seen 'til now near to London – and it fills my soul.

Your latest letter fills me with gladness. It is warm and loving. I sleep with it under my pillow and read it many times over. Truly I should keep it in the icehouse of my brother's friends near Epping. But I shall not part with it – nor leave it where curious eyes might spy it.

My brother's friends own some shipyards near Tilbury and vast lands around Epping. We see a herd of deer – such graceful creatures. The streams in the forest invoke memories of you, your sisters and Branwell at Bolton Abbey. I am so sorry to hear of his continued 'illness.' It is disheartening. It saddens me that you have lost your closeness with him and your shared ventures into fiction. How could he so betray you? I'm certain, my dear Charlotte, that Branwell intends neither to inflict hurt nor to re-create The Strid of wild water between him and his sisters. Yet does his descent from decency hurt all, especially you, my dearest. It's confusing, bewildering, affecting everyone in turn. I send to you all my love, my very kindest warmest thoughts.

Your devoted and affectionate friend,

Nell

4 Cleveland Row, 20 May 1837

Dearest Charlotte,

Since our return from Epping there commences a family discussion about the health of King William, because rumours are spreading through the capital, spiralling with gossip and tittle-tattle. It's being suggested that King William's health has so deteriorated that he may not live one more month. The throne will pass to the Princess Victoria, who is but one year younger than I am. However the Hanoverians on the continent cannot allow succession through the female line, so there will be a divergence of thrones after King William dies.

As an apothecary to the Royal household, my brother has to stay in London for the foreseeable future – I'm unlikely therefore to be home by mid-summer – I hope perhaps for July. John and Mary intend to travel north to place young Edward in school, but they are unable to arrange firm dates until the Royal household gives leave – I will write to you as soon as I know… I must hurry now for the post. I send you all my love and to your sisters, your papa and Aunt Elizabeth when you write to them.

I am truly yours,

Your loving and intimate friend,

Nell

Roe Head, 8 June 1837

My dearest Ellen

The enclosed as you will perceive was written before I received your last – I had intended to send it by this but what you said altered my intention

I scarce dare build a hope upon the foundation your letter lays – we have been disappointed so often – and I fear I shall not be able to prevail on them to part with you but I will try my utmost and at any rate there is a chance of our meeting soon   with that thought I will comfort myself

You do not know how selfishly glad I am that you still continue to dislike London and the Londoners – it seems to afford a sort of proof that your affections are not changed – Shall we really stand once again together on the Moors of Haworth? I dare *not flatter myself with too sanguine an expectation   I see many doubts and difficulties – But with Miss Wooler's leave which I have asked and in part obtained I will go to-morrow to try to remove them –*

Give my love to my sweet little correspondent Georgiana and believe me my own Ellen

Yours always and truly

C Brontë

Dearest Charlie, my very own Charles Thunder,

Well, we missed midsummer, didn't we? What a strange, eventful year of our Lord. Early on the morning of June 20th King William died and Princess Victoria was informed that she would accede to the throne.

All who are connected with the Royal Household have been preparing for the funeral of the King. There is a rumour that the Coronation of Victoria will not occur until a year of mourning has ensued. John is now well established in Royal circles as an Apothecary and, when King George was alive, John was Apothecary to the person, which meant he attended the monarch personally. However when King George died in 1830, my brother played a somewhat lesser role in the Royal household. His financial situation was, even so, quite secure, so that it was possible to purchase Rydings, as you know. [My sister, Ann, writes that she has been happy to stay with the Walker family and hopes to continue there for some years.] Amidst much speculation, through which John has tried to be optimistic, I can now confirm that good fortune attends the Nussey family in London, because my brother has been re-appointed to his original position. I am amazed to think that the new Queen is a younger woman even than you or I. King William has not been respected here – his Royal uncles brought ridicule and scorn on the institution of the monarchy itself. Now everyone is expressing the hope that the enthronement of a young Queen will initiate a new period of expansion for Britain, her industries and commerce, her place in the world.

I write with all this news to you my dearest and with much love and longing myself. You acceded to the throne of my heart a long time ago… I am very excited at my impending homecoming, provisionally set for two to three weeks from now. There will be time for us together at Haworth before your return to Roe Head. I'm all packed far ahead of time. I have many books to talk of with you. Also, I have learned new pieces on my brother's pianoforte. I hope sincerely that I may persuade Emily to play – but she's perhaps too private in her musical accomplishments for such an opportunity to arise. I read your enclosed letter with much sympathy, excitement and interest. I have already purchased Leigh Richmond's Domestic Portraiture, which I shall begin immediately.

Take heart, my dearest , there's no need to *get over the next half year without hope of seeing me'* – Soon, Soon.

Yours and always truly,

Your loving and intimate friend,

Nell

It is a slow, re-establishing time, my autumn of calm quietness and gladness. My longings are over and I'm home again. I allow time for prayer and thanksgiving – that the land around me is beautiful and that it is not London.

It's now my custom to walk from Brookroyd to Roe Head every Saturday; now that my routines are established there's little need for letters between myself and Charlotte. Week by week my walks are solitary, reflective and important because I feel, spiritually, that I need to touch the earth. Charlotte says that in this respect I remind her of Emily, not in my ways of expressing myself, nor in my idiosyncrasies, in which we're not at all alike, but in my love of the native earth, of all things growing therein. Once again the lanes are changing, settling down for our long winter's season in the north.

Journal
Brookroyd, 21 October 1837

A beautiful Saturday, just before All Souls, I take my country notebook and record almost twenty varieties of fruit and berries along my route. Crab apples are visible over the wall of a neglected orchard; they're followed by black bryony, dogwood, and guelder roses with bright hips. Beech trees bearing hairy, hard cases around beech-nuts are laced with alder and hazel. Rowan berries compete for colour with the berries of wild honeysuckle and the dark indigo of mulberries, which fringe the edge of a field, protected by dry stone walls. Sloe berries are deep blue-black fluffed with Old Man's Beard. Wild Honesty rattles with purple and parchment-white seed heads. Elderberries have been garnered from all but the highest branches and as I look up they become clusters of small black marbles against a wild blue autumnal sky.

Passing by a churchyard, I notice that yew trees are once again in berry – the fruits are enjoyed by birds although the leaves and branches are deadly poisonous. Holly and ivy bear abundant fruits, turning from green to red and black.

Walking on towards the school and recalling our girlhood when we'd met at Roe Head, I collect a bouquet for Anne, who likes to draw and paint. Horse chestnuts complete my garland, so I arrive with my arms full of green, gold and russet leaves, with scarlet, blue and crimson berries. Anne thanks me profusely for the wild flowers, with which she's delighted, but our meeting is foreshort-ened because she has stomach cramps and must retire to her room.

Charlotte has consulted with Miss Wooler about Anne's ill health.

'Miss Wooler is unconcerned. She tells me it's Anne's time of the month – as if I knew not already – and I must not over protect her. But how can I help it? Tell me that?'

I recall the decline into ill-health of Emily, the previous autumn. I dare not mention this to Charlotte lest I precipitate a panic.

'Perhaps a day or two in bed will bring a speedy recovery,' I venture, at a loss for words to express my concern at the flush in Anne's cheekbones and the slight aura of fever.

'Oh indeed I hope so, Nell. And your bouquet is beautiful and it will gladden Anne's soul and lift her spirits. When last you brought wild flowers she was engrossed in her watercolours and drawings for days after.'

'She will be so again, I'm certain.'

I don't like lying to Charlotte, who seems comforted. Linking her arm in mine, she leads me around the grounds of Roe Head, recalling the stanzas of Keats' Ode To Autumn. I like to recite poetry to my family in private soirées but no longer attempt so with Charlotte, who considers me un-aware of metre and meaning, which is untrue. Charlotte and her sisters have adopted a superior disdain but I am by now accustomed to such attitudes, therefore am I no longer discouraged by the cutting tone of Charlotte's personal observations. On this warm autumn day, I listen with pleasure as we walk under the old elms resplend-ent in their late October foliage.

'Where are the songs of Spring? Ay, where are they?
Think not of them, thou hast thy music too –
While barred clouds bloom the soft-dying day
And touch the stubble plains with rosy hue;
Then in a wailful choir the small gnats mourn
Among the river sallows, borne aloft
Or sinking as the light wind lives or dies;
And full-grown lambs bleat loud from hilly bourn;
Hedge crickets sing, and with treble soft
The redbreast whistles from a garden croft;
And gathering swallows twitter in the skies.'

Journal

Brookroyd, 12 November 1837

The halcyon days of October do not fulfil their promise. The year, begun with disappointment, turns once more sour upon us, as if cider apples, newly harvested, are lain in error in a barrel of vinegar. Rainy weather persistently prevents my beautiful walks. I again resort to communication by letter, which my brother George delivers as he passes by the gates of Roe Head, en-route to Huddersfield.

Journal

Brookroyd, 4 December 1837

Dense fog un-pleats itself like fabric through the valleys, obliterating the sky-line, casting grey gloom around us, then turns to excessive rain which causes serious floods. Just when I most need them, my replies from Charlotte fail to arrive. I am confused and disturbed.

Brookroyd, 18 December 1837

Dearest Charlotte,

I am writing because I am anxious for Anne's health. I durst not create panic when last I was with you, so did not speak my fears. However, last night, after my prayers, there comes to me, as sleep approaches, an image of my bright autumnal bouquet for Anne, with its green and russet leaves, vermillion and scarlet berries.

I fall into a deep sleep in which I feel Anne's presence, and see her face hovering in front of me. I dream that she's lost somewhere in the fog. Whichever way she turns, on the moors, she can detect no lantern; she wanders without landmark. Eventually she finds shelter under an overhanging rock, where she crouches, cold, pale and ill.

Therefore do I hasten to write, in the early light of morning, trusting my intuition, desiring to enquire after Anne's well-being.

Write to me soon. I send my love to you, as always,

Your very own Nell.

Waiting for a reply, I ask myself whether my dream has deeper significance. Is it not Charlotte herself who teaches that dreams are the night's fulfilment of the day's restless imagination? Does she not sometimes read aloud from her day's writing immediately preceding sleep? By so doing, she discovers that her brain works the night shift, while she sleeps, thus providing her with new people, events, or a fresh twist of plot the next day. More often, Charlotte does not speak of her writings. Usually she's private, keeps them close to her heart. I'm accustomed to a similar total closure from Emily, since our first encounter, even though she's loving towards me, walking with me, making bread together as dear friends – Emily's the most private of all the sisters. Over the years, I learn to accept this closure from Charlotte. If I should dare intrude into Charlotte's personal world I'd run risk of its door slamming. Charlotte is quite capable of closing such a door upon me. She could slam it in my face! Besides, Mama says, 'Even if people have their curtains open, it is very rude to look through someone else's windows.' Perhaps all the Brontë children copy this naturally from their papa. I observe him depart for his own room at night after family prayers. He may read silently behind his closed door, or perhaps write letters or poetry, or perhaps he may pray. I know not. At any rate, it's private and symbolic – a salutary reminder that, for all the family, intrusion is the worst impertinence a friend might perform. It will not be tolerated and this is unlikely ever to change. Usually I dare not risk being frozen out, and therefore I remain determined not to intrude.

I hope and pray that my letter is well received. My dream forced me to write. Perhaps I am foolish to despatch it.

Haworth, 22 December 1837

Dearest Ellen,

My kind friend, thank you for your solicitous note. We are home because Anne is ill. I cannot invite you to Haworth for Christmas – it is impossible until I know that Anne will make a full recovery. I will tell you all my reasons and my news when I next write – expect a letter from me early in the New Year. My love to your family and Christmas Blessings.

Yours always and truly

C. Brontë.

'Scuse the scribble. I trust you are well and not suffering from floods. I heard that three people died in Bradford. The fog seems endless – bitterly cold here. The valleys are frozen solid. How is it at Brookroyd? C.B.

Brookroyd, Christmas, 1837

Dearest Charlotte,

I am very sad to hear that Anne is ill and I send my warmest wishes for her recovery to full health. I miss all of you, very much – please remember me most kindly to everyone in the parsonage. We are well, except for poor Sarah – we have had no flooding hereabouts – but freezing rain then, overnight, heavy snow, falling on frozen ground. I shall paint a picture for you, as best I can –whilst I send Christmas wishes from my home to yours. Brookroyd is a fairy-tale place this year. Drifting snow smoothly swathes our lawns and transforms the conifers into a winter scene of great beauty. Icicles hang from the eaves; the gateposts are snow-capped, and our ornamental trees compete with each other to resemble white Nottingham lace. Sarah says wistfully that the garden imitates a sumptuous gown, fit for a wealthy bride in finest silks and satins. The ice-bound fountain in the circular, frozen pond resembles a three-tiered wedding cake, with silver decorations.

After dusk, the house shines like a lantern, calling us inside to bright fires in every room. Then we gather in front of the parlour hearth, with several long extending toasting forks. Saffron cake is our seasonal rarity, which Mama bakes only at mid-winter because of the cost of saffron, delicious when toasted like fruity slices of bread, thick cut, hot, laden with fresh butter.

Each day, Mama and I browse the shelves of the still room, handling the bottles and testing them against the light, replacing them, picking and choosing through a vast array of pickles and preserves to accompany our festive meals. Mama, Mercy and I are kept busy in the kitchen, making marzipan confectionery, mulled wine, spiced cider, chestnut stuffing, roast gammon in oatmeal, pea soup with bacon and herbs, buttered eggs with smoked salmon and other seasonal delicacies.

By way of thanks for our efforts, my brothers carve a wooden bird table with a sloping roof so that my robin redbreast, who's called Dicky, feeds safely with the many blue tits who belong around Brookroyd. Sarah is unwell again and now rests upstairs most days, so we set her chair by an upstairs window, and we hang curls of bacon rind and strings of nuts on the bird table. We can hear her laughing at the antics of the winged acrobats as we approach along the landing to her room.

65

Throughout our neighbourhood, the parish poor are set to clearing the snow-packed roads in return for soup. They take several days working dawn to dusk, before our lanes are freed and my sister Ann can be fetched home from Rydings. Despite the relatively short journey by carriage, she arrives chilled to the bone, solid, shaped like a chair, with an appearance so amusing that, amidst much laughter at her plight, she's lifted into the house by George and Joseph, who set her down to thaw out by the drawing room fire.

'You must keep her feet from that heat,' admonishes Mama, 'lest you give her chilblains. Do you hear me, Ellen?'

'I hear you, Mama, but she's frozen.'

'Mama, don't fret so,' says Ann, 'I'd rather have chilblains than frostbite. Nellie knows what she's doing.'

We're a merry bunch at home this Christmas. Joseph's still living here, working in our family's manufacturing business. George travels to and from the cloth market in Huddersfield – being next in age to me, we're particularly fond. Henry's five years my senior and, having graduated in the summer of 1835, he's now curate with the Rev Heald in Birstall. I'm delighted he's home with us but concerned about him because he's so unsuited to his chosen profession. He has a fine tenor voice and I accompany him, on the pianoforte, when we entertain the family in the evenings. He never finds so relaxing an audience beyond these walls – public speaking continues to be his cross to bear, Henry's personal tragedy. When he sings for our family his love of music and poetry flows unobstructed through his fine pure voice, bringing tears to our mother's eyes.

Our household's completed this year by Mercy, Ann and Sarah. No one guesses that my festivities are lacking in any way. I miss you and your sisters most dreadfully. We worship separately – you in Haworth, myself in Birstall. We live separately; we wake each morning and sleep each night, separately. The organ music rings from our church and I love my family and my home so I sing with everyone else. But I cannot sing with all my heart. Part of my heart is missing.

My heartiest greetings to you all, especially to Anne for her recovery,

Your loving and devoted friend

Nell

Journal

Brookroyd, 6 January 1838

At last there arrives the promised letter, written on January 4th, explaining that, during Anne's illness at Roe Head, Charlotte has quarrelled most righteously with Miss Wooler, because the latter has appeared unconcerned for Anne's welfare. Charlotte formed a firm resolution to leave Roe Head and Miss Wooler for ever, but has reconsidered and relented after much persuasion from Miss Wooler.

Haworth, 4 January 1838

Your letter Ellen was a welcome surprise even though it contained something like a reprimand – I had not however forgotten our agreement – I had prepared a note to be forthcoming against the arrival of Your Messenger – But things so happened that it was of no avail – You were right in your conjectures respecting the cause of my sudden departure – Anne continued – wretchedly ill – neither the pain nor the difficulty of breathing left her – and how could I feel otherwise than very miserable? I looked upon her case in a different light to what I could wish or expect any uninterested person to view it in – Miss Wooler thought me a fool –and by way of proving her opinion treated me with marked coldness – we came to a little eclairsissement one evening– I told her one or two rather plain truths–which set her a crying – and the next day unknown to me she wrote to Papa – telling him that I had reproached her– bitterly –taken her severely to task &c. &c. –Papa sent for us the day after he had received her letter–

... ...

I was in a regular passion my "<u>warm</u> <u>temper</u>" quite got the better of me – Of which I don't boast for it was a weakness – nor am I ashamed of it for I had reason to be angry – Anne is now much better – though she still requires a great deal of care – however I am relieved from my worst fears respecting her–

... ...

It will want three weeks next Monday to the termination of the holidays— Come to see me my <u>dear</u> Ellen as soon as you can – however bitterly I sometimes feel towards other people – the recollection of your mild steady friendship consoles and softens me – I am glad you are not such a passionate fool as myself – Give my best love to your Mother and sisters, excuse the most hideous scrawl that ever was penned – and believe me

Always tenderly

I reply immediately, run upstairs to pack my clothes, and set off next morning on the seventeen-mile journey through a white landscape. On reaching Haworth, we pause by a bridge below the village, where sacking is obtained, which is tied around the horses' feet. More sacks are lain across the cobbles at intervals up the treacherous incline to the Church, so that the horses neither skid nor plummet back down hill, their carriages and contents hurtling, willy-nilly, to the valley below.

Eventually, I arrive, to be greeted warmly by Aunt Elizabeth, Charlotte and her sisters. Anne is much recovered, with new colour in her cheeks. Emily is in excellent health, and Charlotte's plump, relaxed and happy. Surrounded by my friends and the pervasive smell of new bread from the kitchen, I commence a most contented fortnight's visit at the parsonage.

Each day I spend some time with Anne, reading to her and talking a little, though I don't want to tire her. Although her illness has been gastric in origin, it has affected her entire physique, bringing her, as she puts it, to the edge of the valley of the shadow of death. On becoming extremely fearful and low in spirit at Roe Head, she asks for the Bishop of the Moravian Church to attend her. I remind her that, when I was very young I received my early lessons at the Moravian school with Mary Taylor. I experienced very happy times there. It's a kind and gentle place, from which I have retained a deep respect for the Moravians, and their beliefs. They are dedicated missionaries, having emigrated from Europe to England, where they've founded a church at Mirfield, which is opposed entirely to Calvinistic doctrine and practice.

During Anne's illness at Roe Head, James la Trobe visits her on several occasions, bringing comfort and release from inner turmoil. He is an inspiring, generous person, who reassures her that indeed all sinners who repent may be confident of salvation, pardon and peace in the Blood of Christ.

In the parsonage, after supper, we girls persuade Aunt Branwell to reminisce about her girl-hood in Penzance. For us she describes the house in Chapel Street and the Wesleyan Chapel with its huge portico façade, of which the Penzance Wesleyans are extremely proud. Chapel Street leads up into the town from the parish church of St. Mary, which stands proud against the southerly gales on the 'holy' headland, from which Penance takes its name.

'Mary is the Star of the Sea, from the Latin name, mare.' She pronounces it mar-ray. 'Your mama was named after her, bless her dear heart. She was a bonny maid. She was, so, me 'andsomes.'

From the flat courtyard of St. Mary's, the Branwells can look south to the busy fishing village of Newlyn, but from the end of their street itself, winding stone steps lead down, as steep as any Yorkshire ginnel, to the harbour and quay-side where sailing ships are moored. From thence people and cargoes depart to the Isles of Scilly. In the town itself, up the street past the Old Turk's Head, are new coffee shops where men catch up on the latest shipping news and read the newspapers; and a newly formed Ladies' Club attracts many social activities. To Aunt Branwell, Penzance seems a safe and prosperous town, there at the end of the land. Barely can I imagine the distance of the journey north, the numerous changes of coaches and horses, with overnight stays at the inns en route. There's a causeway in the bay, to the east of the town, across which people walk at low tide to an island named St. Michael's Mount. There, overlooking the full circle of the surrounding countryside, above the wide shallow sweep of the bay, stands a romantic stone building with medieval stained glass windows, which was once a monastery. It's now inhabited by the St. Levens, one of the county's most prestigious families. At high tide the mount is cut off and in winter people are marooned for days on end. Storms batter the low tides across the entirety of their causeway, making return by foot impossible – and it's too dangerous by boat.

We listen, enthralled, while Aunt Branwell tells tales this winter – and I realise that not only from her father's library is Charlotte's imagination being fed. This Cornish aunt has vivid powers of story-telling and she knows some wonderful legends.

'My maids, I cannot be telling you the tales tonight for I am tired. I am old...'

'Please, Aunt, please.'

She sighs dramatically, but we know we've prevailed when she smoothes her skirts and looks into the fire. 'Maybe just the one...'

We wait, silently, hopefully...

'I will tell you of the building of that causeway, but I shall have but this one tale this night, mind, because I'm for my bed.

'There were, in the times before time, in the old days, two giants, a husband and wife whose names are known. Cormoran and Cornelian. Their work it was to carry white stone to build St. Michael's Mount.

'This they had to fetch an extremely long distance, for the mount was originally not built of white stone, not at all. The mount is called carreg-luz-en-kiz, which, in the Cornish language, means the white-rock-in-the-wood. Now, m'dears, the wood refers to the days long gone, when the whole of Mount's Bay was an enormous forest.

'There was another giant also, Cormoran's friend, who lived on Trecobben Hill.'

'What was his name, Aunt?'

'No name. His name is not known. He is known only as the giant of Trecobben Hill. It is not known why. Just the giant of Trecobben Hill. All three giants threw stones and boulders about the place for it was their work to shape and reshape the land. Sometimes they sculpted the rocks with a giant hammer, but they had only one hammer between them, thus did they have to toss the one hammer from hill to hill.

'However, they were not always best friends. Like all friends they argued from time to time and, on rare occasions, overcome with their own strength, they threw the hammer at one another. On one almost fatal occasion it hit Cornelian on her head.

'Nevertheless she did not die and from that time they strove to take more care in the direction in which they threw the hammer.

'Now time was and time was not, that Cormoran was not always gentle in his manner. He was no gentleman. Nor was he gentle in his domestic manner. Then did a situation befall. And it happened one day like this: Cornelian was wearing her strongest apron, wrapped tightly around her huge waist. Like this. And she did take up the loose ends like so. And she strode around the hills gathering the white rocks. Yes was she most weary to the bone with her work. She struggled forwards with all the boulders in her apron. She was frustrated at the distance, the distance with which to carry the white stones. So, when she could not hold all the boulders, then did slip from her grasp the corner of her apron, and out fell some of the white stones, long before she had reached the causeway. She decided she would change her tasks. She would not bear the white stones from so far afield. No, rather than struggle forwards, day after day, night upon night, she decided to make the work easier by using local greenstone, and this she would substitute for white.

'But Cornelian told no one of this change of plan. Neither did she reveal this to her husband Cormoran, nor to his friend, who was also her friend, the giant of Trecobben Hill.

'Time was and time was not, when her husband, Cormoran, heard that she was no longer working as hard as him.

'This made him angry. Indeed, he was so angry that he lashed out with his foot. He kicked her in his rage, killing her and causing her to drop the green stone, which can be seen this day at the Penzance end of the causeway. To this very day.'

70

'Have you seen it, Aunt?'

'Indeed I have. It's there for all to see. But I digress, because the giant of Trecobben Hill had been very fond of Cornelian. He knew she had worked as hard as she could, day after day, night upon night, carrying massive white boulders in her enormous apron. So distressed was he at Cormoran's actions, and so dismayed was he about the death of the giantess, in such a manner, that he helped bury poor Cornelian's body under the Chapel rock, or some say in the courtyard.

'Then he returned to Trecobben Hill, still mourning his friend's wife, and buried his own treasure there, which has not been found unto this day, though many have searched and searched again. Then did the giant on Trecobben Hill die of grief.

'Thus did the giants of the time before time, when the earth was younger than it is now, create the tors and hills of Cornwall.

'And I have heard it said, my maids, that a shape of stones, just south of Hathersage, was also made by a giant striding out across the Pennines, dropping stones in the form of a circle from her apron as she went. It is still called the Apronful-of-Stones, to this day. Thus is my own Cornish homeland linked by old tales with the valleys and hills of these northern shires, shaped by the same words, handed at the firesides, in the depth of every winter, through families, like this, from generation to generation, through the testaments of time.'

Journal
Haworth, 23 January 1838

On one of the brightest days of my visit, Charlotte, Emily and I walk to the snow-covered moors, wrapped in our thick cloaks and wearing warm strong boots, rubbed thick with beeswax. As we make our way carefully beyond the parsonage, everything is transformed by snow. Old trees around Haworth are edged with white, the cobbled stone paths resemble bakers' trays of regimented neat white loaves, and each blade of grass and separate seed-head is frosted in white crystal.

We dare not venture as far as the waterfall because its valley is obliterated by drifted snow, but we gain height across the moors, and eventually, we stand gazing at the clear sky-line, turning slowly, focussing on the horizon, adjusting to the reflected intensity of the light.

Charlotte and I are arm in arm, talking quietly, aware of the vast expanse of glittering moor-land when, spell-bound by the beauty of the distant hills, Emily calls us to her. Raising her arm and sweeping her outstretched hand across the view she exclaims, 'I have insufficient words for these colours! The snow is not white. Its shades, tints and hues defy me.'

We laugh and Charlotte, being anyway very short-sighted, peers at the snow on the nearby heather. But my eyes follow Emily's, exhilarated by her audacity. No one knows and loves her surroundings as intensely as Emily, nor can observe the earth as acutely as does she, not even Charlotte whose powers of description are awesome. The snow-covered landscape is opal with a hint of cream and blue, blending to lilac and back to faintest dove grey again.

Straightening up once more after laughingly acknowledging Emily, Charlotte breathes the clean air in deep draughts. Then, joining hands, we three run forward to the edge of the rise. The doors open in my mind as if my brain has been a bird erstwhile trapped inside my skull. My friends lift the latch and out fly my ideas that have been previously settled there, tamed within familiar walls.

Charlotte's and Emily's minds are not imprisoned – their imaginations can fly like wild buzzards, in all seasons, soaring and swooping. They search for rich language as a buzzard searches for hidden field mice – and neither ever is satisfied because the hunger grows from within.

'Practice, practice, practice!' they cry, as we fall into a game of naming all the shades of white, which previously I have neither noticed nor recorded.

'What do we know that is white?' We begin chanting and listing, variously pointing to a hilly outcrop or the nearby foliage obscured by snow. Colours change as the light moves, the sun slides away, the clouds race and the wintry blue sky blends into the soft creams and primrose of late afternoon.

It's an entrancing game – the first time the sisters have allowed me to enter their private poetry or intimate theatre. Here in this journal, before I forget these words, down the years, I shall, nay I must, recall some of the ways we describe the colours of white, which is not white:

'Beeswax and butter milk; linen cloths and woven silk; woollen blankets heavy as snow; candle wax in lamplight's glow; grey white feather of a collared-dove; tear-filled eyes of a woman in love; Nottingham lace and ladies' gloves; Blessed bread and Noah's doves.

'Lambs' tails and snails' trails; icicles and ice pails; soft cotton night robes; oil lamp glass globes; candle wax in churches; altar cloths and surplices; vestments at Easter; the Star above the Manger.

'Starlight, candle-bright, starry skies and moonlight; full moon and round cheese; clouds are white; wind in the trees; household soap and housemaids' knees; Daisy flowers with summer bees; Lily flowers and snowdrops; spiders' webs and dew-drops.

'Butterflies are cabbage white; church mice have sharp bites; teeth are white; and so are tusks; piano practice is a must. Ho! ho!

'Piano notes are ivories; milk is white – and so is cheese; milk-white; shirt-bright; moonlight; starry-night. Ivory's from Africa; papyrus from Libya; quills write feather light; words on white paper; papers and tapers; papers and Papas.

'Papa's cravat is made of silk – Tabby's jug is brimmed with milk.'

Emily catches hold of my hand and our word game becomes a dance as we laugh and swing around, watched by Charlotte who does not like to dance.

'Porcelain and window-pane, chant the snowy words again. Snow and glow and shimmer at night; Star of the East and sky-blue white. Catch the song and make it white; name the snow that's bright with light. Snow is blue – a tinted hue. I am dancing here with you. I am chanting here with you. I am dancing, I am dancing, I am dancing, here with you!'

She is tall, the tallest of the three of us. Letting go of my hands, as we reel apart, panting with exertion, my breath frosting on the cold air, she opens her arms in her cloak and twirls there, a solitary figure, spiralling across the snowy ground. She loves the earth and she calls it her Mother Earth. It seems to me, there on that white hilltop, that Emily's love of the earth is the same as her love of God.

Her arms are wings, in her cloak. I gasp, hearing Emily's laugher, for if she were not a Christian she could, in this moment, have been a witch.

In this moment I inhale deeply – like children when they know they are breathing happiness. It is in the air around them; it is comprehended; it is named for the first time. I feel simultaneously very young and very old – I love these two women more than I love anyone in my own family. Each of them I love differently. Emily I love like a sister and I wish she were my sister. Charlotte I have loved as a fiancée loves her betrothed.

But it's in this same moment that past, present and future conjoin into one testament. Something I must now name. I must understand it fully, in my open mind, my moment of fusion of water into ice. Ice crystals are many sided and beautiful but transitory. My past dreams will not hold against future mornings, when the sunrise melts them. They will flow away like water down a hillside, and water is always the element that signifies separation between my beloved and me.

It is impossible for me, Ellen Nussey, to become the wife of Charlotte Brontë. God has created both of us in Eve's likeness, female and the same. That cannot be changed and I do not want to change it. To do so would be to defy Providence, which is nigh unthinkable, even with my doors open, my caged ideas flown. I'm ordinary, different from my two friends. Word games flow with ease from their practised, self-trained minds. The gilded cage doors are open, therefore their imaginations rise high as birds – imitated by the one in front of me dancing in her cloak, with her winged arms stretched wide.

There will be no marriage bond between Charlotte and me. It could *be* never. It will *never* be. Never is past, present and future, longer than time. I'm an adult, on the moors, intensely happy with two extraordinary friends, each of whom may develop her individual literary powers. I have no doubt about this. The opening of my mind comes like the Book of Revelation. My dreams of a life with Charlotte will not come true. I know this with astonishing certainty, on this day when the snow is not white.

Brookroyd, 10 February 1838

Dearest C.B.,

I write to you in some distress because I have bad news to communicate to you – my brother William is ill at John's house in Cleveland Row. I have been asked to accompany John back to London to help with the family there.

I wish neither to depart Brookroyd, nor absent myself from the vicinity of Roe Head. It is especially difficult for me to leave when I know that your move to Heald's House, Dewsbury Moor, is imminent – I had hoped to be of help and comfort to you during and after.

But it is not to be. We leave for London at the end of next week. I cannot tell you when I shall be home. I shall miss you most terribly. There is for me a disturbing contrast between my visit to Haworth and the suddenness of the proposed journey to the other end of the country.

I promise that I will write often from London.

In deep sadness.

Your loving friend, Nell.

Roe Head (12?), February 1838

My dear Ellen

We were at breakfast when your note reached me and I consequently write in great hurry – Your trials seem to thicken – I trust God will either remove them or – give you strength to bear them ... ...

I wish I were with you to lighten at least by Sympathy the burden that seems so unsparingly laid upon you

Let me thank you Ellen for remembering me in the midst of such hurry and affliction we are all apt to grow selfish in distress – this so far as I have found is not your case – When shall I see you again? the Uncertainty in which the answer to that question must be involved gives me a bitter feeling – through all changes, through all chances I trust I shall love you as I do now – We can pray for each other and think of each other – Distance is no bar to recollection – You have promised to write to me soon and I do not doubt that you will keep your word Give my love to Mercy and your Mother – take with you my blessing and affection and all the warm wishes of a warm heart for your welfare

C Brontë
Miss Wooler sends her love

Brookroyd, 16 February 1838

Dearest C.B.,

Can you come to the tollgate tomorrow morning, say eleven o'clock, at White Lee? We could talk together for a little while. I have a need to say farewell before my journey – to see your face for one last time before my stay in London.

Please come. Please, if you can.

Your loving friend, Nell.

Cleveland Row, 19 February 1838

Dearest C.B.,

This is a dire, depressing place this spring. It seems that nothing shall cheer this household at Cleveland Row. My usual liveliness of spirit that I experience in springtime, fails me. Barely canst I summon the energy to read to poor William, nor venture out of doors. I'm uninspired by the flowers in the park, and I desire neither to dance nor to visit John's and Mary's friends. I'm uninterested in a proposed day out to Epping and I find but little diversion in my erstwhile pleasure of reading. The rare times I am happy are with Georgiana, teaching her to paint by watercolours and, less frequently, in the basement kitchen, making bread. There are many servants here   I have to insist that I be allowed to make bread for it's considered an unusual request.

I think of Emily – making bread for the family, her German books propped beside her, and the smell of new bread welcoming me on my last visit there. Tears fill my eyes, and I clamp my teeth together, set my jaw down firm in the shoulders of my voluminous white apron, and knead the dough violently, punishing it for the absence of you, my dearest Charlotte and its being the wrong bread in the wrong house.

Write to me soon, I long for your voice, if not in person, by proxy.

Yours, missing you,

Your sadly affectionate friend,

Nell.

Journal

4 Cleveland Row, 21 March 1838

I do not know how it happened that my own health began to fail, but I am dismal and melancholy in a degree most singular. I am utterly without joy. In truth, I'm missing Charlotte, and the pictures in my head are of wild birds flying over the Haworth moors. I do not lie awake at night as she might have done but I wake each morning un-refreshed, redolent with sadness, and cannot be-stir myself.

My brother, William, is now suffering an undefined malady of the brain. He believes that he is a sinful person who deserves not to live. He exists, it seems, under a damp grey cloud, reminiscent of a shroud of clinging mist which slid upon the surface of a doom-laden lake, of which I had once written to Charlotte. I wish I could call upon James la Trobe, who recently helped Anne, but there's no one like him known to my relatives in London. I contrive not to show my disquiet to my family in St. James's. If only I were home in Yorkshire I might obey Charlotte's instruction to daily take exercise, which she holds good for young women – but I do not wish to walk in London's parks. I am dis-harmonious with the metropolis – the greening of the great parks passes me by for I feel lost when out of doors.

William is by turns sad, silent and withdrawn, thus to my sister-in-law, Mary, I voice my frustration with the complexity of his mental state.

'This despicable spectre of Calvinism is again haunting the Nussey family!'

'Hush yourself, Nell. It will do you no good to be so agitated.'

76

'If I could curse, if I dared to, I should curse Calvin himself and all who propagate his detestable beliefs!'

'Nellie, I have never heard you shout in such a manner.'

'I am angry, and rightly so. This spectre has William in its teeth. Like a rabid dog it shakes him until he wishes to die. It is a waste of his skills, and of his whole life, is it not?'

'I agree, my dear. He used to help John with his patients and now he can help no-one. It is very sad. Poor William seems helpless, even to help himself.'

'I am justified in my anger, Mary. He believes in his head that he is too sinful to live. It is such foolishness. William is a good man. What could he possibly have done to harm his own mind in such a degree? He has not committed murder, nor, to the best of our knowledge, broken even one of the Ten Commandments. Yet does he believe that he is so bad in the eyes of God that his life is no longer of any worth. I have witnessed this before, in Charlotte's younger sister, Anne. I do not desire to see any other human being suffer this malady. Yet I cannot prevent it. It takes me to the very edge of despair.'

'Try to get some sleep, Nellie, lest you make yourself ill also.'

'You are very kind indeed to me, Mary. I was brought here to be of assistance in your household and to comfort William. Yet I fear that I have failed in both respects.'

'All of us have failed in our efforts to comfort William. You have tried your best, Nell, and he has chosen not to respond to your ministrations. You must not reproach yourself.'

'I cannot bear to watch him struggling. Someone, somewhere has to take a stand against these poisonous, treacherous notions of sin and retribution. I do not believe in a God of suffering and vengeance. I do not and I *shall* not.'

'Good. I am very glad to hear it. You have a strong spirit, Nellie, and I trust it will bring you through this sad time. Now here is your warm milk. It will help you to sleep.'

4 Cleveland Row, 22 April 1838

Dearest Mama,

I write as your dutiful daughter-in-law, regretfully to inform you that Ellen is very unwell and indeed to report the current situation of the health of our beloved William. We have been, each one of us, most concerned at William's mental state of health. You know already how closely a watch is kept upon him by John, and the distress caused whilst watching our brother William failing to thrive – someone whose life had been full of promise, with gifts from God of a fine brain and a dear, kind heart. But we cannot reach him. He has barricaded himself inside his castle walls. He can peer at us only through slits, or over the top of the battlements, looking down from within those stone-cold turrets, down, down, to where we stand helpless the other side of a deep moat of icy water.

However, we had not – until now – realised the effect of William's state of mind upon Ellen's sensitive soul. Her energy has been depleted daily – and now she can barely stand. John has ordered her to bed for a complete rest, with food brought by myself, or one of the kindly upstairs maids. She is too weak to write and is most deeply distressed at her failure to correspond with Charlotte, with whom she has a vow of frequent letters. We ask therefore that either directly or through your friends you would communicate with Charlotte, passing on Ellen's warm friendship, as always. Despite Ellen's current predicament, I am reassured that she will soon be strong, on her way to a full recovery. Sadly we cannot be confident about the same for William.

I enclose with this letter a note for you from your dear Georgiana and kisses from the children.

Your loving daughter-in-law,

Mary.

Dewsbury Moor, 5 May 1838

My dearest Ellen

Yesterday I heard that you were ill – Mr and Miss Heald were at Dewsbury-Moor and it was from them I obtained the information. This Morning I set off to Brookroyd to learn further particulars; from whence I am but just returned. Your Mother is in great distress about you – she can hardly mention your name without tears – and both She and Mercy wish very much to see you at home again – Poor girl you have been a fortnight confined to your bed and while I was blaming you in my own mind for not writing – you were suffering in sickness without one kind female friend to watch over you. I should have heard all this before and have hastened to express my sympathy with you in this crisis, had I been able to visit Brookroyd in the Easter Holidays but an unexpected summons back to Dewsbury-Moor in consequence of the illness and death of Mr Wooler prevented it. Since that time I have been a fortnight and two days quite alone – Miss Wooler being detained in the interim at Rouse-Mill. You will now see Ellen that it was not

neglect or failure of affection which has occasioned my silence – though I fear you will long ago have attributed it to those causes – If you are well enough do write to me just two lines – just to assure me of your convalescence. not a word however if it would harm you, not a syllable. They value you at home Ellen. Sickness and absence call forth expressions of attachment which might have remained long enough unspoken if their object had been present and well. Mercy told me that George is quite miserable about you and that his anxiety is making him look wretchedly ill   I wish your <u>friends</u> (I include myself in that word) may soon cease to have cause for so painful an excitement of their regard. As yet I have but an imperfect idea of the nature of your illness – of its extent –or of the degree in which it may have now subsided – When you can let me hear all, no particular however minute will be uninteresting to me. How have your spirits been? I trust not much overclouded – for that is the most melancholy result of illness. You are not I understand going to Bath at present; they seem to have arranged matters strangely. I feel impatient to hear your own account of your future plans and prospects – When I parted from you near White-lee Bar I had a more sorrowful feeling than ever I experienced before in our temporary separations   it is foolish to dwell too much on the idea of presentiments– but I certainly had a feeling that the time of our re-union had never been so indefinite or so distant as then. I doubt not my dear Ellen that amidst your many trials – amidst the sufferings that you have of late felt in yourself and seen in several of your relations – you have still been able to look up and find support in trial, consolation in affliction, and repose in tumult – where human interference can make no change. I think you know in the right spirit how to withdraw yourself from the vexation, the care, the meanness of Life and to derive comfort from purer sources than this world can afford. You know how to do it silently, unknown to others - you can avail yourself of that hallowed communion, the Bible gives us with God. I am charged to transmit your Mother's and Sister's love – Receive mine in the same parcel, I think it will scarcely be the smallest share. Farewell my <u>dear</u> Ellen
    C Brontë.

4 Cleveland Row, 7 May 1838

Dearest Charlotte, my dear dear kind friend,

It is a beautiful, loving and caring letter, which reaches me today. It's brought to my room where I sit by an open window – for the weather is turned fine and warm, and together the sunshine and your words bring joy to me again.

You may be relieved from your anxieties over my health. It will return as the summer comes to London, though my brother William's state of body and mind does not show similar signs of improvement.

It seems that he does not have, in his sad life, the love and blessing which are bestowed in mine. I am truly blessed to be loved by so sweet a friend as you – I hold in my heart a steady affection for you and receive likewise from you – did you not say that even '*the most minute particular*' would be of interest to you – to know that is to experience love's fullness to brimming like Tabby's milk jug.

Meanwhile, I am truly concerned for your health and well-being, my dearest Charlie. Heald's House is not the best location – Dewsbury Moor is notoriously damp and the air is unpleasant there. I am further anxious that you are left with sole responsibility for tutorials, when Miss Wooler is at Rouse Mill. I am truly concerned at your isolation and exhaustion. Everyday life should be shared with companions with whom to dine and converse. Isolation is a circumstance that brings you discord – for it invites the onset of melancholy feelings – and it is the affliction of every governess.

Please write to me soon. I trust that my prayers for your welfare will sustain you in the lonely hours after midnight. Think of me at those times and know that I care for you, dearest warm friend.

Always your loving friend,

Nell

Ps. You wrote me once that I am not '*a passionate fool*' such as you. I kiss your letter and sleep with it under my pillow, so that my hair loosed long and softly brushed, ready for night, spreads there-over, like a fan. Do not underestimate my affection for you.

Nell.

4 Cleveland Row, 15 June 1838

Dearest Charlie, my loving friend,

I am heartened to discover that you're in Haworth. Your letter, written on 9th, arrived here yesterday. I had been truly worried, as you know, by the burden upon you of your work, alone, at Heald's House and the consequent exhaustion of the long hours of tutorials and mundane needlework therein. Now the kind summer air will refresh you and I shall rest assured that through the ministrations of your sisters and the ambience of your wonderful, peaceful home, you shall be soon fully recovered from a very hard year of teaching.

I am very sorry to hear of Mary Taylor's ill health. What a time this has been for all of us! But Mary is a strong woman of lively constitution and I am hopeful that this will be a temporary malady. You say that she has no ulceration of the lungs, no cough and no pain in her side – surely these are optimistic indications that she is in no serious danger? Your words paint a homely picture for me – your description of Martha talking without pause makes me laugh and laugh – I can 'see' Mary on the pianoforte – I can hear the laughter and I am joyful for your sake.

Now then, dearest friend, please prepare yourself for some very difficult news which I am now about to impart: My testament of the waters of separation – do I not always imply the meaning of 'waters' in my life in this way? – is drawing to its fateful conclusion. My brother William died here on June 7th. He died by drowning in the Thames.

John has tried valiantly, but unsuccessfully, to protect the whole family from the intimate details of this family tragedy. You will be aware, already, from my earlier epistles that my dear brother longed for death. William told me back in February, when first I arrived in Cleveland Row, that he *wanted* to die. It is obvious to one and all that this was no accident – William intended his own death and proceeded to determine the method of his final Goodbye. He chose the time of his death. He decided upon the location. He carried through his carefully laid plans successfully. My heart is with his spirit where it now abides – a place of peace, forgiveness and hope. My deep compassion to my lovely brother for his terrible winter of the soul extends now to his spirit wherever he may be. He is gone from us. Water was the element through which William met his sad death. I find it hard to forgive all those who purport the religious doctrines of Calvin, which flooded his soul and drowned him in that murky demise.

For sustenance I have your be-ribboned letters and I turn to a purer source – as you advise therein – I daily read my Bible. I dwell among the comforting words of St. Paul in 1 Corinthians 13. They are the most beautiful words on the meaning of love – thus, through prayer and readings, the watery depths of the soul shall flow away from me.

I am no more enamoured of London and the Londoners than ever I was. Old Father Thames laid a claim to my brother – and my poor unhappy William was unable to resist his call. I shall be very pleased indeed to leave this river and this city.

So I give thanks to God that I have now some good news to impart. We leave London next week. We are going to the village of Batheaston – just three miles from Bath – where I shall rest, recuperate, complete my grieving, and become fully well again. Alas, I am not yet allowed to travel north but I shall be safe and happy in my brother Joshua's home. We travel next week through open country-side – think of it – fields with red poppies at the edges of the wheat acres; the sheep on the hills, the lush leafy trees of the woodlands; the pretty villages and thatched cottages along the way.

I shall write as often as I can. Give my love to your sisters, your papa, your Aunt Branwell and to Tabby. I shall pray for you, every evening, at ten o'clock. Think of me when you read the words of St. Paul: 'There is nothing love cannot face'.

Always your loving friend,
Nell.

EARTH (ONE)

Ellen's Journal and Letters
Midsummer 1838 to April 1849

Dearest Charlotte,

Come with me – come with me, dearest friend, on my journey across the south of England. Let me share with you this delight. I shall endeavour to paint the colours, to bring you closer to me.

We depart London very early, soon emerging from city streets, into gentle cultivated countryside, scattered with farms and villages. Rounded hills roll by, lazy and luxurious under the June sunshine. Roadsides are abundant with milkwort, tormentil, heath bedstraw, purple and white vetch and many shades of blue speedwell; and the summer air fills with birdsong from linnets, warblers, thrushes and green-finches. Meadow brown butterflies and small heaths flit in the fields, the banks are fragrant with thyme, and grassy meadows glow red with flowery spires of sorrel.

Much to the surprise of my family, I begin to sing, working my way through the entire repertoire I learned at Roe Head, years ago. So glad am I to be travelling with my friends away from the city – its endless bustle and buildings – that, when not singing, I discover that I'm humming to myself. In my mind I am, perhaps, making my way already home to Yorkshire, but anyway, even though we are not travelling north, I feel home to be nearer once the carriage is bowling along through open countryside. I think of you and your sisters – especially Emily, who so loves the earth and all her creatures. I enjoy every mile of our journey – I become aware that our horses' hooves are taking us across a wide sweep of Salisbury Plain. Never have I viewed such an expansive plateau of arable land. Vast stretches of green, beige and gold fields are laid to wheat, oats and barley, swaying in the summer breeze. There, within sight of the megaliths of Stonehenge, our carriage draws to a halt for our repast of summer fruits, cheese and new bread. Never have I previously seen the monument, and I'm told that it pre-dates the pyramids, at which I am astonished.

Our repast completed, we drive on in full sunshine under a wide blue dome of sky, whilst passing dwellings which are adorned with cottage roses, and hedgerows decorated with elderberry flowers, wild angelica, dog roses and honeysuckle.

We arrive before dusk in the village of Batheaston, where my brother Joshua, who is eighteen years my senior, has been curate since 1834. From the front garden of the curate's residence, we hear a woman's voice warmly welcoming us – of course it belongs to my sister-in-law, Anne-Elizabeth. She hugs me close, arranges for our luggage to be taken upstairs, and escorts me through the gardens and orchards, where is a hammock slung between two apple trees 'so that I can rest and recuperate amidst the dappled light and shade'.

Thenceforth I anticipate many happy evenings dining with my charming companions, giving over my afternoons to repose in the orchards, and slow, quiet mornings catching up on my correspondence with you. Here perhaps I can recover from the tragedy of William.

Give my dearest love to your sisters, your aunt, your papa and Tabby. Tell them I shall see them at the end of summer.

I pray every night for you. Write soon, with all your news,

Your loving, affectionate friend.

Nell

Dewsbury Moor, 24 August 1838

My dear Ellen

I have been waiting a long time for an opportunity of sending you a letter by private hand –but as none such occurs I have determined to write by post lest you should begin to think I have forgotten you and in revenge resolve to forget me.

... ...

When will you come home? Make haste you have been at Bath long enough for all purposes –by this time you have acquired polish enough I am sure – if the varnish is laid on much thicker I am afraid the good wood underneath will be quite concealed and your old Yorkshire friends won't stand that – come– come I am getting really tired of your absence Saturday after Saturday comes round and I can have no hope of hearing your knock at the door and then being told that "Miss Ellen Nussey is come." Oh dear in this monotonous life of mine that was a pleasant event I wish it would recur again. but it will take two or three interviews before the stiffness –the estrangement of this long separation will quite wear away– I have nothing at all to tell you now except that Mary Taylor is better and that she and Martha are gone –to take a tour in Wales. Patty came on her pony about a fortnight since to inform me that this important event was in contemplation – she actually began to fret about your long absence and to express the most eager wishes for your return. I heard something from your Sister Mercy about Mr and Mrs. Joshua wishing you to stay over the Winter   don't be persuaded by them Ellen   you've been from home long enough   Come back–

... ... Write to me as soon as ever you get this scrawl. I should be ashamed of such writing as this only I am past all shame –

My own dear Ellen good-bye if we are all spared I hope soon to see you again God bless you –

C Brontë

Batheaston, 4 Sept 1838

Dearest C.B.,

The summer passes pleasantly here, finding me rested and thoroughly well in body and spirit. My daily life here continues methodically, quietly, and slowly Joshua and Anne-Elizabeth are preparing for their move to Poughill in Devon, where he is to become the new incumbent in the autumn. I have not yet a date for my homecoming but I envisage that it may be not many weeks away.

The good wood is quite visible beneath the varnish – I am the same Ellen, your cherished and affectionate friend, although time changes my dreams, of necessity. Having neither my own money nor independence, I am unable to assert my own needs but my family are extremely kind, gentle people, and I have been happy here. We go into the countryside around the village, where the parishioners have come to know me and invite me into their homes. My midsummer sojourn in Batheaston, though not of my choosing, has been neither difficult nor unpleasant.

In the mornings on waking I pray for the strength to understand my place in the world, a young woman with not a little education but no role assigned to her except that of finding a husband. I know that Polly and Patty are both outspoken about the rights of women to travel and find gainful employment beyond the household, but there is no one with whom to air such views hereabouts. I speak to no one about it.

Although I long for my own income, and to make my own decisions, it is neither in my constitution nor my upbringing to speak out as does Polly nor shout about my needs nor make a public assertion of any nature. These thoughts remain private matters and I ask God to guide me.

However, I read the newspapers every day and I am not uninformed about the outside world beyond the limitations of my circles. I have read of the riots in Dewsbury concerning opposition to the Poor Law. I am glad that your papa voices his opposition and that he is concerned at the sufferings of the families in his parish. In Batheaston the poorer people live in tied cottages on the land; in Bath there are slum houses hidden behind the wealthy streets; and in Bristol the condition of the poor has been always shocking. I am aware of the contrasts – how can I be not aware, when the newspapers shout them to the far ends of the earth?

Nevertheless, in my family there is no single individual, man or woman, with the compassion of your sisters and your papa. Perhaps he recalls his early days in Ireland, about which you have painted so vivid a picture. Of course your poor dear mother and Aunt Branwell have spoken to him of the plight of the poor in the fishing village of Newlyn and the tiny coves like Lamorna and Mousehole. I could listen to your Aunt for hours at a time, as you know.

It is uplifting for me to remain close to the women of ideas like yourself, Polly and Patty Taylor – your consideration for the poor is one of the reasons I love you. Manufacturers like my brothers George and Joseph, and wealthy apothecaries like John in London – and my poor late William – have virtually no contact with the poor. But you and your family minister on a daily basis from the parsonage, where you live within sight and sound of the passing bell, the sewers, the cellar dwellers of Haworth. Indeed your Aunt exclaims frequently on the good fortune of provision of pure water from your well, which, being above the parsonage, is also by consequence higher than the graveyard and therefore un-contaminated by the residents of the tombs! Have I not been in the parish Church when the floor has been under seepage, its attendant 'perfume' not of our choosing! Were we not glad of our pattens, and did we not sing extra loudly as if our raised voices might overcome the essence of putrefaction? The poor of Haworth – and it may be said Birstall, Gomersal and everywhere else in our vicinity, do not live with pleasures and niceties. I accept and recognise that we do not want revolution – God forbid such turmoil and tempest in our northern towns – and we abhor the prospect of rapid, tumultuous social change – yet do I hope that we are compassionate people. Are we cruel human beings without pity for the men, women and children who starve, without shelter in midwinter, reliant on charity or existing in terror of forced departure for the workhouses? Unkind places are they – where our Lord is being mocked – because he would not punish people for their poverty. Are not the workhouses constructed like prisons of which Calvin might have approved? Are they not places of retribution where suffering is laid upon suffering? In my heart I know that your papa is right to oppose them. Yet I was born not into the family background which might applaud the Chartists and their meetings which are being called in various parts of our beloved county. They frighten me, for they advocate turmoil and urgent political change. I cannot embrace such ideas. Apropos of which, my sister-in-law, Anne-Elizabeth, seems changed by her imminent rise in social status. Time will tell – but she adopts some small airs and graces, which she has not evidenced previously. I remain un-impressed by them.

I will write again when I have a date for my return.

Home! How sweet the sound!

May it be sooner rather than later!

Always your loving friend,

Nell.

Batheaston, 5 October 1838

My Dearest Charlie,

At last I am to return to Brookroyd and to you. I anticipate with such excitement our imminent reunion. I do not fear that we shall require many interviews before the old warmth is manifest between us.

I am flitting busily around the house, where my belongings spread themselves in nooks and crannies. Here a sewing box, there an embroidery frame; here a lace collar, there a writing case. We have plentiful space in which to spread ourselves: there are upholstered chairs in various window recesses, where I sit, with my work, following the sunshine around through the daytime. Here is a ribbon, there is a scarf. Now I must gather together these reminders of the many hours resting and recuperating herein.

However, I read your latest letter with some dismay, for you write that Emily has taken a situation at a school near Halifax. I am angry to read of her '*Hard labour from six in the morning to till near eleven at night*'. You are correct to call this slavery. It is a disgrace that any school teacher should be treated thus. My life here, by comparison, is filled with comfort. I am truly grateful to Joshua and Anne-Elizabeth for this time of ease. I wish most sincerely that Emily might rest and be nurtured in such a manner. Yet it is without nostalgia and with no regrets that I visit in turn each room, rescuing a needle case, a handkerchief, a spool of thread. I am ready to come home, more than ready. I am strong again after the sadness of William's departure from this life; and soon I shall see you again, my dearest. No longer shall we have to face each other, as you put it, '*through a letter darkly*'. How I enjoy your witty pun on 1 Corinthians 13.

Oh how it gladdens me to be coming back to Yorkshire. We shall walk again on the moors – is the autumn heather still resplendent in purple raiment there? So, my dearest Charlie, I answer your call *'come come'* – with my heart singing *home home*. God be with you until that day, which is *soon soon*.

Always your loving friend,
Nell.

Brookroyd, 7 December 1838

Dear Miss Margaret Wooler,

It has been my pleasure on many occasions this autumn to walk from Brookroyd, visiting with both my dearest Charlotte and yourself, during her last term at Heald's House. When this term closes, so will her work close. Such changes! Old Mrs. Wooler shall be cared for by Miss Eliza, who will take over the school from you, our trusted mentor and friend. I am most deeply grateful for your kindness throughout my school days and thenceforward, and for the warm welcome which has been always extended to me on visiting Charlotte. Steady friendship is of great significance to me, and I hope always to repay you in generous measure. Not only am I deeply honoured by your friendship, but also I am reassured by your statement that, should ever the need arise, I may turn to you for advice, comfort or support.

I can convey my delight, meanwhile, in anticipation of the festivities this Christmas. By December 22nd, Anne will be already at home, Charlotte will be returned from Dewsbury Moor, Emily from Law Hill, and I am invited to complete the Quartette!

Please accept my most sincere greetings for Christmas, from myself, my mother and all my family.

Your friend and erstwhile pupil,
Ellen Nussey

Brookroyd, 10 January 1839

Dear Miss Wooler,

I write to wish you a very happy New Year, and to send warm greetings from both Charlotte and myself. The hospitality of the Brontës is reciprocated when Mama invites Charlotte to return with me to Brookroyd for New Year. Let me paint you a picture:

We travel one afternoon, as dusk falls. We approach in the gig, laden with gifts from her aunt and sisters, as Charlotte wishes me a year of good fortune. I hold her hand, responding with my hope that the coming year shall signal a happy time for both families. Brookroyd welcomes us as if it is an enormous lantern, whose rectangles of gold shine across the snow-covered garden.

Thus do we celebrate the beginning of 1839 calmly, and before we sleep, we listen to an east wind sifting snow against the casements. It's a soft sound, snow on snow. With our window drapes open, moonlight fall across our room, its quality of light evoking lost legends, ancient magic and classical myth. I think of you then, dear Miss Wooler, the fire nights – may I call them that? – when we walk round your room – and I promise myself that I shall let you know that we are both happy and well.

Please accept my sincere wishes for the health of Mrs. Wooler and your sister, Miss Eliza.

Your affectionate erstwhile pupil,

Ellen Nussey

Brookroyd, 15 January 1839

Dearest Charlotte,

Your visit ends all too soon and then I succumb to the mild fever, which is doing the rounds. Mama's apothecary, who lives in Birstall, routinely prescribes beetle juice, of which you may perhaps disapprove, its being an eighteenth century remedy, administered daily for a fortnight to create blisters which draw the fever out. The malady is rapidly subsiding, although my skin remains sore and inflamed, but is soothed by Mama's herbal healing salve. Also the apothecary suggests caustic – Mercy was treated in similar fashion last autumn, and thus understands the effects of blister beetles, and is very sympathetic to me.

Your visit was so very short – *Please* come and see us again soon. Mama invites you for a *prolonged stay* here at Brookroyd. I am almost well again now. Write to me soon,

Your loving and affectionate friend,

Nell

My dear, kind Ellen

I can hardly help laughing when I reckon up the number of urgent invitations I have received from you during the last three months – had I accepted all, or even half of them – the Birstallians would certainly have concluded that I had come to make Brookroyd my permanent residence – When you set your mind upon a thing you have a peculiar way of hedging one in with a circle of dilemmas so that they hardly know how to refuse you – however I shall take a running leap and clear them all –Frankly my dear Ellen I cannot come – Reflect for yourself a moment – do you see nothing absurd in the idea of a person coming again into a neighbourhood within a month after they have taken a solemn and formal leave of all their acquaintance–? However I thank both you & your Mother for the invitation which was most kindly expressed – You give no answer to my proposal that you should come to Haworth with the Taylors – I still think it would be your best plan – I should have been at Lascelles-Hall before now if Amelia Walker had not made a mistake about the Huddersfield Coach from Bradford – I go to-morrow – Oh dear! I wish the visit were well over – I wish you and the Taylors were safely here, there is no pleasure to be had without toiling for it

I feel rather uneasy about the continued application of blisters you have had to undergo   does it not produce great weakness? Was the Caustic ordered on account of soreness left by the blisters –or for the removal of inflamation – it appears to me a strange kind of remedy in your Case – When you come here we will give up Medical prescriptions and try what exercise and fresh air will do – I have desired Branwell to make inquiries about your donkey–&c.

You must invite me no more my dear Ellen until next Midsummer at the nearest. I know you will call me a stupid little thing for refusing– but no matter I trust to get a reconciling kiss when you come to Haworth

All desire to be remembered to you Aunt particularly – Angry though you are I will venture to sign myself as usual – (no not as usual, but as suits circumstances)

Yours under a cloud
C Brontë

Dear Pegasus,

You fly with your words over all my obstacles. I understand that you cannot come. I do accept it, so although I may be angry, which is in truth a cover for my disappointment, I cannot *stay* angry with you. I shall reciprocate your reconciling kiss when I come to Haworth – I shall try to persuade my family to release me at the end of February. Meanwhile, I have news from Henry. You know already that he took several months to recover from the riding accident last autumn, and that it affected his head and therefore his ministry most severely. His new living, in the rural diocese of Chichester, now comprises curate-in-charge for the villages of Donnington and Earnley. It seems that living in Earnley vicarage suits him very well. He has proposed marriage to Margaret Anne Lutwidge, daughter of his erstwhile vicar in Burton Agnes, near Burlington. If she is his choice, we all hope she will accept – and make him happy.

Thank you for asking Branwell to procure a donkey for me during my visit to Haworth – but I doubt that it will be necessary as I am stronger daily. I fully intend to *walk* beside you and your sisters on the moors. I'm laughing at the thought of you leaping – and although I am not so confident as you with puns, I endeavour to amuse you,

so I bray goodbye
Donkey-Nell

Brookroyd, 6 March 1839

Dearest Charlotte,

I'm so sad not to be visiting Haworth as planned. They simply won't release me yet, which they say is on account of my health.

However I write without delay or ceremony because you may have heard from Henry. I know not how he achieved this audacity – except that Margaret-Anne Lutwidge refused his proposal, whereupon Henry reflected upon his friend and companion whom he had met through his young sister – and wants you for his wife and to start a school in Earnley with him.

I could anticipate with pleasure being close to you – to visit you under your own roof, and stay a long time there – for would I not be always welcome in Henry's home? Yet I do not feel about you the way I should about a sister by marriage. You know my feelings for you. How would I sleep peacefully, imagining your hair splayed across Henry's pillow, when so recently had it shone wild in moonlight across mine own?

Nevertheless we have discussed the future for women without independent means – and I shall accept whatever decision you make, knowing your integrity and honesty, both with my brother and in your heart.

Write to me soon – *Please* come to Brookroyd when you can
Your loving friend
Nell

Journal
Brookroyd, 14 March 1839

Today – a letter from Charlotte. Much news. Anne is gone to work for the Inghams – Anne's school friend, Hannah, is Mrs. Ingram's sister. Charlotte refuses my brother Henry, very courteously, very gently. Such a long letter.

So I sit now by my window, reading and re-reading…

Haworth, 12 March 1839

My dearest Ellen

When your letter was put into my hands – I said "She is coming at last   I hope" but when I opened it and found what the contents were I was vexed to the heart. You need not ask me to go to Brookroyd any more – Once for all and at the hazard of being called the most stupid little Wretch that ever existed – I won't go till you've been to Haworth. –I don't blame <u>you</u> I believe you would come if you might   perhaps I ought not to blame others – but I'm grieved.

... ...

You ask me my dear Ellen whether I have received a letter from Henry – I have about a week since – The Contents I confess did a little surprise me, but I kept them to myself, and unless you had questioned me on the subject I would never have adverted to it – Henry says he is comfortably settled in Sussex that his health is much improved & and that it is his intention to take pupils after Easter– he then intimates that in due time he shall want a Wife to take care of his pupils and frankly asks me to be that Wife. Altogether the letter is written without cant or flattery – & in a common-sense style which does credit to his judgement – Now my dear Ellen there were in this proposal some things that *might have proved a strong temptation – I thought if I were to marry so, Ellen could live with me and how happy I should be. but again I asked myself two questions –"Do I love Henry Nussey as much as a woman ought to love her husband? Am I the person best qualified to make him happy –?– Alas Ellen my Conscience answered "<u>no</u>" to both these questions. I felt that though I esteemed Henry – though I had a kindly leaning towards him because he is an amiable –well-disposed man   Yet I had not, and never could have that intense attachment which would make me willing to die for him – and if ever I marry it must be in that light of adoration that I will regard my Husband ten to one I shall never have the chance again but n'importe. Moreover I was aware that Henry knew so little of me he could hardly be conscious to whom he was writing – why it would startle him to see me in my natural home-character he would think I was a wild, romantic enthusiast indeed– I could not sit all day long making a grave face before my husband – I would laugh and satirize and say whatever came into my head first – and if he were a clever man & loved me the whole world weighed in the balance against his smallest wish should be light as air—*

Could I– knowing my mind to be such as that could I conscientiously say that I would take a grave quiet young man like Henry? No it would have been deceiving him – and deception of that sort is beneath me. So I wrote a long letter back in which I expressed my refusal as gently as I could and also candidly avowed my reasons for that refusal. I described to him too the sort of Character I thought would suit him for a wife – Good-bye my dear Ellen – write to me soon and say whether you are angry with me or not – .

C Brontë

Brookroyd, 19 March 1839

My dearest Charlotte,

You ask, my dear friend, whether I am angry with you. In my clearest words, No, I am not angry. I had no wish that you would marry Henry – for I do not think that marriage can create happiness where there is no passion. For myself, I shall never marry. I know where my source of passion may lie – and that's enough knowledge to last me through all my life. Now to other things – have you heard from Polly? She says the Taylors are going to invite you to Gomersal and will invite me while you're there. Meantime is the season not beautiful? My blisters are all healed perfectly and my cough and cold are gone – I always feel stronger in body, brighter in spirit, come the spring. There's plenty of sunshine and our gardens are a source of joy once more.

Write to me soon. Is there any news of your going out? Have you found a situation yet?

Remember, a moonlit room, your hair upon my pillow.

Yourn,

Nell

Haworth, 15 April 1839

My dear Ellen

I could not well write to you in the week you requested as about that time we were very busy in preparing for Anne's departure – poor child! She left us last Monday   no one went with her – it was her own wish that she might be allowed to go alone – as she thought she could manage better and summon more courage if thrown entirely upon her own ressources. We have had one letter from her since she went – she expressed herself very well satisfied – and says that Mrs. Ingham is extremely kind, the two eldest children alone are under her care, the rest are confined to the nursery—

... ...

for my own part I am as yet "wanting a situation – like a housemaid out of place"–bye the bye Ellen I've lately discovered that I've quite a talent for cleaning–sweeping up hearths dusting rooms – making beds &c so if everything else fails—

... ... I will be nothing "but a housemaid"

Setting aside nonsense – I was very glad my dear Ellen to learn by your last letter that some improvement had taken place in your health – for occasionally I have felt more uneasy about you than I would willingly confess to yourself – I verily believe that a visit to Haworth would now greatly help to restore you – and there can be no objection on account of cold when the weather is so much milder. However angry you are I still stick to my resolution that I will go no more to Brookroyd till you have been to Haworth – I think I am right in this determination and I'll abide by it. it does not arise from resentment but from reason. I have never for a moment supposed that the reluctance of your friends to allow you to leave home arose from any ill-will to me   justice compels me to say that I think the wish to keep you near them in your then precarious state of health was quite natural. but now that you are better that argument does not hold good. With regard to my visit to Gomersal I have as yet received no invitation– but if I should be asked though I should feel it a great act of self denial to refuse yet I have almost made up my mind to do so – though the society of the Taylors is one of the most rousing pleasures I have ever known. I wish you Good-bye my darling Ellen & I tell you once more I want to see you –Strike out that word <u>darling</u> *it is humbug where's the use of protestations? –we've known each other and liked each other a good while that's enough*

    C Brontë

Brookroyd, 19 April 1839

Dearest Charlotte,

    I am so sorry to cause more disappointment, for you are right there is no good reason why my family will not release me. They insist I must remain here on account of my health – in my turn I make the rejoinder that it is NOT precarious now and the air in the hills would be beneficial. Despite my protestations, they continue to cosset me, fussing around and entrapping me, which is now posing to me a most serious frustration. I wish you a very happy birthday and I want to *see* you. Across the seventeen miles from my home to yours, on a mild night you may hear my voice – it is hee-hawing like a frustrated donkey, all alone in a fenced-in field.

    Yourn

    Nell

Brookroyd, 25 June 1839

Dearest Charlotte,

    I am so sorry that my last letter to you was sent to the wrong address – the Sidgwicks at Stonegappe in Lothersdale –You will be wondering why you have heard nothing from me – and in your lonely, isolated situation that will create more sadness, which I am trying to avoid. I do not know when it will be collected or forwarded to you. So I hasten to send this one. I'm pleased to receive a long letter from Emily, who tells me of your latest epistle from your new situation – and sends your address – the summer residence of the Sidgwick family at Swarecliffe, near Harrogate. But I'm not pleased to learn of those dreadful children '*riotous perverse and unmanageable cubs*'. How can these people commend such behaviour in their young ones? Times are indeed changing are they not? Neither you and I would e'er be allowed such turbulence and my brothers never so behaved nor would they entertain such manners from their 'cubs'! I think it not just that any governess should struggle in such conditions. You may take comfort from this being a temporary post. Soon, this time will end and then I have permission to stay at Haworth. Nowadays, I often hide my true feelings from my family, in case they conjure up more reasons for my imprisonment here. But I must speak not of entrapment – my life, nothwithstanding its frustrations, is sheer luxury and idleness compared to yours as governess to the Sidgwicks.

I am angry also in this regard – that you have no respite from your labours to enjoy your new surroundings. I am truly sorry about your hours of coarse sewing – bondage to the needle as well as the brats. I've a mind to arrive in the gig, demand a bed, sit and sew with you until all is done, and bring you home.

Let's be thankful that it is a temporary post, and soon it will be over.

Together, soon, soon,

Your ever devoted,

Nell

Brookroyd, 10 July 1839

Dearest Charlotte,

Your letter written on 30th has arrived safely here – oh my dear girl, how horrible does this situation seem to one who knows your love of freedom and your sensitive and caring soul. I should like to slap that Sidgwick-woman very hard around the face : I can see the red mark I should make. Rarely do I feel violent but I cannot have her scolding you in a stern manner with harshness of language. How dare she! So angry am I at this insult. You are a beloved tutor, experienced and dutiful – never do you shirk or lack in courage. So, this is what going out means, is it? Hours of labour for people who are not worthy and care not a stuff for their governess. I am righteously furious on your behalf. The pen fair singes the paper with it!

However, come the end of July your trials there shall be over!

Then, my Charlotte, my weary, hard-working friend, things will change.

How? Why? Because I now convey news about which I am restless with excitement. I have the most wonderful chance – a circumstance come upon us!

I am to plan a holiday by the sea and permission is granted to invite you for my companion. Say you can. Say you will come! I am offered three weeks away, possibly in Cleethorpes. But for my part, I ask you, where shall we go? When can you travel? How long may you be with me? You who, when hedged in with a circle of dilemmas, '*shall take a running leap and clear them all.*'

Write soon. Please say 'yes'.

Your affectionate and very devoted

Nell

Journal
Brookroyd, 1 August 1839

If I'm to believe Charlotte's letter at the end of July, the excitement is driving her "*clean daft*". She says she may only get a week away with me, at most a fortnight. Her family talks of travelling to Liverpool, which I think is a strange choice, although I have heard that people take to bathing there in August. But anyway she's set upon a holiday with me and will '*bear down opposition*'. She wonders whether I'd like to join them in Liverpool, because Cleethorpes is unlikely to be agreed by her family. I reply, best I can, suggesting three weeks and again requesting the East Coast.

Journal
Brookroyd, 4 August 1839

She suggests Burlington and says: '*the idea of seeing the SEA – of being near it – watching its changes by sunrise Sunset – moonlight – & noonday –in calm – perhaps in storm – fills & satisfies my mind.*' I can barely wait.

Journal
Brookroyd, 11 August 1839

Letters speed between us, as we try to make and re-make our arrangements.

Journal
Brookroyd, 15 August 1839

It seems her aunt and her papa have been creating impediments. Until finally we must recognise that her aunt has never formally agreed.

Charlotte cannot go. I know not whether to crash about in my room, making a mess, stamp my way around the gardens, or slam into the earth with a heavy spade – so violently disappointed. I dare not cry. I shall not allow myself to cry.

Journal
Brookroyd, 3 September 1839

I have a plan. I have money from Richard in Leeds. Tomorrow I shall go in the gig directly to Haworth and take them all by surprise.

I shall simply be there. I shall insist that they release Charlotte and we shall have our holiday together. Never have I been so determined about anything. I shall not be bullied by her aunt or her papa. I shall be myself, Ellen Nussey, who knows who she loves and what she wants.

Journal
In transit, 4 September 1839

They agree! It's a warm and sunny day. Charlotte laughs, holding my hand in the gig. I whisper in her ear: 'We can do this. Just watch me!' Our journey from Haworth is comprised in part by train and in part by stagecoach.

Easton, 12 September 1839

We're kidnapped! Henry's curacy at Burton Agnes is not far from Burlington. He hears by post from my family at Brookroyd and he arranges an abduction! We're in the farmhouse of the Hudsons in the hamlet of Easton. It is very pretty indeed and we have, of course, our own room and shared bed, but this is not what I intend!

By day we walk to the fir clad slopes of Boynton, which is but a mile away, or more frequently we stroll the three miles to the cliffs, where we watch the sea for hours. With its changes of moods, and colour, its roughness or its soft, sliding sounds when calm, we are entranced.

Journal
Burlington, mid October

At last after a whole month we are allowed to rent lodgings in Burlington, although visited each day by the Hudsons, who are kindness indeed, carrying dairy produce and fresh bread and vegetables. I suppose we are naïve, for our meagre finances cannot cover our costs, so we are grateful, anyway for the provisions – and the providers.

Yes. We have this one miraculous week – my darling declares that she will never forget these experiences. Overcome with emotion at the ocean's vastness, Charlotte desires sometimes to absorb its beauty and power in solitude, storing up images which will never wear away.

In the evenings, the 'Parade on the Pier' is the greatest absurdity – for it is packed with so many people that they must walk in regular file, round and round, to secure any movement whatsoever. We laugh at their antics, enjoying ourselves thoroughly as spectators.

On our first night here we take ourselves to the cliffs by moonlight – but we discover a terrible fear – for we cannot walk as women alone in the night. We repair to our lodgings whereupon we hear the sound of a Ranters' meeting in the chapel across the street.

'Nell, it's so wild! Listen to the wails and shrieks. Let's go and look. I want to go in, find out what's going on.'

'Think on though, Charlie,' I intersperse quickly, 'these people are sincere – they believe in their religious impulses – and should be neither ridiculed nor criticised by strangers in their midst.'

'Oh, Nell how very frustrating! But, perhaps you're right. Let's sit by the open window and watch as they all troop out.'

We blow out the candles whereupon the lights from the house opposite reveal to us the street below and the people, still singing loudly as they depart the chapel.

She is bright-eyed and laughing. 'I'll never forget this holiday away with you – so many people and pictures. It's been quite a spectacle, hasn't it?'

'Time with you, yes, it's like a dream,' I reply, storing it all in my heart, for who knows when may I have this chance, with her, ever again?

Dearest Charlotte,

I did not hasten to answer your last letter, though received a good while since. We're busy with family discussions concerning the state of the mills. The Chartist uprisings prove a considerable threat to Joseph, Richard and George – the entire woollen industry is embroiled in an era of trials and tribulations. Liken to other mills in Yorkshire, we continue to be worried about our financial plight – we are plagued by rumours of businesses going bankrupt hereabouts.

We have come through this difficult year with both the mills still operational but are vulnerable to the vagaries of supply and demand. We rely on raw materials, for the coarse carding process. If one mill 'goes under' then others will of necessity follow suit. It's estimated that there are now a hundred thousand people out of employment in the Leeds area – I pray nightly for the poor families. The weather turns worse and I imagine the children crying from cold and hunger. When last I was in Haworth, we walked down the hill, past the basement dwellers and you spoke of your papa's concern for them, especially when street water seeps into their hovels. I take comfort always that your drinking water is from the well situated above the parsonage – thereby unlikely to suffer contamination from foulness and night soil further down the hill. Now that these uncertain times surround us, how much worse it is for the poor among us.

The two lasses, who reside here doing the heavy work, are from decent hard working families in Gomersal. I question both of them – they are distant cousins, the one recommended by the other – and both have parents still in work. The father of one is a smithy, the other a charcoal burner. They are satisfied with their lodgings in the attic, which we have warmed these past weeks with a small fire, else the ice forms on the pitcher, and they must break it before their ablutions. Mama gives permission for warm water to be fetched from the kitchen.

Brookroyd Mill has provides well for my family – which circumstance I hope and pray will continue. In regard of my own future, financial uncertainty of my family does not make me desirous of marriage to a rich and wealthy husband, in the un-likely event one should materialise before my surprised eyes. I think I shall never marry. Speaking of that institution, Mercy writes from Earnley, where she keeps house this winter for Henry, and says he longs to find a wife. Poor dear man, I yearn for his happiness. You may hear from him – you're a kind friend with whom he wishes to correspond. Mercy and Ann intend to keep house for him in rotation.

The Nusseys' problems are not merely financial. In truth, the triangle of brothers who run the mill is not equal. George, though the youngest, has many health problems at present. Joseph, notwithstanding that he's the oldest of the three, is by no means wisest – he continues to imbibe alcohol in ever greater volumes. The ensuing responsibility, which befalls Richard, is enough to bend him low to the earth.

This letter is not intended as complaint. I am happy in my own way, although I intend to seek a situation as a governess, if it's possible. I wonder if Miss Wooler might advise me, and shall be glad to receive any wisdom from yourself on the same subject.

Bye the bye, I hear wondrous reports of the merriment caused by the new curate William Weightman in the Haworth area. The parishioners roundabouts find him most agreeable and amusing company, which news comes via all at the Red House. When next I visit I shall anticipate with pleasure his company and hearing him preach. I have no more news for now but intend to impose my presence upon you, if you'll have me. Write to me soon and tell me which dates would best suit you.

Your loving and affectionate friend,
Nell

Brookroyd, 22 December 1839

Dearest Charlotte,

I am so sorry to hear of your troubles – how hard it must be for Tabby, who likes be busy, to bear the pain and incapacity of an ulcerated leg. I am glad she is able to reside with her sister – but how sad that she feels at last obliged to leave you. Tabby is the very heart and soul of the kitchen. I imagine only too well you would rather share the household duties than employ a stranger in your midst. It's shocking to learn that you shall search by and by for a new situation. Mama knows not of any households wanting a governess at present. I am communicating frequently and kindly with Mama about 'going out' – I hope you will give me assistance and encouragement in this plan. She is unhappy with my suggestion but is sympathetic to my need to be independent, by which I'm taken surprise. However Mama has not yet broached with my brothers this sensitive subject. Heyho, Charlie, I am unsure how best to proceed from this point. Any advice on your part shall be most welcome and I wonder, should I approach Miss Wooler also for information? This is written in utmost haste, to reach you by Christmas. Also, is January 10th still convenient to your family for my visit to Haworth?

Blessings of this wondrous season upon you, my dearest, and all
your family.

My affectionate love towards you, always,

Nell

Brookroyd, 4 January 1840

Dearest Charlotte,

A new decade has begun and with it, I hope for a period of industrial peace for the county of Yorkshire, indeed for England. As to the Nussey family – we appreciate your kind wishes for a better year than last. I sincerely hope so! Thank you for your 'hasty line', confirming January 10th but at present my sister Sarah is ill and I must postpone my visit until next month, for which I am deeply disappointed but resigned to accept the fact of it.

I'm interested to learn of Branwell's new employment in Ulverston. As you rightly acknowledge it will be hard for him to settle but I hope it works out well for him. I am so very sorry to change my visit – you said '*don't change your day*' but please don't be angry – I must return now to Sarah's bedside, but hope to rearrange my visit for just before Valentine's Day. I hardly believe it's the decade of the 1840s. I will be twenty three in April! I shall not scold you for bad writing – so long as you write – that's what matters!

I am missing you, my dearest friend.

Your loving and affectionate
Nell

Journal
Haworth, 14 February 1840

My 'end-of-winter' visit comes at last. Here I chat with everyone, make bread in the busy kitchen, slide seamlessly into the fabric of my friends' lives. I simply adore to be here – I could be happy to live here always, sleeping with my beloved friend again, listening to the clatclatclat of Aunt Branwell's pattens on the stone floors, noticing the familiar tickticktick of the grandfather clock on the stairs. This peaceful and contented visit brings me intense happiness and joyfulness. Today there arrive Valentine Cards, from our curate here, our funny and friendly 'Celia Amelia'. Each one of the sisters and myself – the Quartette – is in receipt of such, although their provenance is disguised by Celia Amelia walking ten miles away to post them. We guess the origin most easily, although it must remain secret from Charlotte's aunt and her papa. In return we write poetic verses upon a card, which we all sign and despatch forthwith. I'm pleased especially to talk quietly with Anne, whose ordeal at the Inghams is over – she is not to return and now seeks a new situation. There is a possibility of her going out again this summer for contact has been made with the Robinsons of Thorp Green, near York. I am so very attached to Anne, my most gentle of friends – my heart is glad of witness now that her health improves. She's not strong, but is recovering, not only from the Inghams but also from the shocking news of the death of her school friend, Anne Cook, back at New Year.

Brookroyd, Vernal Equinox 1840

Dearest Charlotte,

Every morning on rising I go directly into our gardens, where the lawn edges are abundant with daffodils, which bloom earlier this year than ever have I seen in the north. Truly, they sing a golden welcome home. I daily take exercise – I hear your voice approving me – by clearing the borders, and long reconnoitring walks. I'm allowed to go riding again by myself, what joy for me, the wind in my bonnet, the wonderful skies – everywhere it is the same picture – green shoots and fattening buds. How I love this time of year.

All is well here – my brothers discuss with me the state of the workforce in the mills – they are calm and the Chartists pose no insurgence at present. Long may it be so. From Earnley, Henry writes that he has again visited the sea, which rolls inwards on pebble beaches in Sussex & they rattle in the outflow like trees in the wind on the moors. He has hopes of marriage to Miss Follett, although he has not received her answer to his proposal. However, my sister Ann writes from Earnley, with most disturbing turns of phrase. I am surprised at Ann's vehemence – I feel estranged from her after reading her haughty words. She declares that Miss Follett dresses neither with fashion nor good taste. She expresses the opinion that Henry should give up his romantic attachment because this lady brings no dowry. Henry, for his part, insists Miss Follett's honest – a good person with whom he intends to pursue the prospect of union. Ann's caustic rejoinder is that Henry needs a more worldly wife – one who could entertain local squires and gentry, there being many in the hinterland of Chichester. Write & tell me your considerations on this subject. I shall trust your judgement, most sincerely.

Now then, I have something to tell you, rather than you hear this from anyone else. Someone is residing in this area, temporarily, who was known to Henry whilst at Magdelene, Cambridge. My suspicions are that he was sent by Henry to make courtship to me. This attention is being paid to me currently by the Rev. Osman Parke Vincent, a young curate, who was hoping for a curacy near to Henry, but was unsuccessful. Mr. Vincent prefers the south and expresses his eventual intention of making his ministry there. He is a gentle & kind person, who seeks out my company. Pressure builds like a pan boiling on the range. My whole family wants me married off, justifications being that 'it's only your happiness we are thinking of, Ellen'. Not a week passes but Mama gently, nay insistently, chides about my 'old age and single state'. Were I to be downright rude or distantly cold to Mr. Vincent the disapprobation of my family would descend like carding fluff in the mills – I should be covered by its clouds, unable to breathe or smile beneath its smothering layers. So I remain calm, attempt to appear serene, my conversation charming & my countenance pleasant. It is a façade, an act, for which you might commend my thespian qualities.

In truth, my dear Charlie, there is no response in me & I have no great respect for Mr. Vincent's abilities as a curate. Perhaps there is a shadow cast by the glittering success of our William Weightman – our naughty, playful 'Celia Amelia' – I do not mean in romantic attachment, but rather in his force of personality, the charisma with which he attracts and holds his congregation. I see little future in my friendship with Mr. Vincent, though he would wish for one, but his company has been not unpleasant, since my return from Haworth. Meanwhile, I miss you, Charlie, and I miss the walks around your home. I miss the days with you, the nights with you. Remember me to your sisters, Aunt, Papa and Tabby.

I miss you, Charivari, and the warmth of your embrace.

There being little more to report I shall sign this as usual,

Your loving and affectionate friend,

Nell

Brookroyd, 10 May 1840

My dearest Charlotte,

I have something to tell you, pertaining to Mr. Vincent. All through this springtime, as we walked under bowers, and the canopies of new leaves opened above and around us, I have been encouraged by my family to spend all my time in his company.

In truth I was lonely, and his friendship has been gentle, and sustained. But at last I was persuaded by my inner heart to be open and forthright. I had with him a conversation yesterday which I rehearsed for days previous. I didn't want to lose his friendship, for he is known to Henry and has become familiar with my brothers during his dinners at Brookroyd. He has been a not infrequent guest at our table.

I do not believe that he will give up on his courtship but my heart is calmer, my soul lighter in weight since my last meeting with him. I spoke of families to him in general terms. I told him of my brother John, my sister-in-law Mary and their children. I told him of my schooldays – our triangle – you, me, Mary – conversations with my female friends. I didn't speak of marriage (or say that I would never marry anyone) – for he might have felt I was fishing for compliments or, at the worst, a proposal, furthest from my intentions. Rather did I try to convey what my female friends mean to me, my joy of writing letters to you and your sisters, my most contented times being when I'm in your home at Haworth. It was not an easy thing to attempt – I was trying to convey something of my interests, something of my needs. However there is no language for my needs, there is no world for my intentions, no recognisable shape for my desires.

I have no desire whatsoever to marry Mr. Vincent. Nor, indeed, anyone. You are the only recipient of my words, on this subject. I cannot speak of this to Polly, however much do I admire her mind. We are set worlds apart, she and I, in this experience, despite our affection for one another. Perhaps your Emily would understand – my intuition tells me so, but ne'er may I divulge to her my innermost thoughts – I may not allow her spark of intelligence inside my private life, my days, my nights. Only to you, can I reveal my thoughts, my wishes. As for hopes? We are growing older and even our hopes must change, n'est-ce pas, ma chérie?

I am not sad, except in the missing of you. My days are full, very busy in the household, each moment filled with my family's expectations.

Around me the land is very beautiful, the shire-horses ploughing, the earth waking up. How can one be sad at these wild skies, the call of the curlews? No, I am not sad. Until…until I attempt lexicon for my feelings, this strange and fragile world of my language with you, a world with no words for what I need to say.

Your devoted friend,

Nell

My dear Ellen,

I read your last letter with a great deal of interest. Perhaps it is not always well to tell people when we approve of their actions, and yet it is very pleasant to do so; and as if you had done wrongly, I hope I should have had honesty enough to tell you so, so now you have done rightly, I shall gratify myself by telling you what I think...

If I made you my Father Confessor I could reveal weaknesses which you do not dream of – I do not mean to intimate that I attach a <u>high</u> <u>value</u> to empty compliments, but a word of panegyric has often made me feel a sense of confused pleasure which it required my strongest effort to conceal – and on the other hand, a hasty expression which I could construe into neglect or disapprobation, has tortured me till I have lost half a night's rest from its rankling pangs. Do not be over-persuaded to marry a man you can never respect – I do not say <u>love</u> because, I think, if you can respect a person before marriage, moderate love at least will come after; and as to intense <u>passion</u>, I am convinced that is no desirable feeling. In the first place, it seldom or never meets with a requital; and, in the second place, if it did, the feeling would be only temporary; it would last the honeymoon, and then, perhaps, give place to disgust or indifference, worse, perhaps, than disgust. Certainly this would be the case on the man's part; and on the woman's –God help her, if she is left to love passionately and alone.

Our letters are assuming an odd tone. We write of little else but love and marriage and, verily, I have a sort of presentiment that you will be married before you are many years older. I do not wish you to reciprocate the compliment because I am tolerably well convinced that I shall never marry at all. Reason tells me so, and I am not so utterly a slave of feeling but that I can <u>occasionally</u> <u>hear</u> her voice. God bless you.

CBrontë

Dearest Charlotte,

I write in haste to invite you to Brookroyd. Can you come next week? I am most agitated and enthusiastic awaiting your reply.

Longing to see you,

Ellen

Dearest Charlotte,

I am deeply disappointed but I must accept that you are to visit Gomersal – the continuing illness of Polly and Patty's father is so distressing for the family – your presence there will cheer every one up – and I shall walk over to meet with you at Gomersal church.

Au revoir,

Ellen

Haworth 2 June 1840

My Dear Ellen

Mary Taylor is not yet come to Haworth – but she is to come on the condition that I first go and stay a few days there – If all be well, I shall go next Wednesday—I may stay at Gomersal until Friday or Saturday and the early part of the following week I shall pass with you if you will have me – which last sentence indeed is nonsense – for as I shall be glad to see you – so I know you will be glad to see me –This arrangement will not allow much time, but it is the only practicable one which considering all the circumstances I can effect – Do not my dear Ellen urge me to stay more than two or three days because I shall be obliged to refuse you   I intend to walk to Keighley – there to take the Coach – as far as Bradford – then to get someone to carry my box –and walk the rest of the way to Gomersal – If I manage this I think I shall contrive very well – I shall reach Bradford by about five o'clock – and thus I shall have the cool of the evening for the walk   I have communicated the whole arrangement to Mary Taylor – I desire exceedingly to see both her and you

Goodbye

CB

CB

CB

CB

CB

CB

Dearest C.B.,

I am joyful that you will come YES! Mama says she will be delighted at your intended visit. As indeed shall I. So, you intend to walk – three and a half miles from Haworth to Keighley and five and a half from Bradford to Gomersal. Well done, in advance. I pray for a beautiful summer's evening for your walk.

Soon, soon
Your loving and devoted
EN
EN
EN
EN
EN

Brookroyd, 16 August 1840

Dearest C.B.,

Here at last is a long letter – hopefully to catch us up. Where to begin? Perhaps first upon our friends and their romantic involvement. I'm daily talking with Polly, indeed holding her while she weeps. She blames herself, for she allows herself to reveal her feelings for Branwell, who flirts with her for his own amusement. Now she is most cruelly rejected, which leaves her distressed in the extreme. She asks me directly about Mr. Vincent, am I not being courted by him. I tell her I think I will likely marry no one, I am myself, she may call me Mrs. Ellen – or Mrs. Menelaus – which amuses her, and now we're both laughing together, our friendship closer than it's been of late. With Branwell I am frustrated, nay exasperated. The gap in his work since his dismissal by the Postlewaites in Broughton has been filled with Polly – to Branwell's gratification and Polly's detriment. He has a charisma most dangerous – t'was ever thus, was it not?

Celia Amelia continues to write poetry to all the young ladies of the district and beyond, including myself. You are aware already that he flirts outrageously, but he is not dangerous, only playful – as you already sensibly comment: '*Mr Weightman is better in health, but don't set your heart on him   I'm afraid he is very fickle – not to you in particular but to half a dozen other ladies.*' No, I didn't set my heart on him – I have no male person to whom my heart belongs.

It's my heart, it belongs to me. I shall stay unmarried. You, also, my dear C.B., may call me Mrs. Ellen. How did I become so wise, so young?

I hear from Anne – a delightful letter – She seems settled with the Robinsons, for which you must be equally thankful – I wonder when the Quartette shall be again re-united? Today, our dear Vicar of Birstall, Mr. Heald, is at Brookroyd. You will recall that he's our distant cousin through my sister-in-law Mary. We love him for his gentle ways – he is talking intimately with poor George, who leaves for Scotland tomorrow. My sad brother abides with a mental state of instability and we long for the return of his erstwhile buoyant spirits. During his Scottish sojourn, we pray that the bright clean air and beauteous mountain scenery will lift his soul. I end hastily – I wish to write more but I have a million things to do around the house. Au revoir.

Your loving and, always, devoted friend,

Nell

Brookroyd, 17 November 1840

Dearest Charlotte,

I read your latest letter and the embedded advice therein with profound sympathy and interest. It seems that the old triangle, of Mary Taylor, you and me, is a wondrous protection against romantic humbug – humbug is your phrase, which is a happy acquisition. It holds such sweet toxicity. Through talking with both of you, all these years, I have gained more knowledge and insight into how marriage may be an entrapment for women of our generation. The institution of marriage offers, by itself, no protection whatsoever for the unwary. Nor may we take comfort from a potential husband being an ordained member of the Church of England. We must rely on thorough knowledge of the man himself – by which I mean – to know in advance the reliability, steadfastness, good behaviour and integrity of any man who may parade affection and a conjoined future.

Your letter is graphic in its explanations – I do empathise with Mrs. Sarah Collins. In approaching the parsonage for a prolonged discussion of her plight, Mrs. Sarah Collins is indeed fortunate to experience the combined wisdom of you and Emily. You understand the intimacies of a clergy household, and are well placed to offer both advice and temporary sanctuary – two hours in your dining room, taking tea and revealing her tribulations, provides considerable comfort and support to her. In years to come, after she has left this appalling man and his threatening, bullying habits, she will recall your kindness and, in the larger significance, the fact that you believe her. This is the most valuable gift of her desperate circumstance. Her evidence is truly noted, recorded in the memory of others. She receives the acceptance of truth. I honour you for so doing, on her behalf. This poor woman now finds herself shackled to a profligate, drunken, extravagant man, notwithstanding that he is a Clerk in Holy Orders.

This is a warning, as indeed perhaps you intend it. The Collins' travesty of a union, in which he is the bully and she, the victim, is a metaphor for everything undesirable in the institution of marriage. If one does not know or trust one's betrothed, better stay unmarried to the ends of time. Once the ceremony has occurred one is a canary in a cage. I shall pray that the outcome of Sarah Collins' story shall be positive. She has the courage to leave, and in the forthcoming years I hope to hear of her success. I pray that, through her own endeavours and strength of character, she will raise herself and her son from brutality and poverty.

As to my own circumstances, I do not know Mr. Vincent, despite these many months of attention. For all I know he drinks in secret, and is dishonest and unreliable. How I could I know otherwise, for he reveals not his true self to me – rather does he confide in Henry and seek information from our relatives. This bodes not well, and in truth I feel disgust towards him on occasions. I'm aware, as indeed are you, my dearest friend, that my brother Joseph imbibes alcohol, and your brother Branwell likewise, nay worse perhaps. Now then, I ask you, is not Mr. Vincent less known to me than either of these brothers?

Meanwhile, I have no prospects, no money, nothing to inherit – therefore Henry wishes me to marry *someone*. Kindly as he is, my brother fails to comprehend that, years hence, I could be placed in jeopardy, as is poor Sarah Collins at this current time. Write me soon and give me of your most honest appraisal.

Always your dear, trusted friend,

Your very own affectionate,

Nell.

Brookroyd, 24 November 1840

Dearest C.B.,

I thank you for your reply, which assiduously I peruse, to scrutinise every word, every feeling expressed therein. Indeed so long a letter have I but rarely received from you, for is it not several pages? Your frustration with Mr. Vincent – that he trusts me not with his feelings, but rather that he relies on

Henry, who transmits the dilemma to you, is well founded. Round and round the mulberry bush does my clerical gentleman dance, or so I envisage from both his behaviour and your reply. The dance completed, the music ceased, we may be none of us the wiser as to his personality, or his intentions. When I re-read your long, detailed letter of 20th November, I feel nothing but love, respect and admiration for you – and a diminishing sense of nothing for Rev. Osman Parke Vincent. He continues to court me, sometimes by letter, but I am a strong woman, and I will make a sensible, reasonable decision, when the time comes. I shall employ my brain, just as you and Polly would advise. Be not disturbed by any of Henry's missives concerning the very same Mr. Vincent. Remember, C.B., that you may trust me, always, to be *your* devoted friend,

    Ellen

Journal
Brookroyd, 8 December 1840

Mary & Martha's papa has not long to live. We shall be surprised if he sees out the year. Polly and I talk for two hours during my visit to the Red House. Mary prophesies that the family will now scatter to the ends of the earth. They try so hard to love their mother, but none are happy at home with her, because sadly, she is already a sour, bitter, disagreeable person. In anticipation of their beloved papa's demise, Martha and Mary are determined that they shall not stay longer than necessary in the Red House. They mean no disrespect to their mother, with whom they will live for several months after their papa dies. Time will help them all face the truth – the unbearable unhappiness which seeps in damp layers throughout that house.

Polly and Patty speak of attending a finishing school in Brussels, and Polly's already considering teaching on the continent, and, later, emigrating to New Zealand within the decade. After their father's demise it's likely that John and Joe shall move to the cottage by Hunsworth Mill. However, William, the youngest brother, is already hoping to precede Mary to the antipodes, by emigrating within a couple of years from now. He will be there sooner – so Mary may join him when she is ready. She is a very brave, adventurous woman. I am very proud of her determination and to be known as her friend.

Journal

Brookroyd, 28 December 1840

Poor Mr. Taylor is gone. We are all to attend the funeral. He has suffered so badly for a full year that we cannot but be relieved – the end of his earthly journey.

Journal

Brookroyd, 31 December 1840

So ends 1840, a year in which my attitudes to my future have consolidated, rather than changed. I have not heard the last of Mr. Vincent but I shall not marry him. It is Charlotte Brontë who holds the key to my heart. I know of no female within my world, who lives and loves as I do. But, as to the future – I have some wonderful female friends, to whom I can turn for guidance: if Mary Taylor can be so strong, and Charlotte can be so brave, it behoves me as the third of Miss Wooler's young lions to hold steady with my lantern, even in the winter's weather. Charlotte Brontë holds the key to my heart – it is Charlotte Brontë with whom I shall live, or shall remain an unmarried woman, residing in my family home, where my brothers are kind and there is no equivalent to the notorious Rev. Collins, to make misery of my days and violence of my nights.

Brookroyd, 26 January 1841

Dearest C.B.,

In this matter of Mr. Vincent, you may be reassured by this letter. Recent correspondence from Henry exonerates you completely. I do believe you – no underhand dealings were employed by you – Henry wishes to find a husband for me, but you are not involved in his conspiracy to have me married. I have heard from Henry to this end – it's clear that the correspondence between you and my brother concerning Mr. Vincent does in no way implicate you. So that's the end of it – Your feelings are illustrated most eloquently in your letter written on 3rd. You advise that if I were to marry, I should 'marry well' or better stay single. Your words are so direct – an arrow to its target. *'I'll never come and see you after you are married.'* The truth of your real feelings rings louder than church bells on a Sunday morning, even though you choose to soften the sound of discordant clanging, by playing with my name – Ellen Helen Eleonora Nell Nelly Mrs. Vincent.

Now then, let us lay this matter to rest, for once and for all. Please listen to me – Charlotte, Charlie, Charles Thunder, Chiarvari, my sweet friend. *I shall not marry Mr. Vincent.* Please absorb this information. I may continue my correspondence with the same gentleman, but shall do so only as a friend. *I shall not alter my decision.*

Meanwhile, I hear from Polly and Patty Taylor that you may have found a situation – or shall do so very soon. Write me with your new address when you have it, and with all other news. Do you know already that Polly Taylor intends to emigrate to New Holland or New Zealand – what do you think about it?

I am yours truly and always,

Your reassuring friend,

Nell

Brookroyd, 10 March 1841

Dearest C.B.,

How glad am I that the spring is coming and the days grow lighter.

My heart likewise grows lighter for I shall come to Upperwood House at Rawdon, to see you. I know not whether it be a breach of etiquette – for a governess to ask a friend to visit – nevertheless, I have beguiled George into bringing me in the gig on Saturday 13th and I shall stay for an hour or two if it's allowed.

I am in receipt of a pretty, decorated silk and lace card for Valentine's Day from Celia Amelia. I laugh most heartily, thinking how hard must he work on his 'poetry' and how many dozens he does send. At least now with the penny post he must pay postage himself and not charge it to the recipient. N'est ce pas?

I shall close now and see you soon.

Expect me around two in the afternoon.

Your loving and affectionate friend,

Nell

Brookroyd, 18 March 1841

Dearest C.B,

How short is our visit! I try to not grumble for I see how difficult is your situation with Mrs. White. She expects so much sewing from you – already your eyes are very tired.

Currently the atmosphere is not harmonious at Brookroyd – Mercy is at her most difficult, being simultaneously capricious *and* cantankerous. She has taken to ordering me about the house. At present it seems that I can do no right for doing wrong. It makes me weary in the extreme, most saddened and forlorn. I am also rather frightened. Mercy is fearsome in her rage. I have never before felt this in her presence. The trauma doesn't quite depart, although I sleep without nightmares all through the night, which is a blessing. Mama endeavours to bring peace and calm to the household – she tries to reassure me that it's not my fault – and to explain about women's problems – for women of Mercy's age – but it doesn't make my older sister any the more likeable or peaceful of temperament!

I miss you profoundly, although I accept that you must maintain this employment at Rawdon. When summer comes along, you will be able to take the children on walks and teach them in the countryside. It will allow escape from the house. Do take heart, my dearest, and remember that Spring Equinox is herald of summer. Look to the sunnier days ahead. Is it not also a time of balance – so shall our spirits be lifted – we shall feel more contented when there is more sunshine.

Please write soon and do not forsake me.

Your affectionate friend,

Nell

Brookroyd, 29 March 1841

Dearest Charlotte,

Thank you so much for your latest letter. You say that you shall not forsake me – Oh how heartened am I when I read those words. You ask for sympathy and attachment in some quarter – you may find it in *this* quarter whenever and howsoever you may choose.

I am writing with an invitation from Mama – can you come and see us on Easter Saturday, the 10th April? Mama sends this message, saying, 'We shall bake your favourite apple cake – and all manner of morsels for your delight.'

Is that enough to persuade you to come?

George will fetch you in the gig.

Your loving friend

Nell

Dearest Charlotte,

How wonderful to see you at Brookroyd even if only for one day. We have May Day celebrations here in Birstall, throughout today, with dancing around the maypole, to the delight of all the children. The booths are decorated with ribbons and flowers – there's a fortune-teller although Mama forbids me to partake. I think of your aunt and her stories, the dancing in the Cornwall of her youth and her songs such as Way Down to Lamorna. It's a merry time for everyone today, except George, who is 'under a cloud'. I know not how or why this cloud descends, even in bright weather, and amidst a crowd of familiar faces. Polly teases him. She calls him the Noah of Birstall: 'Bring your own rain, why don't you?' This hurts his feelings most dreadfully and off he stalks, sulking, at which she's distressed for she means only to ruffle him and shake him out of it. The Taylor brothers are settled now in the cottage next to Hunsworth mill and, together with Polly and Patty, we weave in and out of our May Day throng. We wear our new muslins, so warm is the sunshine.

I am sorry indeed that your employers would not release you for today – to visit and attend our village fair. What harm would befall the children, without their governess, for just one day?

I talk with George and Joshua about becoming a governess, but they are adamant that men – brothers, husbands, fathers – are the rightful earners – my suggestion appears to be hurtful to family pride.

So must I again quieten myself for the present. Bye the bye – I can come on Saturday 15th to Upperwood House, arriving in the gig at about 2pm. Let me know if this will be convenient.

Your loving and affectionate friend,

Nell

Brookroyd, 27 May 1841

Dearest Charlotte,

Excuse the brevity but I can come on Saturday afternoon, next, 29th.

Write by return and tell me this is possible.

These visits, albeit brief, are so good for us – they cheer us up – I feel that without these commas, our paragraphs are long, far too long. When I come to you, I can hold you, rub your back, laugh with you, and watch your face. The shine returns to your eyes when we share one another's presence, e'en for so short a time.

Soon, I shall see you

Nell

Brookroyd, 13 June 1841

Dearest Charlotte,

I hope most sincerely that Mr. and Mrs. White return in time for you to go home and see Anne. If the worst happens and you miss her, I will go to Haworth to visit and report back to you on her health & etc.

I know that is poor substitute – I shall pray for all to work out well for you. There is not much news from here, notwithstanding a visit to The Red House, where Polly and I talk for a long afternoon. She regrets that she cannot accept the Irish position – and that her brothers and mine feel similarly about our going out to become a governess. They are wrong but we cannot change them.

Write and tell me where you will be on Saturday, 26th.

If you're not in Haworth I will come and see you in Rawdon.

Your loving and affectionate friend,

Nell

Brookroyd, 3 July 1841

Dearest Charlotte,

Yes I should love to come to Haworth and see you on Tuesday next, 6th. I am so excited I can hardly breathe. I can stay ten days – I have permission. I shall arrive by the gig about twelve noon.

Soon. Soon.

In haste

Nell

Brookroyd, 5 July 1841

Dearest Charlotte,
Your hasty note with the change of times has arrived safely.

I shall be with you on Thursday 8th.

I plan to arrive as before about twelve noon.

I am jumping up and down.

Barely can I wait the extra two days.

Soon. Soon.

Your loving friend

Nell.

Haworth, 19 July 1841

My dear Ellen

We waited long – and anxiously for you on the Thursday that you promised to come – I quite wearied my eyes with watching from the window – eye-glass in hand and sometimes spectacles on nose—However you are not to blame—I believe you have done right in going to Earnley and as to the disappointment we endured why all must suffer disappointment at some period or other of their lives—but a hundred things I had to say to you will now be forgotten and never said—there is a project hatching in this house – which both Emily and I anxiously wished to discuss with you—The project is yet in its infancy – hardly peeping from its shell ... ...

... ... To come to the point – Papa and Aunt talk by fits & starts of our – id est – Emily Anne & myself commencing a School–! I have often you know said how much I wished such a thing – ... ...

– Much inquiry & consideration will be necessary of course before any plan is decided on ... ... Can events be so turned as that you shall be included as an associate in our projects?... ... ...

... ...

Write to me as soon as you can and address to Rawden—I shall not leave my present situation—till my future prospects assume a more fixed & definite aspect—Good bye dear Ellen

CB

Dearest Charlotte,

I write first of all with my apology – I am sorry most sincerely that you waited so long and anxiously for me on the Thursday that I promised to come to Haworth – and I was so very pleased to receive your long letter written on 19th inst. It showed, to my utmost relief, that you understood the *reason* for the suddenness of my departure.

Sometimes my whole family unites, settles upon a plan for my life, or even my next few months – hey presto – they act upon it.

This time, they insist that I accompany Henry – admittedly a far more attractive prospect than travelling such a distance by myself. Notwithstanding that my family know all my plans – time with you in Haworth – if Henry is ready to leave, my arrangements account for *nothing*. Once again, is it not my intercourse with you that is relegated to the shadows?

I am disappointed, most especially, not to be with you during your initial discussions of your school. At last, my dearest, this possibility may be brought closer to reality. I am so excited by this – I read your letter to myself over and again. As to your request for help – yes – of course I shall in due course and with cautious regard for discretion, ask for my sister Ann's advice about housekeeping. As to the geography – I think that Burlington is a fine idea. There are indeed several schools in that area other than Miss Clarissa Jack's academy at Prospect Place. Nevertheless, the location is nigh perfect and I well remember our delight with our lodgings in Garrison Street. It seems only yesterday that we lodged and loved therein, though it is almost a full two years since. I can but affirm that my dearest wish would be to housekeep 'our' school – myself as one of the Quartette – I would be willing to work day and night, night and day, towards its success. Were it to become my residence, my home, my workplace, I would be the luckiest person in the world.

Oh yes, please convey to Emily and Anne that I wish to be '*an associate in your projects*'. I agree that it is too soon to know how best I become involved. But I *am* involved.

My dearest, we have born with patience and fortitude the separations of our daily lives, yet do my deepest feelings for you remain constant, although I am aware that the maturity of my middle twenties invokes the necessity of realism. During these past few years our positions have changed in the wider world – you have been encouraged to 'go out' and earn a living as a governess. I durst not mention even such a possibility in my family. My 'going out' is a notion inconceivable within my circumstances. I enclose a letter from Mary Taylor fairly bubbling with enthusiasm for her studies with Martha, in Belgium. She says that she has written to you and sent a packet. Did you receive it?

How would you feel about increasing your languages? Surely Mary's enjoyment of Brussels – and further studies – must light a spark? And would it not be useful for your school?

Write me soon and – especially – let me know how Anne fares with the Robinsons.

My love to you,
Your affectionate friend,
Nell

Earnley Rectory, 10 October 1841

Dearest Charlotte,

I am yours, yet my sleep comes not easily to me. There is created in me some considerable disturbance from those morsels of news that fly like bats beyond my window, in the dark where I cannot see them, only hear them as their faint squeals disappear into the distant night.

I refer to rumours, which reach me in Earnley, that Miss Wooler invites you to take over Heald's House in Dewsbury to run as a school. Yet following your previous letters to me, I assume – perhaps with arrogance on my part – that I shall receive intelligence of such changes from you, not from a third party as if it means nothing to me. I am somewhat distressed – more so daily – about the miscommunication between us. Are you taking up school at Dewsbury? Is it not an inappropriate and damp location? Are there not rumours of consumption therein? What transpires of plans for Burlington? And why am I not to know of any changes, hints or doubts?

In the meantime I think that whispers will reach you about the further attention being paid to me by Mr. Vincent, which I do not intend to encourage. Of course, I look to my future and I recognise that it might be *prudent* to marry. Yet I cannot marry without love, nor find in my heart a place for anyone else. My heart is given already to someone very dear to me. You know the true identity of the recipient.

Your devoted and bewildered friend,
Nell

Dearest Charlotte,

I hardly know how to answer. Please forgive the petulance of my last letter. It is some considerable comfort to have, albeit tardily, some information from you about the proposal from Miss Wooler. I do not mean my letters to berate you – perhaps I'm isolated here in Earnley, and perhaps I miss you more than I declare. I have a new friend here, name of Mary Gorham. She's the daughter of a gentleman farmer who came from Kent – and the family moved here in 1831.

The Gorhams are kind, generous people, known through being parishioners at Henry's church, being only one mile from Henry's home. Mary is nine years younger than I, a sincere person, whose friendship helps me feel more at home hereabouts. Also, I hear from a friend in Yorkshire, a Miss Swithinhurst. I enclose her details on a separate scrap of paper – and ask you to speak on her behalf to Mrs. White, as she seeks a situation near Bradford.

I am relieved that you shall not take up the offer from Miss Wooler of making a school at Dewsbury Moor. It is both a damp and an inappropriate place. Far better to try for Burlington as mooted in other discussions. As to your interest in going to Brussels, it is what I had envisaged – an excellent plan. Oh how I wish that I would be permitted to travel to Belgium next spring with you. It hurts me however that all these plans are made without reference to my knowledge of them. I feel abandoned by you, indeed, abandoned.

Mr. Vincent has openly proposed. I have equally openly refused him. Now that's the end of it. Write again as soon as you can and tell me that you really care about me. Rawdon seems so far away from Earnley. I need to see you and be held by you.

Nell

Upperwood House, Rawdon, 2 November 1841

Dear E. N!

Let us dismiss business matters first – and then quarrel like cat & dog on private concerns afterwards – Mrs White has already five applications from ex-governesses under consideration –I believe she has nearly completed a bargain with one – It would therefore answer no good end to propose the lady you mention – had there been the remotest chance of success I would have done my possible to oblige you –

Now let us begin to quarrel ... ...

The plain fact is I was not   I am not now certain of my destiny – on the contrary I have been most uncertain – perplexed with contradictory schemes & proposals– my time – as I have often told you is fully occupied – yet I had many letters to write which it was absolutely necessary should be written – I knew it would avail nothing to write to you then to say I was in doubt & uncertainty – hoping this fearing that – anxious eagerly desirous to do what seemed impossible to be done. When I thought of you in that busy interval it was to resolve that you should know all when my way was clear & my grand end attained   If I could Ellen I would always work in silence & obscurity & let my efforts be known only by their results – Miss Wooler did most kindly propose that I should come to Dewsbury Moor & attempt to revive the school her sister had relinquished – she offered me the use of her furniture for the consideration of her board –at first I received the proposal cordially & and prepared to do my utmost to bring about success – but a fire was kindled in my very heart which I could not quench – I so longed to increase my attainments to become something better than I am – a glimpse of what I felt I shewed to you in one of my former letters – only a glimpse– Mary Taylor cast oil on the flames– encouraged me & in her own strong energetic language heartened me on– I longed to go to Brussels ... ...

Dewsbury-Moor is relinquished... ... ... My plans for the future are bounded to this intention if once I get to Brussels... ... ...When we two shall meet again God knows   Believe me my dear Ellen though I was born in April the month of cloud & sunshine I am not changeful– my spirits are unequal & sometimes I speak vehemently & sometimes I say nothing at all– but I have steady regard for you– & if you will let the cloud & shower only pass by without upbraiding – be sure the sun is always behind – obscured but still existing. Write & say all is forgiven   I'm fit to cry

CB

Earnley Rectory, 11 November 1841

Dear C.B.,

I trust that you know my feelings for you – there is no need to cry. Please don't be distressed, but rather accept that our separations make our plans and life's chances not easy always to convey. Forgive any lack of charitable attitudes on my part – I have no excuses – I am not able always to accommodate to change as rapidly as others around me. In truth I am very pleased for you and Emily about the possibility of Brussels – I shall write to her to convey my delight that she may be your companion there. You should not be away alone from England because the comfort of at least one of your sisters is essential for your well-being. Believe me that I am your sincere friend, who will always love you. I pray for guidance from Almighty God, and the strength and wisdom to accept all the changes and chances ahead.

I shall be home soon, and shall hope to see you at Brookroyd after you have finished with Upperwood House. Until then, my family begs to be remembered to you and Henry says to send his warm wishes and considers you a dear friend.

Your loving and affectionate friend,

Nell

Brookroyd, 12 December 1841

Dearest Charlotte,

Thank you for your letter written on 9th. I am worried about your health – not my own – for you write that you have not a moment to yourself all day and un-free from your labours to sleep until midnight or after. How can they treat you so? In every house hereabouts with servants they are allowed more respite from work. I should hire a gig and arrive out of the dark, lights a-blazing, storm up to the door and demand your freedom. Be unafraid, 'tis but a dream. Do not think I am a meek, gentle person. The health of my friend is of the utmost significance to me. For myself, I am at last home from Earnley Rectory and glad to be so. I am now well and pleased to say also that Mercy is fully recovered. However we continue to nurse Mama, whose fatigue lingers on. But there is no sickness here that might carry contagion and we would be truly grateful for a visit from you to Brookroyd. Mercy has written an invitation – she is at present housekeeping here in the absence of my sister Ann – and persuades me to enclose her invitation with this letter. During the time that you're home, I shall try to persuade my family to release me. I long to stay with you at the parsonage once again. What are the twenty things to tell me? I hasten to know. How I miss being able to speak with you, by the fireside or between the blankets. It seems so long since last I enjoyed the sound of your voice.

Write me soon and inform me of your arrival home – your letter says you must work at Rawdon a week or two longer – but of course you will be allowed home by Christmas – it would be unthinkable, else.

Remember me to your papa, your aunt, and your sisters

Your loving and affectionate friend

Nell

Dearest Charlotte,

You find me in my most melancholy mood. Forgive me for my continued absence from Haworth. They will not release me. I am too useful here. I accept not one of the reasons why it is impossible for me to visit Haworth before you leave with Emily and Polly for Belgium. I long to share good conversation face to face with you before your departure – with intensity of distress I bite back my rage. I dare not release my bitter rejoinders. The tangle of this family's skein is impenetrable. The threads are entwined, knotted, and may not be un-ravelled. At least, not by *me*.

I endeavour to bear the frustration of my dreams with fortitude – I resolve to pray for increased patience. I try to think of the future, to hold onto its hopes, its possibilities. Beyond these months of our separation, when you will travel, study abroad and meet new friends, there is surely a little hope for me. I pray that your improvement in foreign languages will bring nearer, in God's good time, the fulfilment of your school. I know you intend to amuse me, lift my spirits, by painting the picture of our Celia Amelia '*looking out of the corners of his eyes*' to win Anne's attention in church, but indeed it made me sigh – no, not for *him*, rather for the loss of 'the Quartette', your company, my separation from Haworth and those I love. Don't tease me therefore – about Celia Amelia – '*He would the better of a comfortable wife like you to settle him.*' I'm no 'comfortable wife' for any man. I'm clear in my mind about my course of action – to be a 'spinster of this parish'. A little while longer and verily I shall be named an old maid.

I shall read the newspapers which you must promise to send to me – for the French language – bright, light, refreshing – sounds like a babbling brook upon the moors in early summer – its sparkle shall carry away even the most melancholy of days.

Believe if you can – since I failed *again* to come to Haworth – that I *am* your devoted and affectionate friend.

Nell

Journal
Brookroyd, 6 June 1842

There is coldness now, where once was warmth between my sweetheart and myself, since the commencement of her sojourn in Brussels. Perhaps, of necessity, coldness arrives and lingers on. We have not talked face to face for months. In each separation, it is I who fails to travel to Haworth despite her pleas. A few sparse lines from Charlotte penned with a letter from Mary and Martha in April comprises my only communication. She is gone – and I should dissolve into the blue ocean that now lies between us were I to give myself up to more grief and sorrow on account of her. I ask myself, should I have married Mr. Vincent? My most significant change during last winter was my decision not to marry anyone. Perhaps I should have enjoyed having my own children. Perhaps he would have been a steady, reliable husband – I think not. My having made my choice – not to marry – the relief of having made it, illuminates its validity. However, if my brothers were to hear these words, they'd tease me – my words seem irregular, singular, over-philosophical for a 'slip of a lass' like myself. But I am proud of my refusal, each moment of every day. Most women of my years are focussed on nothing else except marriage, husbands and procreation. Moreover, Charlotte shows in her letters that she half expects me to take that predictable route. I did not. I shall not. My decision sits comfortably inside me – it saves my sanity, for it rejects a mediocre opportunity and I choose to be complete by myself. The relief washes over me like the waves that crash the distant shores where my beloved Charlotte now resides.

Today – ironically since I have 'let go' of my need to gainsay the future – a glimpse thereof opens up for me. 'Tis always the way of it. Today I receive a pretty little note from Mary Gorham, my young friend from Sussex. She does not mention Mr. Vincent, for which I am grateful. She is a forward-looking young woman, and, despite the nine years between us, I have a comfortable feeling that we shall grow to be steady friends. Without new friends, I would be lonely in Yorkshire – with the Quartette and the sisters from the Red House all dispersed – therefore I need new friends, here in this country, to lift me from the past and occupy me in the here and now. So be it.

To Mary Gorham
Brookroyd, midsummer, 1842

Dear Mary,

How very kind of you to write – to say that you're thinking of me because I may feel bereft now that my friends are gone away. Your most timely note, with its sympathy and understanding, is of great comfort to me now that my local friends are dispersed. Only Anne is in Yorkshire, the rest being across the German Ocean.

In truth I do feel lost, nay abandoned, but that feeling I endeavour with prayer and strength of will to overcome. Being once again without my dearest Charlotte, I ride into the hills these summer days, where I contemplate the possibility of henceforth making myself happy as a way of 'being alive'. I have already lost one brother, William, from his decline into melancholy. I have another, my dearest George, who suffers mental malady – therefore do I look around me at the people I have known all my life and form the conclusion that happiness is not a feeling that is bestowed upon one, externally by circumstance, from outside and beyond. Happiness is a way of living. It's a way of *staying* alive. My mind takes a philosophical turn this summer and, as I enjoy writing letters, may I share with you a few of my observations?

As to my surroundings, I live in the midst of the working people – the mill workers, farm hands, and so forth. Some of the poorest mill-workers in our vicinity are not the most miserable with each other. I witness mill girls, arm in arm laughing. I notice the men, who work long hard hours, gathering in bunches, sharing a joke. There are suffering people in Birstall parish, sick people I visit through our church, yet in whose presence the happiness is tangible. By contrast, I evidence that some of the wealthiest, luckiest people I have ever met, like Mary & Martha's mother, are unwilling to communicate happiness – or even kindness – to those around them.

I must be strong with due regard for my present circumstances, and must remain firm in my decision not to find a husband, or leave home, or begin a family of procreation. I hope you will affirm my strength of purpose in enjoyment of my daily life *as it is*. Am I not a most fortunate woman, loved dearly by the members of my family, known in my neighbourhood, self-sufficient in my love of life? I enjoy simply being alive. We are not wealthy folk – the income throughout my family has to be hard-earned – but I am economically very secure, albeit not independent – I am warm, well-shod, fashionably-clothed and never hungry. My garden at Brookroyd is a treasure-trove; the moors beyond the mill valleys are mine, on horseback – surely there can be no more spectacular way to view my homeland? I take comfort in the familiarity of my surroundings this summer, and I trust my intuition – which tells me that Charlotte and Emily shall be studying for half a year, then abiding in Brussels for a further half year. Mama is persuaded to find me a local tutor for French conversation, if I may not leave Brookroyd to study or travel abroad. I quote the Brontë sisters and the Taylor sisters, to press my point. I read to Sarah, whose health continues to decline, and assist Mercy with the housekeeping when Ann's not at home. Shall you write to me, as my new friend, and paint for me a picture of your life in Sussex? I should enjoy very much receiving an epistle from you. Meantime, please convey my kindest regards to your dear family, whom I thank again for their kindness last autumn.

Ellen Nussey.

Journal
Brookroyd, 30 June 1842

Martha Taylor is home, temporarily, from the continent – her delightful visit here brings news from Brussels and confirms my intuition – the sisters shall stay for six months longer. I am encouraged to renew my contact with Charlotte, by Patty, and it's grand to see her. Just grand.

Brookroyd, 10 July 1842

Dear Charlotte,

I am persuaded to write to you by Martha, and indeed it is now a pleasure to anticipate the renewal of our correspondence. I am much stronger now – for the months have taught me brave lessons, which I have been determined to learn. I pray to God about the quantity of time available to me, and the quality of life I live within it, since none can know how long we have on this earth.

In the spring I shuddered at the coldness of draught – did it not sweep into Brookroyd from the eastern shores of Yorkshire, borne on the decks of the ship that took my friends across the windswept German Ocean? After your departure, I fell into the danger of wasting my happiness, allowing disappointment, like a tubercle, to fester inside me. Now I am calm. I declare, maintenant, I am happy here at Brookroyd. I have ceased my rage at separation, my silent anger with everyone around me. Perhaps I make a 'virtue of necessity'. I would accept the justice of that assertion.

This summer, I am not hunted for the purpose of marriage by my family, or their friends, they on horseback with hounds baying at their feet, 'find Ellen, find Ellen', bring her back, make her stay here, make her go there. I shall not be the vixen of their hunt. This summer, I take respite from my erstwhile aspirations and my tantalizing, nay phantom-like, dreams. I accept that Brookroyd is my earth and in its familiar woodland I take comfort in my lair. But also, my dear friend, *because* I am alone here, is not this summer *truly mine own*? Can my solitude be transformed into my freedom – albeit transitory – on horseback on the moors? We are as one, my horse and her rider – we belong together – our rides are exhilarating. Yes, for I have permission from home.

Is not our West Riding very beautiful? I take my chances to laugh aloud in the wind – I revel in the fullness of each hour. After much prayer and contemplation I make again my own purpose – so that my time again has hope within – I shall not sink into hopeless waiting for my friends' return, nor for my sweetheart's reciprocity, nor for some future moment, unspecified and unattainable. My life is saved. Do you comprehend me, Charlotte? Give my love to Emily, and to Mary Taylor.

Your friend,
Ellen Rider-Fox

Journal
Brookroyd, 18August 1842

Our first hint of autumn – so early? Golden leaves on silver birch, glittering through late afternoon, shimmering like golf leaf upon a cathedral altar. I am too young for my own autumn, but calm quiet settling of the earth is my own calm. As the angle of the Lammas light changes, and the first russet bracken clothes the moors, I gather my feelings like a flock of sheep; protect them inside me, like a sheepfold on the moors with a sturdy gate; delegate their care to no-one; expose them to neither the vagaries of climate nor the fluctuating fortunes of fate. My life must be my own, and my heart can belong to no-one but myself. I have not seen Charlotte nor heard her voice for over a year. Transformation has taken place: a singular transformation of the heart and soul. Although Charlotte shall continue to be the most important friend in my life, she is no longer the secret fiancée whom I have loved and lost. I have a sense of relief – the end of yearning.

Journal
Brookroyd, 29 August 1842

Cholera. Suddenly, a virulent epidemic sweeps across Britain and Europe and touches the very stones of Haworth. Cholera descends upon our friend William Weightman – our Celia Amelia – the curate of Haworth – his suffering is abominable.

Dear Mary,

Thank you for your latest letter in which I am most relieved to read that cholera has not invaded your village, and that all your friends are well. Not so hereabouts. In particular the area around Haworth is affected – our friend William Weightman [our beloved Celia Amelia] died after a fortnight's suffering. He was buried on 10th September and, today in the Parish Church, Charlotte's papa led our memorial service with deep emotion in his voice: '*We shall remember him for his preaching and practising which was neither distant nor austere, timid nor obtrusive, not bigoted, exclusive, nor dogmatical.*'

I am deeply sad for this indeed is the autumn of shadows. My brother George is again home, but his spirits are troubled. I shared with him many good times during childhood and he was always my riding companion. I hear from Mary Taylor that she is going to teach English to children among the mountains, trees and waters of Germany – a place called Iserlohn. She says that Charlotte and Emily are well: '*not only in health but in mind and hope*' – but I haven't heard from Charlotte since July.

I hope that next time I shall write with happier news,

Your friend,

Ellen Nussey

Brookroyd, 30 October 1842

Dear Anne,

I am sad in the extreme to receive your letter informing me that Aunt Branwell died yesterday – I loved her dearly and shall always listen for her voice in the tales of Cornwall. She was so welcoming, so kind to me. I trust that your faith will sustain and strengthen you in this tragic bereavement.

My mother, my sisters and especially myself send our love to you and all your family. Mama and I shall attend the funeral on November 3rd, and until then shall pray for all your family at this time of deep sorrow.

Yours very sincerely and with affection,

Ellen.

My dear Ellen

You will have heard by this time the end of poor Martha; & with my head full of this event & still having nothing to say upon it, or rather not feeling inclined to say it, I scarcely know why I write to you. But I don't wish you to think this misfortune will make me forget you more than the rest did; having the opportunity of sending you a letter postage free I just write to tell you I think of you ... ...

I am now staying with the Dixons in Brussels. I find them very different to what I expected. They are the most united affectionate family I ever met with... ... ... I shall finish my letter after I have seen Charlotte. Well I have seen her & Emily. We have walked about six miles to see the cemetery & the country round it. We then spent a pleasant evening with my cousins & in presence of my Uncle & Emily one not speaking at all; the other once or twice. I like to hear from you & thank you very much for your letter. Remember me to your sister Mercy & your Mother, & to all who inquire about me, ... To Miss Cockhill Mary, & all the Misses Wooler, particularly to Miss Wooler, Miss Bradbury & The Healds.

Mary Taylor.

11 Rue de la Regence

If this letter should not reach you for some time after the date, it will not be because it has been delayed on the road but because an opportunity did not occur of sending it sooner by a private hand.

Mary Dixon wishes me to begin again to express her kind remembrances to you & your sister.

Haworth, 10 November 1842

My dear Ellen

I was not yet returned to England when your letter arrived – We received the first news of Aunt's illness – Wednesday Novbr 2nd – we decided to come home directly –next morning a second letter informed us of her death. We sailed from Antwerp on Sunday– we travelled day & night and got home on Tuesday morning – of course the funeral and all was over. We shall see her no more – Papa is pretty well   we found Anne at home   she is pretty well also – You say you have had no letter from me for a long time – I wrote to you three weeks ago

– When you answer this note I will write to you again more in detail – Martha Taylor's illness was unknown to me till the day before she died – I hastened to Kokleberg the next morning – unconscious that she was in great danger – and was told that it was finished, she had died in the night – Mary was taken away to Bruxelles – I have seen Mary frequently since – she is in no way crushed by the event – but while Martha was ill she was to her, more than a Mother – more than a Sister watching – nursing – cherishing her – so tenderly, so unweariedly – she appears calm and serious now – no bursts of violent emotion – no exaggeration of distress – I have seen Martha's grave – the place where her ashes lie in a foreign country Aunt – Martha- Taylor – Mr Weightman are now all gone – how dreary & void everything seems – Mr Weightman's illness was exactly what Martha's was – he was ill the same length of time & died in the same manner – Aunts disease was internal obstruction. she was also ill a fortnight

Goodbye my dear Ellen

Brookroyd, 16 Nov 1842

Dearest Charlotte,

I was so distressed on your behalf to hear of your many bereavements this autumn. I am so very sorry that such sad circumstances call you home. It must be of some comfort to you to know that Mary is safely being cared for by the Dixons in Bruxelles. They are good, kind people and will help her through this saddest time. I am glad that you were able to visit the grave, for that would be a peaceful place to pray for Martha, but how sad that she was taken so young, and in such a manner.

We have lost another dear friend in Celia Amelia. Dare I now call him so? How strange that we shall never again hear him preach, nor enjoy the sound of his laughter.

And, especially, we have lost your Aunt – I loved Aunt Branwell very dearly and I shall miss her most sorely. She was a good, kind woman of a most generous heart, amusing us so with her stories, an inspiring raconteur. Shall her tales live on, somehow in your poems and prose? I dare to hope so.

We have been separated, you and I, for over a year, and I long to be with you, yet cannot leave George who is gaining strength but slowly. It was *not* cholera, but some form of inward melancholy, which takes toll of his body as well as his mind, appearing as a sickness of the soul. Believe me I would love to meet with you, and we extend a warm sincere invitation from my family.

Write to me soon and let me know if you can come.

Always yourn,

Nell

Dear Ellen

I hope your brother George is sufficiently recovered now to dispense with your constant attendance – Papa desires his compliments to you and says he should be very glad if you could give us your company at Haworth for a little while – Can you come on Friday next–? I mention so early a day because Anne leaves us to return to York on Monday – and she wishes very much to see you before her departure – I think George is too good-natured to object to your coming – there is little enough pleasure in this world and it would be truly unkind to deny to you and me that of meeting again after so long a separation – do not fear to find us melancholy or depressed – we are now all much as usual – you will see no difference from our former demeanour   Send me an immediate answer

CB

Give my love & best wishes to your Mother & Mercy

Tuesday morning

Brookroyd, 24 November 1842

Dear Charlotte,

Forgive me but I cannot leave George, because Ann is away at present and Mercy is fully occupied with housekeeping. Besides George, we have daily attendance with Sarah whose incapacity continues, as always, to debilitate and frustrate her wishes for a 'normal' life.

Please therefore hasten here to see us and please give my most sincere regrets to Anne, with whom I should have delighted in talking prior to her return to Thorp Green.

I await your urgent reply.

Ellen

Subsequent letters are transmitted most hurriedly between us, trying desperately to make arrangements. Finally Charlotte pens a few lines to *'break though ceremony, or pride, or whatever it is, and like Mahomet go to the mountain which won't or can't come to me.'* She can be fetched from Bradford very early next Tuesday. I am joyful.

Brookroyd, 26 November 1842

Dear Charlotte,

Tuesday will suit fine because my brother Richard does not require the gig for Leeds market – rather he will wait until Saturday. So I shall collect you at the coaching-inn, Bridge Street in Bradford with the gig – half past eight is not too early. Yes – if the mountain be Brookroyd House and you be Mohammed then so be it – Mohammed comes to the mountain.

Allelujah.

Your friend,

Nell

Journal
Brookroyd, 5 December 1842

How is it that we weave together as if never separated? How can I explain the swift dexterity with which we mend our broken threads? For seven days and seven nights, Charlotte enters my life, telling the truths, speaking about Martha, Celia Amelia and Aunt Branwell, hearing about the twists and turns our lives have taken, sharing blanket talk and confidences, making little jokes and anecdotes. I learn of the details, which she may not convey in censored letters, about her dislike of Madame Heger and her adoration of the head of the household, Monsieur Heger.

'I witness your excitement, Charlotte, you're a little enamoured of him. He is but seven years your elder. Does he mean more to you than an employer?'

'Perhaps. I crave scholarship. To learn to fly, like a gosling wanting and needing to stretch my wings. Praise for my studies makes me bright inside. Like a lantern that waits for its candle to be ignited in a dark winter.'

This is cruel. I am silenced. I am not the lantern bearer. I cannot be. Fate intervenes. Separated for a full year, by the dictates of my mother and my elder sisters who often refuse to release me for trips to Haworth both before my departure for Earnley Rectory and Charlotte's first departure for Brussels, I have undergone a moor-change, a metamorphosis of heart.

She says, 'Come back with me, to the Pensionnat. I have money from my Aunt Branwell. I will pay for you. Come with me for six months.'

'With you? To Belgium?'

'I desire not to be alone in Belgium. Of course I shall go, shall teach the younger ones. You could do likewise. You were as clever as I at Roe Head.'

'The offer is so generous, Charlie,' I say, unconsciously letting slip her old name. I hesitate. 'I should have a problem persuading my family.'

'They are holding you on too tight a rein, my filly. When will you demand your release? Why do you permit them to take advantage of you in such a manner?'

'I urge you to not decry them like that.'

'Forgive me. But will you ask them?' I am silent. She repeats the question: 'Will you?'

'Yes. Yes, I will. I would like to share time with you in Belgium. I should like that very much. I will ask.'

I lie beside her as she slumbers but I do not sleep. My eyes rove around my dim room, on the chests where are kept my spare cloaks, on the drawers where I store my clean undergarments, on the sashes of the windows, where the open drapes permit the moonlight to bathe the chamber. At school I was her peer, her equal. She loves to learn, and all good students like to have excellent tutors. Monsieur Heger towers now above and beyond our dear Miss Wooler. He has Charlotte to himself, demanding and receiving her full attention. I hope that she shall suffer no indiscretion on his part, when she returns – returns alone – of this I have little doubt. Does some instinct guide me to the truth? Is it female intuition that tells me to pray for guidance for her? I do not know. But as I lie there, I have a premonition of trouble – not on my own behalf – but on behalf of the friend who now lies sleeping peacefully beside me, in whose handwriting I have letters, very dear to me, wherein she refers to herself as my child.

My child – if that is what she is – has need of a nurturing sea in which to absorb light and colours to feed her mind. She's thirsty as a sea sponge, thirsty for stimulation of her demanding intellect. She needs to inhabit blue beautiful translucent seas, swaying with soft undercurrents and swirling with a myriad of incandescent fishes. Many times have I heard Aunt Branwell's tales of the oceans

– tall stories from exotic shores brought by sailors to the port of Penzance. If I do not accompany Charlotte, whose mind shall it be that shall feed her own? I durst not dwell on these uncertainties. Without the comfort of her sister Emily, who is now the housekeeper for Haworth, to whom will Charlotte turn for discourse? In the absence of familiar companionship, what stranger might approach to hold this lantern steady? Madame Heger? I hardly think so. They do not share a desire for intimacy, quite the contrary. Monsieur Heger? Does he have the potential for attraction? Might he call forth from her in her loneliness some inappropriate response? She is not always discreet. Indeed her letters to me during our closest years brim near over with passion.

I feel so much the senior to Charlotte at this time. Perhaps it's that my own dreams are gone, scattered as leaves upon the wild heather, while I ride fast into the wind upon the moors.

Charlotte appears shining and lively when she recounts aspects of her new tutor. I dare not trust him – I do not know him. I fall asleep eventually, having found no reassurance within the shifting shadows of my comfortable, moonlit room.

Journal
Brookroyd, 15 January 1843

Having no wish to lie to Charlotte, I ask Mama and Mercy about my accompanying her to Belgium. However, the means I employ reveal the lack of intensity with which I pursue my request and indicate that I'm not serious in my intention. Moreover, I wait until after my lovely visit to Haworth where I stay several nights. After my return I write to thank Charlotte and Emily for their wonderful hospitality, whereupon two or three short letters speed from here to there concerning dressmaking and my choice of costume for our fashionable evening of local celebrations, which Charlotte refers to as our 'Birstall rout'.

I choose the timing most discerningly to broach the delicate subject with my family.

'Charlotte wishes me to accompany her to Brussels,' I venture, over dinner, 'at her own expense, and I promised her that I would put this proposition to you. But I'm conscious of my duties here at home, now that Ann is away and Sarah grows no stronger despite our care of her, does she?'

My mother looks at me very kindly, and for once, Mercy's face is gentle, not stern as she listens to my mother's reply.

'What are your wishes in this matter, Nellie?'

'My wishes have changed, Mama. There was a time when this would have been an exciting dream, but I do not yearn to reside in a foreign city, nor travel to foreign shores. I am satisfied with my life at Brookroyd.'

'So, you're happy here at home, Nellie?'

'I am, thank you, Mama. I have many friends in this vicinity and…I enjoy my French conversation with my tutor locally, which enables me, through your generosity, to communicate fluently with the sisters at the parsonage. It is sufficient. I'm grateful to you…and my riding provides me with solitude, which I crave.'

'Then the matter is closed, is it not, and…' my mother turns to smile at Mercy, adding, 'and, the outcome meets with everyone's approbation?'

Mercy nods, smiling at me, commenting quietly, 'That is true.'

'Thank for listening to me, Mama, I shall communicate to Charlotte immediately, for she leaves by the end of this month.'

Brookroyd, 24 March 1843

My dear Charlotte,

I am writing particularly to comment on the people mutually known to us and the awakening of the countryside around me. I am enjoying very greatly the company of Joe and John Taylor and have made several journeys to visit the little house by Hunsworth Mill.

One reason for my increased volume of letters is my concern for your solitary state, and maybe I am not a little guilty, because my absence contributes to your aloneness. No, you may not tease me about my friendship with Joe and John – nor the long lost O.P.Vincent – nor draw letters with the sea between us and bubbles describing 'the chosen one'. How foolish you are, my dear friend, when I am determined in my chosen path – I am destined never to marry. Bye the bye, there are rumours floating around Yorkshire that *you've* met someone you intend to marry – I have been hard pressed in our locality to squash such rumours – so I must ask you straight out – bluntness being our Yorkshire manner hereabouts – if they're founded upon any truth at all. Are they? Though in my right mind I can't imagine this to be true. What *I think* has happened it is that people cannot understand that you might return across the German Ocean just to teach – so they impute some more hidden motives. Rumours might reach your ears about Joe or John and likewise you may chuckle into your kerchief – and waste not one ounce of precious sleep over such nonsense.

Joe Taylor intends to travel with Polly on the continent until June or some-time such and then Polly can return to teaching her little German lads. He will deliver letters and I shall ask Emily whether she wants to use him as donkey-packhorse. I will write again soon –

I'll send more silly gossip, sounding like an old, wrinkled woman

Yours,

Ellen prune

Journal

Brookroyd, 28 April 1843

Today a long letter arrives from Charlotte – it's clear that she's suffering mo-notony and uniformity of life, and also that she is very lonely without Emily – or myself – but she compares her place there with her place at Mrs. Sidgwicks or Mrs. White's, and is thankful.

... ... *'Is there ever any talk now of your coming to Brussels? During the bitter cold weather we had through February and the principal part of March – I did not regret that you had not accompanied me – If I had seen you shivering as I shivered myself – if I had seen your hands and feet as red and swelled as mine were – my discomfort would just have been doubled'.*

Charlotte has no intention of marrying someone in Belgium – it seems I was right and I do know her very well, after all…

'Not that it is a crime to marry – or a crime to wish to be married – but it is an imbecility which I reject with contempt – for women who have neither fortune nor beauty – to make marriage the principal object of their wishes & hopes & the aim of all their actions – not to be able to convince themselves that they are unattractive – and that they had better be quiet & think of other things than wedlock–'

Brookroyd, 24 May 1843

Dearest Charlotte,

We all miss you most terribly in Yorkshire. I hear from Emily, who says Anne will be home in a couple of weeks. She asks me if I could think of coming to stay with you for half a year, but I think you know my answer, which will be as it was in January.

I have to tell you that my sister Sarah is grievously fragile in health. We have a chair for her in the garden where she reclines by the rose bowers, listening to the bird song. On sunny days I read to her but she hears little of my voice, because she drifts into semi-consciousness. Perhaps my voice is too dull but I think not. Rather do I think she sees Elysian fields wherein she might rest and lie in the eternal sunshine, surrounded by everlasting wild flowers. Please do not be distressed: I am telling you so that you comprehend that, like Mary Taylor over Martha's death, '*I am not crushed by this*'. The doctors think that Sarah may be with us only one more month, nay, less. We are sitting with her 'around the clock' – an extra bed in her room allows rest for whomsoever is taking the nightshift. We want her to be always cherished, each minute of each remaining day.

At Haworth every one is very well although Hannah Dawson is gone and Emily is left with Hannah's little sister. So Emily continues to seek a strong woman to do all the work – I'm glad to know that Tabby has returned and is staying although she's too old for heavy work. Seventy-two – that's a good age isn't it – does not the Bible allow us three score years and ten? Tabby is but a little older than my mother, who asks me to send love to you.

Picture me on the moors, on a beautiful day such as yesterday.

I ride as far as your waterfall, desiring to write poetry. I feel close to the earth, but I shall not burden you with poetry – I shall leave that to your sisters. I would be shy of writing it to you in any case. [Or as the mill lasses say, 'any road up' – do you not miss our dialect? I would. Does it not call you home from all those foreign phrases?] I stay a while by the waters, because they're 'summat of yourn'. The sky is huge, a blue dome above me. I rest awhile, my horse tethered, cropping steadily. The water wears away at its rocks, as water does – I am not worn down, nor worn away by Sarah's demise. I am very strong: my health is wonderfully vibrant this year. Whenever I ride on the moors, I become a moors-woman – I become once again calm, neither resigned nor negative, but accepting of my land, my location, my whereabouts. Emily understands – that upon the moors my heart rejoices – for *heart* is the anagram of *earth*. When Sarah leaves us, which will be very soon, we shall commit her body to the welcoming earth. Mama was forewarned of this when Sarah was born. I shall have known my sister for a quarter of a century, which has been my privilege and honour. She has been always at home, always my friend. This is not how I have felt for Mercy – but that is also changing because she is kinder now, and I wonder if she treasures me more, as Ellen, not just a workhorse. I understand your love for Emily and Anne, and theirs for you, and the tragedy of Maria and

Elizabeth – their young lives foreshortened and your heart bruised. On the moors I pick wild flowers and cast them upon the waters, watching them as they flow onwards, out of my sight. As indeed will Sarah.

When will you come home? Will it be after your half-year?

Write to me very soon,

Nell

Brookroyd, 22 October 1843

Dearest Charlotte,

Your kind letter of 13th reaches me safely by George Dixon.

Mama and Mercy remain in deep mourning for Sarah, my sister. Our household is a sad and gloomy establishment, deeply afflicted by our double bereavement – my second cousin, also named Sarah Nussey, died after a sudden illness on 21st July.

I am now home from Haworth – shall I paint one of my pictures? You may imagine us – myself and Emily, by the fireside, such a comfort – to talk quietly, to read your latest letters – and for me, a respite from Brookroyd. Emily and I converse long and earnestly about you. Isolation ails you in Brussels – the wrong medicine for the soul. We wish you would come home although we expect not for your return – until a situation opens. To come home and not work would be impossible – therefore do we discuss 'the school' and our hopes that it may yet transpire. Our shared companionship warms my heart – even though my visit is but a day and a night.

You may imagine me also with friends in Harrogate – they take the waters – there is much talk in Yorkshire of the efficacy of hydropathy, which, having originated on the continent, will be familiar to you rather than to me. The remedy of hydropathy is becoming popular in Ilkley – it is suggested that poor George might benefit thereof. You need not worry about my health, dear Charlotte. I am very well in mind and body. In Harrogate I indulge only in *drinking* the water – certainly I do not desire to be wrapped in wet cloths or plunged into chilly baths. Can you imagine anything less agreeable?

At home, there are promises for George's recovery, certainly of his physique, but perhaps not his mind. We are therefore resigned to his occasional treatment in private asylums in York.

I hear again from Mary Taylor – we write more frequently to one another at the present time. She continues to make good money in her most irregular profession. I cannot imagine teaching boys – but Mary is different from me, always, in her outspoken attitudes and charisma. I admire her! Similarly do I admire you – I respect the courage with which you continue your employment in Brussels. Nevertheless, Mary and I plead with you – please be honest with us – together we are concerned that you will sink into a low state, brought on by loneliness and monotony – and being so cold, so very cold. This is indeed shocking to us. It is inconceivable that no fires exist at the Pensionnat, in *October*. I'm certain I'd conjure a rare tantrum and *order* them to be lit. Cannot you just see me, tossing my curls and stamping my foot!

Come home soon. You write: '*I have much to say Ellen – many little odd things queer and puzzling enough*'. Letters are no substitute for you, by the fireside, feet on the fender, your hearth or mine. Come HOME, Charlie, and SAY them!

Your loving friend,
Ellen.

Earnley Rectory, 29 December 1843

Dear Charlotte,

A note, in haste – Henry is suffering with influenza, so I am called here to nurse him. I shall spend the New Year here – please write, for I am longing to hear from you. I am devastated to be absent on your return.

I am sad, so very sad. Forgive me please.

Your loving friend
Nell

Haworth, 23 January 1844

My dear Ellen

It was a great disappointment to me to hear that you were in the south of England – I had counted upon seeing you soon as one of the great pleasures of my return home   now I fear our meeting will be postponed for an indefinite time … … … When do you think I shall see you Ellen – I have of course much to tell you – and I daresay you have much also to tell me   things which we should neither of us wish to commit to paper   I am much disquieted at not having heard from Mary Taylor for a long time – Joe called at the Rue d'Isabelle

with a letter from you – but I was already gone– he brought the letter back with
him to England

I do not know whether you feel as I do Ellen – but there are times now when
it appears to me as if all my ideas and feelings except a few friendships and
affections are changed from what they used to be – something in me which used
to be enthusiasm is tamed down and broken – I have fewer illusions – what I
wish for now is active exertion – a stake in life – Haworth seems such a lonely,
quiet spot, buried away from the world – I no longer regard myself as young,
indeed I shall soon be 28 – and it seems as if I ought to be working and braving
the rough realities of the world as other people do – It is however my duty to
restrain this feeling at present and I will endeavour to do so   Write to me soon
my dear Ellen

and believe me as far as it regards yourself
Your unchanged friend
C Brontë

Earnley Rectory, Candlemas, 2 February 1844

Dearest Charlotte,

There is a gift in each strange circumstance, is there not? Here Henry is improved in health and brings to me, as ever, the gift of music. I recognise, with
some surprise, just how much I miss his voice when we are parted. I adore to
hear Henry singing. What joy this brings me, I now allow myself to admit. I
have many friends hereabouts among his parishioners – the country people are
extremely hospitable to me. I have frequent invitations to Mary Gorham's house
– where also there is so much music – I am quite exhilarated by this experience
– glad of heart once again.

Yet am I saddened to learn of the failing eyesight of your dear papa. I endeavour to understand how you must feel – that your duty calls you to stay
home – my duty is to housekeep for my brother even though it coincides with
my friend's return to Yorkshire!

You write that you must deny yourself the chance of starting a school while
you are needed in Haworth. Always remember that I am your friend and will
trust your judgement in these matters. We shall talk at length about your plans
when I return to Brookroyd, which is set for the end of this month.

Consequently, Mama, and my sisters write to invite you to stay with us in
March, at your earliest convenience.

I have so much to say to you.
I am always, your loving friend,
Nell

Journal
Brookroyd, 11 March 1844

She is here! And shall stay two weeks! Her visit is likely to be interrupted by turbulent weather – currently we have strong winds and intermittent showers. We hope to partake of one or two good walks, but the greatest gift is being together again. On the wettest days, a shared fender shall be again ours – where, with our feet up, we can communicate once again face to face.

Allelujah!

Journal
Brookroyd, 13 April 1844

Today the announcement is made in the Leeds Intelligencer that Henry is licensed as curate of Hathersage and Derwent, under the Rev. John le Cornu, who is in very poor health. And already Mary Taylor is home from Germany.

Edgbaston, Birmingham, 12 April 1844

Dear Ellen

Many thanks for your welcome to England – How did you smell out so speedily that I was come? I shall see you & ask you this & a thousand other questions in about a fortnight & then I hope to see C.B. too. I am going to stretch the house at Hunsworth & make it hold three or four people to sleep whereas I understand that now it holds only two (strangers). Wish M. Carr much happiness for me, she will be married before I see her again. I have nothing to write & live in hopes of seeing you so I will not crack my brain to find anything.

Remember me to your Mama & sisters.

Yours M. Taylor.

To Mary Gorham
Brookroyd, 10 May 1844

My dear Polly,

How are you? And thank you for your latest letter. Life is extremely pleasant and busy here. Mary Taylor's as good as her word – the little cottage at Hunsworth, inhabited by John and Joe, Mary's bachelor brothers, is as busy as the mill in whose shadow it crouches. Mary and I meet many times and with Charlotte too, when she stays with Mary. I am writing to invite you to Brookroyd to meet with my friends – Mama says you are very welcome indeed in our home. Do please say that you may come. On 22nd of this month Mary Taylor returns across the German Ocean – I shall miss her, but this year promises a delightful summer throughout which my family and I shall frequently travel between Birstall and Hathersage, where Henry is now curate of St. Michael and All Angels – a beautiful location. The church, church hall and vicarage are high on a hill above the other dwellings, with spectacular views – the church itself holds brasses of the famous Eyre family who are wealthy owners of land around the area. I anticipate with much pleasure my future walks throughout the lovely countryside with you. Write soon, and tell me when you can come.

Then I shall hear all your news.

Yours affectionately,

Ellen Nussey

To Mary Gorham
Brookroyd, 21 May 1844

My dear Polly

I should just like to know how many reproaches (of course unspoken ones) have passed your mind since my last letter – Be generous & forgive me, I feel I have sinned <u>though</u> <u>not</u> <u>willingly</u> – I would have written but could not – I have been in a perfect whirl of engagements for the last 3 weeks – In the first place we have been paying visits to Brides, & meeting them in company –I have been also to Hathersage, & lastly Mary Taylor has been staying with her Brothers 4 miles from here – I said my adieu to her last night –She crosses the German Ocean again tomorrow   Miss Brontë has been a few days with Mary – I have been a good deal there too, & had the satisfaction of meeting Mary in nearly every visit she made – It was a grievous disappointment Mary that you did not come, for I *had resolved you should make up the quartette.– When I had certain information of Mary's arrival I set off with my youngest brother at 9 o'clock at night to see her, & there I found Charlotte Brontë also, both, were walking & talking with all their might in the garden, it was so dark when I joined them, that we could distinguish nothing but figures approaching & so afraid were we each of saluting a wrong individual that we cautiously peered into each other's faces – then, all at once a bless you burst forth in all the power of friendship & affection.*

One of Mary's brothers accompanies her to Germany and they attend the great musical festival at Cologne next week.

My journey to Hathersage only occupied 3 days – I am going again there bye & bye ... ...

The Church itself is very pretty, a good size, & most enchantingly situated – happily there is a good probability of the interior being entirely remodeled –The Magistrate of the place has his plans drawn, & every thing in readiness for the good work of renovation – but the old Vicar will have nothing done, nor, will he hear of an additional curate being had, though there is wanting nothing but his consent. The country is very very beautiful I went to the top of one hill & and I quite longed for the time when Mary Gorham could join me in climbing the rocks & hills, & tracing a course for ourselves among the heath, on the moors, or along the banks of the Derwent ... ...

... ...
My Sister joins in kindest love & I remain
My dear Mary ever yours affectionately
Ellen Nussey

To John Nussey, Cleveland Row, London
Brookroyd, 30 May 1844

Dearest John,

I write to you in secret, nay would be mortified were our dear brother, Henry, to know of this missive. I spent many happy weeks with him in Earnley, and I want him near to us, Hathersage being within easy reach from Leeds. So we wait anxiously for Henry's future to be negotiated. Henry is happier than I have seen him for many years – the family in the north is more than pleased that he has returned. However you will have heard already [from Henry, himself, or from Mama] that the health of Rev. le Cornu is failing – rumours are that he will not be in this world for much longer. What then is to become of Henry?

This living is in the gift of the Duke of Devonshire. Could you speak for Henry within the circles in which you move? It would be my dearest wish for Henry to stay on in Hathersage and Derwent – he worked very hard whilst in Earnley and would make a committed and worthwhile contribution to this incumbency.

I know not whether other members of our family have written to you, but dearest brother, if this is an admissible request, if within your powers to assist with this bestow, if within your conscience to plead this cause – I ask you to consider speaking, for Henry's sake.

Give my love to Mary and the children,

Especially my dear little Georgiana,

Your affectionate sister,

Ellen

Haworth, 23 June 1844

My dear Ellen

Anne and Branwell are now at home – and they and Emily add their request to mine that you will join us in the beginning of next week – write and let us know what day you will come and how – if by coach we will meet you at Keighley – Do not let your visit be later than the beginning of next week or you will see little of A&B – as their holidays are very short, they will soon have to join the family at Scarborough Remember me kindly to your mother sisters and Mr George – I hope they are all well

admire my writing in haste CB

Brookroyd, 25 June 1844

Dearest Charlotte,

Yes I can come. It seems that this summer is to be happily shared between Haworth, Birstall and Hathersage. I shall come by the gig direct to Haworth on Monday 1st July, arriving in time for lunch.

It will be wonderful to stay once again in your home.

Give my love to all,

Your affectionate friend,

Nell

If there could be a bridge across the German Ocean, soaring high above the crashing seas, it would be no less a miracle than the un-dreamed bridge from our previous separations to this companionable summer. Estrangement and intimacy might be perilous contradictions, but strangers, in one another's deepest emotions, we are not. Charlotte is now a woman who has travelled across the sea – water and waves will be henceforth always important to her. Sea routes are not uncharted territory to us; and we have weathered some serious storms. Now, like a sailor returning to land, she reaches for familiar safe harbour. I find, which is not what I anticipated, that I am willing.

In the dark of her room, she whispers: 'It seems that we are re-tracing well-known patterns, Nell.'

'Thus do we re-map our belonging. I had expected neither this re-connection nor re-discovery.'

'We are not strangers, Nell, to such patterns as these.'

'At Brookroyd, "patterns" is an everyday word. We're merchants in cloth, after all.'

'Hold my hand, Nell. Our patterns are hand-made.'

'Truly,' I smile into the dark: 'Hand-made at home.'

'Our bridge, Nell, across our night sky, until we touch the earth safely and sleep.'

Whilst with Charlotte, Anne and Emily, we four discuss the possibility of their school – but with a change of plans. Rather than a new establishment, they may invite pupils to stay for their board and lessons in the parsonage itself. Branwell seems in good spirits – he's tutor to the son of the Robinsons, with whom Anne's the governess.

Only one person's communication overshadows my visit to see Charlotte. There's a curate known as Mr. Smith, who hovers around me, paying attention, and smiling ingratiatingly. I do not entirely enjoy his company and do not mention him in my subsequent letter to Charlotte.

She replies to mine, letting me know that he enquires after my money. He shall no doubt suffer a disappointment in that respect. I have no money, nor am

I likely ever to inherit any. This is of no consequence – for I have already settled on my life exactly as it is.

Brookroyd, 4 August 1844.

Dearest Charlotte,

Thank you for your kind information and your family's concerns for my welfare following the [unwanted] attentions of the said Mr. James William Smith. I haven't referred to him in my letters because I see right through him – that he is indeed a fickle person – and woe betide the unfortunate woman to whom he plights his troth.

I urge you to understand that I am happy just as I am. I believe there is a greater plan than ours – for our happiness – which is understood perfectly by the Almighty in his great wisdom.

When I was very young, I gave my heart to another, of my own free will – and gladly. Last year, through circumstance beyond our control, we sustained our year-long separation, and during the year in question, I became a woman of this earth. It is my own phrase. In former times, with more dreams and less realism than nowadays, I formed the obsession of becoming the housekeeper for a school, one of a Quartette, the right hand person to one of the tutors therein – but the designs of the Almighty are not mine to know, nor mine to change. An establishment *separate* from your home in Haworth seems now the most *unlikely* outcome of our youthful dreams – I know that you cannot leave your papa – and I cannot leave my mother. Yet my life is sustainedly happy, the more so because when I visit you at home, I share my sleep with you, which would be not possible were I to live nearby – why so? – because the circumstances of my relocation would be marriage and my [hypothetical] husband would expect his new wife neither to share your bedchamber, nor walk around the dining room table, long after your papa's bed time, arm-in-arm with you talking into the night.

My life – as it is – belongs to me more certainly than if ever I were married. I shall not marry. I am content with our life as we live it now.

Mama and my sisters urge me to invite you to join us all at Hathersage for our celebrations and Henry's investiture. The short interregnum, which must necessarily follow the death of Rev. le Cornu, will end soon when Henry becomes the new incumbent. So, my dearest, be content with life *as it is* now. I am – the more so because I am once again –

your most affectionate friend,

Nell

My dear Charlotte,

Many attempts have I made this autumn to find pupils for your school at the parsonage. I send letters enclosing your prospectus to all the families I can think of – to no avail. I will continue to distribute your information as widely as possible. Let me know what else may I do, in this respect.

I write also with news that Henry has successfully proposed marriage to Emily Prescott. She is very wealthy, the daughter of Mr. Richard Prescott of Everton in Lancashire. Now then, happiness is all underlined. <u>He</u> is very happy. <u>They</u> will reside in Hathersage, which makes <u>me</u> delighted. <u>She</u> is wealthy so <u>my</u> <u>family</u> is satisfied!!

Someone else – but not a person – also makes me laugh and therefore very happy, witness, my lovely little bitch Flossy junior. Not for one moment do I regret accepting the gift, whom we shall re-name O'Calamity. She makes a day bed in my best muslin and decides to wear around her neck my very own lace bertha. O'Calamity is my canine friend, very funny, sympathetic and intelligent. I love her dearly and I wouldn't be without her.

I'm in haste for the post, and to pass on Mama's invitation to you and Anne for Christmas here at Brookroyd. Can you come? It would be merry fun to share with you the festive season.

Your affectionate friend,
Nell

Haworth, 14 November 1844

Dear Ellen

Your letter came very apropos as indeed your letters always do

... ...

We have made no alterations yet in our house – it would be folly to do so while there is so little likelihood of our ever getting pupils – I fear you are giving yourself far too much trouble on our account –Depend upon it Ellen if you were to persuade a Mamma to bring her child to Haworth – the aspect of the place would frighten her and she would probably take the dear thing back with her instanter   We are all glad that we have made the attempt and we are not cast down because it has not succeeded. ... ...

I cannot, dear Nell, make any promises about myself and Anne going to

Brookroyd at Christmas –her vacations are so short she would grudge spending any part of them from home –

The Catastrophe, which you relate so calmly, about your book-muslin dress lace bertha &c. convulsed me with cold shudderings of horror– you have reason to curse the day when so fatal a present was offered you– as that infamous little _bitch_ *– the perfect serenity with which you endured the disaster –proves most fully to me that you would make the best wife, mother & mistress of a family in the world – you and Anne are a pair, for marvellous philosophical powers of endurance – no spoilt dinners – scorched linnen, dirtied carpets – torn sofa-covers squealing brats, cross husbands would ever discompose either of you – You ought never to marry a good-tempered man – such a union would be mingling honey with sugar. Mr Smith now would have been a good contrast to you as far as temper goes –marrying you to him would have been like sticking one of his own white roses upon a black thorn cudgel.*

With this very picturesque metaphor I close my letter –Good-bye and write very soon

Yours C Brontë

I have received two French Newspapers this week which I shall return to Hunsworth – I am very glad of them

Brookroyd, 22 November 1844

Dearest Charlotte,

Your last letter made me laugh and laugh – you so exaggerate my minor calamity with Flossy junior. I do imagine you '*convulsed with cold shudderings of horror*' but I assure you it is an un-warranted concern. I don't mind whatsoever mischief she brings – she is completely loveable. Now as to myself and Anne being two of a kind, with '*marvellous philosophical powers of endurance*', that is a great compliment to me – one which I shall treasure. However, do not wish upon me a sugar husband, nor one for Anne. I have not yet discussed with Anne my decision never to marry – she may do as the Good Lord sees right for her – and perhaps a good-tempered, kindly husband will come along for her. Meanwhile, I laugh and laugh, just as you intend I shall, at the idea of your marrying me off to Mr. Smith – '*like sticking one of his own white roses on a black thorn cudgel*' – simply because he is bad tempered and I am not. Good tempered or bad I need no husband to complete me. However, I treasure your sense of humour. Therefore do I read *that* paragraph out loud – to Mama, Ann and Mercy, and have them laughing along with me. We are glad he is gone, but Ireland is not far enough. As to the roses – I urge you to cherish the metaphor – you may use it in your writings – you may use anything of my life that you wish. I shall never ask you – nor into that closed mansion shall I ever pry. Just tell me that you will write, for it's the very essence of your soul. Anyone who is your friend – anyone who loves you as indeed do I – knows that through your *writing* shall you find your way through your *life*. You know this. Go forward without regrets about your school. Turn again to your powers of imagination – your Hell and High Water powers. Write, write, and write.

Your affectionate friend,

Nell

P.S. I understand that Anne has so little time at home – that you desire not to leave Haworth –& cannot therefore visit us for Christmas. So be it. I am nowadays quite resigned to the vagaries of separations – & their concomitant disappointment, are not you? E.N.

P.P.S. George is ill again. It is a mental malady. Please pray for him – lest it develop.

Brookroyd, 8 January 1845

Dearest Charlotte,

Thank you for your kindly letter about my brother George. We believe his mental illness is the consequence in this instance of an accident, incurred when he fell from his horse in severe weather, just before Christmas. Until that time his recall was perfect, but now his memory seems to fail him every day. He is unable to reason, to connect together the influences around him. Do you know the children's game where dots are joined to make a figure? He cannot join the dots – I do not mean literally but rather, metaphorically. His lack of facility for reason curtails all means of work, which is the more terrible an affliction in that he is fully conscious of what is going wrong for him. This is the bitterest part of his lot. He knows that he has the mental malady. His suffering is acute, but he is polite to each one of us, and we attend to him with devotion. We shall take him to Harrogate and then to Burlington. I will write when I know my plans.

Your affectionate friend,

Nell

Dearest Charlotte,

Firstly I have no further report of Mary since the Louisa Campbell left Gravesend – but shall write as soon as I receive news. She is so brave – New Zealand is so far that words fail me – this is an amazing adventure, is it not?

My journeys are puny by comparison – despite the very cold weather, my return from Burlington in the open gig, being seventy miles, has not harmed my health, but, as you request, I will try to 'take care of myself'. All right, I accept your instruction! I shall obey you! I won't do it again! But take heed. If I am to obey you – you shall also obey me. I shall instruct you later herein – be warned that I shall not take NO for an answer. As to my brother George – I take comfort from his regular habits – he never was a profligate nor drinking man – we shall hope that this gives ground for a full recovery – yet his return to health after the fever and inflammation is very slow.

However, amidst all the distress of George's circumstances, there is another brother whose plans bring much joy into our family at the present time. I refer of course to Henry, whose wedding to Emily Prescott is set for the beginning of May. We shall go to Everton, which is but one mile from Liverpool. I am to be a bridesmaid, which is rather more to my liking than the term old maid – hey-ho! I shall be soon in Hathersage to help with housekeeping and to make preparations for Henry's new bride, so you may expect letters immediately upon my arrival.

Now then, here beginneth my sermon.

I recognise that we all have Duty – a valued philosophy by which to lead our lives. You are right that you must be at home – your papa's well-being depends upon it. That is your duty – just as mine is to travel when necessary with George and care for him. Your papa's failing eyesight brings great frustration to him – as well for those who love and care for him. He has always been a scholarly man – this removal of his greatest pleasure – to read his Bible & study all the books from which he gleans such wisdom, 'doth smite him truly with the afflictions of Job'.

Yet I cannot endure your pining away at home and myself stay silent upon the subject. All those hours – are they not times wherein you might partake of an occupation that brings its own rewards – satisfaction of a task well done – the inward joy that follows your struggle for excellence? I refer to your writing – be it either poetry or prose. Please obey my instruction of setting down to write 'something of significance' – thus pass through melancholy. You said, '*I feel as if we were all buried here*'. If those are your true feelings, so be it, but could you not *write* about them? Are there not so many others, in your situation, for whom those words would have true meaning?

Meanwhile, my dear friend, do not be desperate, or melancholy. Listen to what I have to say – and then obey me! Has not your writing been always, always, always your life blood?

I enclose the French newspapers, which have been sent from Hunsworth, and I shall try to write often since my letters are so important to you in this state of melancholy.

Your ever affectionate friend,

Nell

To Mary Gorham

Hathersage, 26 May 1845

Dear Polly,

I have been here since April keeping house for Henry and preparing rooms for his new bride. The wedding having been postponed, it took place finally, last Thursday, 22nd at St. George's Church in Everton, near Liverpool. Now I am here by myself, and I wonder whether you would like to visit with me here for two or three weeks? It is so beautiful hereabouts. So thickly carpeted are the woodlands and riverbanks with bluebells that their intense blue shimmers a foot above them, colouring the air blue, in every direction. The weather is warm and sunny – we could climb in bright sunshine up to the highest of the edges, looking down over the whole valley. I would like you also to meet Charlotte, and have written also to invite her.

Do please say that you'll come!

Your affectionate friend,

Ellen Nussey

Hathersage, 15 June 1845

Dear Charlotte,

I am so disappointed to receive your reply to my invitation. Polly was hoping to meet you – I am very sad that in the event, you shall not join us – I feel a cold chill at your refusal. A coldness for myself, and on behalf of your papa and his failing eyesight, now so bad that you may not leave him alone, even for one

153

day. Could you visit Hathersage when Anne and Branwell come home from the Robinsons?

We are planning to visit Chatsworth and to travel through the Peak District to the ruins and the caves. When eventually Polly returns to Sussex, I shall be forlorn – for it is a delight to have another woman to talk to.

You ask about Amelia, George's fiancée, with whom I am rather friendly. Should I enter a regular correspondence, I wonder? I should welcome your advice. Amelia Ringrose's family are related to the Taylors and have connections with the business interests of the Taylors in Amsterdam. The obituary that you mentioned was not for Amelia's father – but one of her uncles. Her father is Christopher Leake Ringrose, a ship owner in Hull. George meets the family through his trading contacts – but I am truly concerned over my poor brother's deteriorating mental health and how that shall affect their engagement. I am anxious not to interfere, for I am certain Amelia doesn't know the full story about George's condition. Please say you may come – I remain most hopeful of seeing you here.

Write to me very soon.

Your affectionate friend,

Ellen

Haworth, 18 June 1845

Dear Nell

You thought I refused you coldly did you? It was a queer sort of coldness when I would have given my ears to be able to say yes, and felt obliged to say no.

Matters are now however a little changed, Branwell and Anne are both come home. and Anne I am rejoiced to say has decided not to return to Mr Robinson's—her presence at home certainly makes me feel more at liberty— Then dear Ellen if all be well I will come and see you at Hathersage ....

C Brontë

Write soon   Come to Sheffield to meet me if you can

Journal
Hathersage, 6 July 1845

She is come! With her sleeping beside me, we have begun an intense and happy three weeks, while Henry and his bride are visiting Mama in Birstall.

Today I'm finishing a long letter to Mary Gorham, while Charlotte packs her belongings for her return to Haworth – but she turns to me, appearing so sad that I open my arms, and we stand, she encircled, whilst a strange foreboding clouds her heart. I say, gently, 'What troubles you?' She replies, 'I don't know. I feel a deep sadness – I'm near overwhelmed – something's wrong, at home.'

'A premonition?'

'Perhaps. Something about Branwell – I fear disturbing news awaits me.'

'Shall you return sooner than planned?'

'I think not. This will pass. We are arranged for the 26ᵗʰ. Let it be.'

Hathersage, 2 August 1845

Dear Charlotte,

My heart is with you in your distress that Branwell has been dismissed from the Robinsons and is now drinking heavily – presumably to descend into amnesia, to overcome the horror and shame of the events. So the summer continues, but my peace of mind eludes me because likewise I am anxious for my brothers – Joseph is drinking – and George is unstable. Letters journey between my family and Amelia Ringrose – I enclose a few lines penned recently by her. As always your advice is sought and welcomed. I send love to your papa, Emily and Anne. I shall return to Brookroyd sooner than expected. Henry's bride is rather cool at present – there's little encouragement to prolong my sojourn – I wonder is my usefulness out worn now that the refurbishment is complete?

Write to me soon,

Nell

Haworth, 21 August 1845

Dear Ellen

I shall just scribble a line or two in answer to your last as you wished me to write soon.

Things here at home are much as usual – not very bright as it regards Branwell – though his health and consequently his temper have been *somewhat better this last day or two – because he is now <u>forced</u> to abstain.*

Poor Miss Ringrose's note interested me greatly – your position with regard to her is a difficult one – and I feel it hazardous to advise you – I can only say that were you or I either of us in her place we should be most anxious to know the <u>truth</u>. Still if you do tell her all Ellen – convey your intelligence in careful and guarded language – above all remove from her mind the idea that she is the <u>cause</u> of this disaster – otherwise the news would be too dreadful.

... ...

You must be sure and not leave Hathersage until Joe Taylor has paid his visit– and tell me how he looks and what he says – if he comes out in the colours in which we have seen him he will be a strong dose to Mrs Henry –

I am not, just at present, disposed to augur so well of her as I was –It seems most astonishing to me that she should not be most desirous to retain you

Write again very soon CB–

Hathersage, 24 August 1845

Dear Charlotte,

I waited at Hathersage to welcome home Henry and Emily, and embrace her as my new sister. Yet it is not easy being around the newlyweds – I would rather stay in my room than be a nuisance or interfere in their homecoming, but there are times when their shows of near intimacy in front of me are an embarrassment and I long to absent myself. I can find no time alone for confidential intercourse with Henry, so find myself trapped into silence about family finances. My brother Joseph is now drinking too much and unlikely therefore to be useful in the running of the mill. Our family at this time employs over eighty mill workers in roughly equal proportions at the Birstall-Smithies Mill and Brookroyd Mill. George has not revealed to any of his sisters the economic aspects of the two mills, and now that he is often ill and away from home, our monetary uncertainty is of the utmost concern to me. I am tired, I will add to this tomorrow.

I am ready to go home.

Yourn

Nell

Dear Charlotte,

I write quickly to say that I am going home to Brookroyd – I am sorry indeed that you cannot invite me to Haworth, but I understand only too well how sadly the actions of our brothers are affecting our households.

I have not yet seen Joe Taylor but will endeavour to do so. You are right in your suggestion to speak to him. He is a man of commerce and trade. He will understand our concern at the effect of the current state of George's health on the future of our mills. I shall seek his advice as soon as.

Give my love to your sisters and papa.

Ever your affectionate friend,

Nell

Brookroyd , November 11th 1845

Dearest Charlotte,

Having allowed an interminable time to elapse between my last letters, I'm determined that I'll answer yours of 4th November without undue delay. It is my intention to stay calm amidst the turmoil of our household brought upon us by George's mental illness and Joseph's consumption of alcohol. I continue with my French conversation tutor, which helps my state of mind, and so the French newspaper from you is of considerable interest and I'm most glad to receive it. You do not say with what you are 'preoccupied' at present though 'very busy'. Durst I hope that you have turned to your writing and are making new poetry in these winter evenings? The light draws in so quickly now that I long for mid-December when I know that the sun reaches its lowest and the light will surely return. Then I pray there will be light for the whole family of the name of Nussey.

In answer to your enquiries about Amelia Ringrose – she continues to be uncomplaining and sincere in her letters to me. I enclose another for you to read – but I hope that slowly, very slowly, she begins to realise that George will continue to remain in the care of the doctors at Clifton House in York. Meantime, our family has heard that Joe Taylor is taking the waters in Ilkely – and I had a thought of inviting him here together with Amelia Ringrose – since their families have been interwoven for many generations. My poor brother George is incapable of providing Amelia with the marital happiness she desires. I shall give their invitation due attention and shall hope to see Amelia in happier circumstances in her future. Now then, Charlie, you must not accuse me of match-making. I have liked Joe Taylor for many a long year and have not varied in my affections or respect for him as you have. As to Amelia – I am sad that George cannot make her my happy sister-by-marriage. Of course, Amelia has not yet given up on my brother – but she will have to, eventually. I have intuition around this match for her with Mary's brother. You mark my words!

Meanwhile, how sad am I on reading your angry words about Branwell. It is entirely understandable that no other railway engineers will offer him employment after his prolonged absences due to drinking and carousing whilst at Luddenden Foot. I accept your decision that while he is at Haworth I shall not come – but I miss your company. Therefore does it frustrate me to be separated from you by the actions of the reprobate brothers in our lives. Apropos of which, my brother Joseph is a trouble to us all – because of drink he is entirely without hope. Mercy makes me laugh – her face when she speaks of Joe resembles the strictest school-teacher faced with the naughtiest child. Her shoulders are set down hard like a woman going into battle. She keeps all her rage inside her shoulder blades, and sharpens her tongue on them overnight. Imagine our back-kitchen – Ann, Mama and me watching – while Mercy skins rabbits, speaking bitterly about Joe and covered in blood. Our kitchen's a stage and my sister's Lady Macbeth!

I hope you are writing. I pray for your words, whenever I pray for you, which is always, every night at ten o'clock.

Give my love to Emily and Anne and your papa.

Remember that I will always be

Your friend,

Nell

P.S. Tell your sisters not to worry – we have found good homes for all but one of Flossy junior's puppies so now she can rest and recuperate after her litter.

Leeds, 6 December 1845

Dear Charlotte,

I'm staying with my brother Richard's fiancée, Elizabeth Charnock, in the quiet confidence that she shall indeed become my sister-by-marriage. Mercy and Ann are at home nursing Joseph, who is now exceedingly ill. Dissipation is the cause. Joseph suffers enlargement of the liver, his illness being self-inflicted and nothing of his sick room involves contagion. Therefore on my return I'll hope for a visit from you to Brookroyd. Do let me know when you may come.

I anticipate with such pleasure our meeting after these weeks,

Your affectionate friend,

Nell.

Journal
Brookroyd, 12 December 1845

Nothing from Charlotte. Intuition informs me that she's involved with her sisters in writing and copying their work. But I need to see her.

My notes are becoming shorter and their tone is changing from frustration to annoyance. I await a reply to my latest.

Haworth, 14 December 1845

Dear Ellen

I was glad to get your last note, though it was so short and crusty. ... ... Do you scold me out of habit, Ellen, or are you really angry? In either case it is all nonsense. You know as well as I do that to go to Brookroyd is always a great pleasure to me, and that to one who has so little change and so few friends as I have, it must be a <u>great</u> pleasure.

Journal
Brookroyd, 15 December 1845

Charlotte says that she does not always feel in the mood or circumstances to take this pleasure – and certainly wants very much to see me and shall do so sometime after New Year's Day – perhaps at the end of February or beginning of March. However, she's unwilling to stand on ceremony with me or my mother and sisters because she knows us all too well. She'll invite herself and if the timing doesn't suit me I'm to tell her so with quiet hauteur. She says she should like a longer letter next time, with full particulars and that '*in the name of Common Sense*' we should have '*no more lover's quarrels*'. She signs herself only, '*Good-bye. C.B.*', but I am comforted by a warm, kindly post-script, '*My best love to your mother and sisters*'.

Brookroyd, 15 February 1846

Dearest Charlotte,

At last the snow departs though but a series of flurries, for we have a mild time of it this winter 'down here in the valleys'. Snowdrops lift their heads in the banks under our trees, such a pretty sight, truly heralds of spring time – and of your visit – I hasten to assure you that next Wednesday 18ᵗʰ shall be a fine, fine time for your arrival, though I shall of course endeavour with all my charms to persuade you to stay longer than one week. Barely can I wait for our walks in the woods, where we shall search for early buds on the great trees around my home. The coach for Birstall leaves Bradford at four fifty five, so if you're there at the Talbot by 4.30p.m., you shall have a comfortable lapse of time – and only a little wait. Bring your warmest cloak – don't forget, mind.

Soon to see you – give my love to all

In haste

Nell.

Journal
Brookroyd, 18 February 1846

Charlotte's preoccupation during this time is her father's increasing blindness, and over dinner, Mama suggests that we might prevail upon Dr. William Carr for his expertise in the field. He's married to my first cousin Sarah Nussey, and her husband being of great renown in our area, my family has no difficulty in persuading Charlotte to obtain advice about the deteriorating eyesight of her dear papa. This confuses Charlotte as there are so many Sarah Nusseys in my family. She says, 'I thought she died, same summer as your sister?' I reassure her, 'No, that was my second cousin – you remember, Isabel's sister? Their father is my first cousin, John Nussey of White Lee.' Charlotte nods, in recognition.

Journal
Brookroyd, 23 February 1846

With great cordiality, Charlotte and I are shown into an oak panelled room on the ground floor of Dr. William Carr's home in Gomersal. We are given comfortable leather armchairs in a room lit by long windows onto the extremely large garden, where snowdrops have turned to green after early flowering. At the windows hang deep russet velvet drapes, yet pulled back so that the springtime light comes slanting in. It slides across an old oak floor upon which sets a heavy woven imported carpet, I think from Turkey, inset with birds, in dark russet and very dark brown. Perhaps Charlotte, less materialistic than I, might not have so observed these furnishings, but they delight me, for their effect of warmth, sobriety, and integrity. On the other hand is it not Charlotte who encourages my gifts of observation? Any-road, I feel safe in such environs. I have always enjoyed the company of my cousin and her husband – of course our families were brought close during our shared bereavement, summer of '43, when we lost my sister Sarah, whom they had dearly loved.

Dr. Carr's a distinguished looking gentleman of sixty-two. He has deep blue eyes and a ruddy complexion, with the best head of thick white hair I've seen on any man of his age. But it's his firm handshake and trustworthy smile that impress Charlotte this afternoon. She is able to speak to him in full confidence about all her papa's symptoms. She takes her time to recount the onset and progress of his eye troubles – the cataracts that beset him with problems in his ministration to his parishioners in recent years. At home she feels he should not be left without the attention of one of his daughters.

Dr. Carr listens very carefully then consults some pages in each of two different leather-bound tomes from his glass-fronted bookcases; then advises Charlotte that Rev. Brontë should wait until the cataracts become hardened, at which time an operation could be both possible and successful. With this hope for a future recovery of her father's eyesight, Charlotte is much heartened. We walk home arm-in-arm just as the sky fades to magnificent sunset, with a flock of starlings swooping and roosting, hovering, in great circles, caught in deep silhouette between us and the cerise, orange and scarlet streamers that now merge and blend above the distant hills.

'I feel I can stay with you a while longer, now that I can return with this news,' she says. 'I'll write to Emily and Anne directly: can you cope with me until the second of March?'

'No. You're too much trouble. You must leave tonight.'

'You are a tease, you filly.'

'It's good news, isn't it?'

'The very best. Though Papa will have to wait a while, and that'll be a further trial for him.'

'Your poor papa, it isn't fair that he must suffer this waiting.'

'But the operation – the proposal – gives me grounds for optimism. God will give him his eyes back.'

'Your papa will read again – so your prayers are to be answered.'

'Renewal. He will experience renewal. It's all I ask, all I could ever ask.'

Brookroyd, 28 May 1846

My dear, dear C.B.,

We have corresponded but intermittently since your return to Haworth, but when I outline our circumstances I trust that you will forgive me. Not only is my mother in the poorest of health, which has continued throughout most of the spring and early summer – poor Mama requires considerable nursing – but also we are exhausted by the effect upon us of Joseph's 'condition'. His slow decline is like the ebbing, retreating, steadily out-going tide. The doctor says it's only a few hours now until Joseph departs this life.

I have been witness to my mother's grief, wearing away at her already frail health, a steady aggravation, a daily, nay hourly, incipient attack on our senses. Tell me, Charlie, am I wrong to use the word *violence* for this circumstance? To my mind this depravity is an insidious form of violence, as a result of which, my heart hardens further towards all dissolute men. Never in my life have I been so relieved at anyone's imminent departure. This death is different both in kind and intensity from my loss of our darling Sarah – a lovely, warm, generous person, and a good friend to me. Joseph, supposed to be a true Nussey – hard-working in the woollen trade on behalf of the whole family – has relinquished instead all sense of responsibility or duty. We have watched him drink the proceeds of all our work. He has been an abominable burden at home. Yet perhaps my grief shall be foreshortened for another reason – I have no doubt that he will be given a chance in Heaven, time to think over and repent his actions, for that is the Moravian doctrine, which permits me to take leave of my dissolute brother, and give my full attention to the ones I love who are still alive.

From your letters this spring, and our conversations when during your visit, it appears that Branwell now reels in zigzag fashion along the same path as Joseph has so deliberately staggered to his chosen end. I erstwhile mourned the loss of this wonderful brother – from the amazing man he was during my childhood, wise, kind and amusing, to this stranger who weights the household with sorrow, weariness and anger. Loss, there has been so much, Charlie, this man being lost to me so long, long ago. Now it is with the greatest relief at the removal of an intolerable burden that I write to you. Joseph's earthly journey is almost over. At his funeral we shall pray, in the hope – nay, trust – that the next stretch of his journey will bring to him Revelation and call forth from him Repentance – it does not occur whilst he abides with us here on this earth. Write to me soon; tell me how you fare with Branwell. Till then I pray for you and your sisters for strength for endurance alongside your dissolute brother.

Yourn

E. N.

Haworth, 17 June 1846

... ... Branwell declares now that he neither can nor will do anything for himself – good situations have been offered more than once – for which by a fortnight's work he might have qualified himself – but he will do nothing – except drink, and make us all wretched –

Do not say a word about this to anyone dear Ellen– I know no one but yourself to whom I would communicate it–

... ...

I should like to hear from you again soon

Believe me yrs

CB–

Brookroyd, 29 June 1846

Dearest Charlotte,

I have news from the brothers at Hunsworth Mill that all is well with Mary Taylor and indeed her decision to leave this country and go to New Zealand has been entirely successful. Joe Taylor invites me to their house during Ellen Taylor's visit – for of course none dare disobey my sister Ann's exclusion of visitors from our house while my mother is in mourning. Apart from you, my dearest one – Ann states most emphatically that you are welcome here. Joe openly admits to me that he and the brothers send money to Mary to help her whenever they can. He intimates that he would discuss with Richard some financial help for our mills – but I durst not press for details.

Such are the problems financially for our family this summer that I once again have put to them the possibility of my becoming a Governess. I write to you, dearest Charlotte, to ask your advice.

My brother, Joshua, visits my mother and pays his respects – which is of some comfort to Mama, but he neither stays long nor issues forth an invitation to the vicarage at Oundle – it is six years since I spent that long and treasured summer at Batheaston. Joshua calls in at Hathersage en route south and urges Henry and his wife to come and see my mother – but you know what Emily is like – she cares not one jot for any of us, and he does what she asks. Then there arrives a most extraordinary letter saying that Henry cannot come because he cannot afford it and we cannot either – it's pure fabrication – which makes me very angry though I durst not write a scold's note to him lest Emily read it and make matters worse. Just listen to his voice: '*we must beg to be excused on a/c of the expense to both yrselves and us*'. Have you ever heard the like? I rue the day he married that woman. The dislike which hovers now between us is, believe me, perfectly mutual. Meantime, Mama is happier when I am home, and we have always been such friends, she and I. I love her most dearly and yet would enjoy time away from here, a chance of independence, to take the burden of my keep away from the family's coffers. What should I do?

I hear a rumour – strange it is – for I know you felt coldly towards your papa's new curate on his appointment last year, yet it goes around that you may marry him? Marry Mr. Nicholls? For why? Does not Miss Wooler laugh – within the twelvemonth – at your long epistle urging women never to marry? So, I write to you to hear your truth in this whisper. I long to hear your voice, but letters must suffice for a while. What news of your papa's eyesight? Have you heard from the surgeon in Manchester? Tell me all – and give me the benefit of your wisdom, as one who 'went out' many moons ago.

Ever your affectionate friend,
Nell

Brookroyd, 25 August 1846

Dearest Charlotte,

I hasten to write to you as soon as your Manchester address is known to me, for it must indeed seem strange when up-rooted like a mountain rowan replanted in the streets of a large city. Yet shall you remain green and lively, berries in full colour approaching with joyfulness the harvest of autumn – the restoration of your papa's sight.

On Monday – beside a vase of fresh flowers in my room – I kept alight two beautiful beeswax candles and said prayers for your papa and the happiness of his restored sight. What a wonderful thing it will be when he can see his beloved daughters again.

As to nursing him – I have no personal experience with eye operations but I asked Mercy and Ann for advice. The patient should be kept very still and no light whatsoever allowed to enter his eyes until they are fully healed – so the bandages should be changed by the nurse as near in the dark as possible. The leeches will remove the inflammation. You should assist him when relieving himself to keep his head still at all times, and he must sleep sitting up, so hold him steady when leaning him forward to change the pillows. Obviously wrap a towel around him when feeding him with broth and you are right to cut the meat and allow the minimum of chewing. I am sorry he will be bored and frustrated with being unable to read – but by dim candles you could read to him, could you not, so long as no light may creep under the bandages. You have all the healing herbs, which you carried with you – the teas and tisanes will render him strong again.

I enclose on a separate page some hints from Ann for your housekeeping as requested; she advises you to purchase good fresh vegetables for the nurse and perhaps some boiled ham. My mother makes a wonderful high tea with a plate of ham and good fresh bread sliced with parsley for garnish and perhaps some piccalilli. Though as to the piccalilli, you must first check whether or not the nurse likes mustard, else she will find the ham overpowered. There is a box on its way to you with several small jars of Mama's best onion and red currant preserve, which is most delicious when taken with cold meats of all varieties. I shall pack it carefully with jars of pears in their own syrup and quince jelly, and in between the jars, I'll wedge some parkin, wrapped in muslin. The jars should travel well if packed in straw and you must let me know if you receive them safely. For an extra treat I send some apple cake, which is very soft and easy on the mouth when your teeth are sore. I'm most sorry indeed that they have been painful – but try oil of cloves, which I pray should ease your discomfort. For the nurse, you might make jam roly-poly with custard, because it is good household economy and very filling.

Thank you for your kind words *'What would I not give to have you here'*, but remember that you are very strong, and when your courage fails you, you can turn to the Almighty to replenish your weary soul. He is always with you, by your side, caring for you. Again, thank you for kind words about my letters to Amelia. I am glad I wrote the truth both about George's illness and our family's financial affairs.

I hear from Mary Taylor – and I enclose her letter for you to read. She says that another is in transit to you – have you received it yet? Joe Taylor is flirtatious in the extreme with several of the young women in Birstall – the Pilkington sisters – there are five of them all within six years of one another – do you remember them when you visited? The gossip is whizzing about like August wasps throughout the valley. One young favourite is merely seventeen, that's Sophia – she being the prettiest, but her older sister, Margaret, who is nineteen, has a singing voice like a nightingale.

I'm sometimes invited to the cottage by the mill for tea – Joe says he's bored already of being the centre of attraction – I expect he will put an end to the theatricals by the end of harvest and the lasses will fall away like autumn leaves blown by September winds. I tell him about my friend Amelia Ringrose, who is no longer betrothed to George. Joe agrees it should be pleasant to spend time with someone as intelligent and sophisticated as my friend no doubt is. So I have to plan their introduction – I am sure she shall be a far better match for a mature man like Joe.

You are daily in my thoughts. I hope the box arrives soon, and you enjoy its contents, which are packed with love.

You are always on my mind, in my prayers,

Give my love to your dear papa,

Your affectionate friend,

Nell

Brookroyd, 8 October 1846

Dearest C. B.,

Your papa is home! I'm glad to read your letter of September 29th. How is he? When will he read again to his congregation? His beautiful Irish tones reach through the whole building – I do love to hear him reading the lessons – no one else can match him, certainly not poor Mr. Nicholls, though I am sure he does his best. But your papa is a hard act to follow – would it not take a more charismatic man than Arthur Bell Nicholls to compete with his presence in his own church?

We attended Richard's and Elizabeth's wedding in Leeds, which was a wonderful family event. He has married into so much wealth that maybe we feel more secure from this time onwards. Elizabeth is a lovely person – I am so happy for them both – they're residing in Woodhouse Lane, Leeds.

She is so delighted to become 'Mrs. Richard Nussey'.

Several changes are taking place in our household this autumn. My mother has a lodger, Mrs. Noble, whose fear and dislike of men is becoming already apparent; and we're trying to accept that George must stay in York under the care of Dr. Belcombe. A doorknob twists, a footstep falls, I turn in expectation of George, but it isn't him. It cannot be. I instruct myself to become accustomed to this.

I write here with a suggestion, one which will take you by surprise as much as it has astonished and thrilled me. I refer to a proposal by Richard to find two or three pupils to board in Brookroyd. The house is nigh empty since George left, followed by Joseph, then Richard. Of course the money brought by Mrs. Noble, our lodger, is useful – though the price is rather high in terms of the choice of body – we find her personality most tedious, which makes for a less harmonious atmosphere throughout our home.

I would be so overjoyed were you to join me as co-tutor. Could you work here and live here with me? We could share the tuition and re-awaken nightly that pleasure which we have forgone during these long separations. I hardly dare dream of this – it feels like an unsolicited gift from God. If we found ourselves together at last I should think a miracle had happened, not in the Holy Land but in my own homestead.

Write me soon and tell me you will come, you can come, you may come. Please say Yes, if you possibly can.

Yours, in anticipation of much happiness,

Yourn

E.N.

Journal
Brookroyd, 16 October 1846

Charlotte begins her reply by assuring me that any project which involves her leaving home is impracticable. She pays sincere attention to the details of how to charge for pupils and how to cost the whole venture, for my sake not for hers. She urges me to take courage and try the matter for myself and let my sisters keep house, whilst I attend to the schoolroom.

My keen disappointment mists my eyes and I place the letter aside.

My mind repeats three words, like a fairground whirligig: *She says No. She says No. She says No.*

Is this only about her papa? Is there something else which I am not allowed to know? Her sisters are all at home – are there plans which do not include me? Are they writing – should I not be pleased if they are? Have I not urged Charlotte to put pen to paper? So why must I sense betrayal?

It's a wild windy day and I don my walking boots and bonnet, wrap my warmest cloak against the wind and run from the house with her letter in my pocket. Tears whip across my cheeks as the wind catches tendrils of my hair, pulling out hairpins and blowing the strands around my face like a lion's mane. *She says No. She says No. She says No.*

I run east from the house along the lane towards Batley Hall, then turn north following the dry bed of an old stream leading into some favourite woodlands. I know the track so well because I used to ride here frequently with George. I miss his warm friendship – he would hold me while I weep.

Presently I arrive at a small copse of old oak trees, of which one has a low branch curving under its own weight almost to the ground, thus making a seat of sorts. Here I sit and allow my legs to swing, like a child, catching russet leaves underfoot with my heels. In the copse there's no breeze, for it's so sheltered that barely a breath of wind creeps around my feet. Previous years' leaves have built layers on the ground, scattered with acorns, while new arrivals continue to spiral, earth-bound, from huge overhanging branches, like wrinkled brown snowflakes.

Calming down, earth, earth, down to earth, I want now to understand how Charlotte must feel, she who has taught me about Duty – she will not leave her papa even though Emily and Anne are now at home.

Disappointment is a bitter food. It is always indigestible, thus creating a hollow feeling however full we are after repast. Held in the arm of the oak tree, I cry in solitude, grateful for the lack of prying eyes and unquestioning acceptance given to me by the secluded, enclosing place.

On returning I take tea with Mama, who guesses that I've received a negative reply, and holds me, rubbing my back in a firm, circular manner.

'That feels good, Mama.'

She looks at me kindly, asking no questions.

'She says No.'

'Would you like a change, a rest, far away from here?'

'Where would I go?'

'You can stay with Joshua, in Northamptonshire.'

'Soon?'

'I think so, Nell. This is a hurtful circumstance for you, and I am angry with Richard. He's the cause of this disturbance. He must take more care before he raises people's hopes. He has not thought through his notion of a school here at Brookroyd. Did not the Brontë sisters find it impossible to procure pupils – you tried your very best for them, as I well recall.'

'I will go. Just as soon as it can be arranged. I should love to visit Joshua and his family.'

Now, by candlelight, I return to C.B.'s long letter of 14th. I read on:

'were I an isolated being without ties or duties connected with others I should probably with pleasure and promptitude have cast my lot in with yours – and struggled to double the £20 which I should scruple to share – But if I could leave home Ellen – I should not be at Haworth now – I know life is passing away and I am doing nothing– earning nothing   a very bitter knowledge it is at moments – but I see no way out of the mist – More than one very favourable opportunity has now offered which I have been obliged to put aside– probably when I am free to leave home I shall neither be able to find place nor employment – perhaps too I shall be quite past the prime of life – my faculties will be rusted – and my few acquirements in a great measure forgotten –These ideas sting me keenly sometimes –but whenever I consult my Conscience it affirms that I am doing right in staying at home – and bitter are its upbraidings when I yield to an eager desire for release–'

She writes of her selfish folly in returning to Brussels the second time; asks to hear from me again soon; and finishes by telling me to bring Richard to the point and make him give a clear not vague account of what pupils he really could procure. Speaking from bitter experience, Charlotte warns that people often think they can do great things in that way until they try, but that getting pupils is unlike getting any other sort of goods.

Now, amidst bitter tears of regret, I shake myself into common sense: the dream of a life with Charlotte has returned like a phantom of the night, and will depart, as phantoms do, by the break of day.

Haworth, 13 December 1846

Dear Ellen

I hope you are not frozen up in Northamptonshire – the cold here is dreadful   I do not remember such a series of North-Pole-days– England might

really have taken a slide up into the Arctic Zone –the sky looks like ice –the earth is
frozen, the wind is as keen as a two-edged blade –I cannot keep myself warm –We
have all had severe colds and coughs in consequence of the severe weather... ... ...

You say I am "to tell you plenty" –What would you have me to say – noth-
ing happens at Haworth –nothing at least of a pleasant kind –one little incident
... ... the arrival of a Sheriff's Officer on a visit to Branwell –inviting him
either to pay his debts or to take a trip to York –Of course his debts had to be
paid –it is not agreeable to lose money time after time in this way but it is ten
times worse –to witness the shabbiness of his behaviour on such occasions–

... ... I have not heard of any further tidings from Mary Taylor –I send you
the last French Newspaper   several have missed coming –I don't know why
–Do you intend paying a visit to Sussex before you return home? –Write again
soon –your last epistle was very interesting–

I am dear Nell
Yours in spirit & flesh
CB–

Oundle Vicarage, Northamptonshire,
31 December 1846

Dearest Charlotte,

Thank you for your Christmas greetings in your letter of 28th.

As in our West Riding, Christmas here extends right through till Epiphany on
6th, so the decorations and festivities are still continuing in the vicarage – often
we have guests, wine and food. So your Christmas greetings are timely and most
welcome here.

However, the longer do I reside in Joshua's home, the more clearly do I understand your previous isolation as a governess, for these people, though family,
have become strangers over the past few years.

When I stayed that long summer at Batheaston with Joshua and Anne-
Elizabeth, I was younger, exhausted and in need of rest, solitude and relaxa-
tion. I sewed out of doors, took my repose in the orchards, where a hammock
was placed, and enjoyed meeting the local people. Here it is different, not only
because it is winter. I am lonely in Northamptonshire, and try as I will, I cannot
accommodate myself to the false imitations of the gentry, which now I perceive
the focus of my sister-in law's daily life. Like yourself with the Sidgwicks [or
the Whites], I am without money, in a social world where money seems the

purpose of existence – or at least necessary for the upkeep of mores and traditions unfamiliar to me. Anne-Elizabeth is cold towards me – her temperament now matches the weather beyond her front door. The Joshua Nusseys have been elevated by his incumbency at Oundle. My brother is no longer a young curate, and Anne-Elizabeth has embraced such airs and graces as do affirm her low regard for Joshua's youngest sister. It is made obvious that I am un-advanced in position, unequal in social standing in this superficial world hereabouts.

During this extended visit the house is kept chilly – there are not enough fires, except when guests are imminent and then only in the entertainment rooms – and I long for the homely hearths of Brookroyd and Haworth, with the kettle on the hob and everyone laughing. No one here proffers a sisterly hug around my shoulders. Gold would I give for one of my mother's back rubs. Joshua is kind but too busy and, besides, men inhabit a remote universe, far away from our women's world.

Your letters bring comfort across time and space – as I open each one and re-read them many times over, a warm hug comes, like a shawl. I am most sorry to hear, however, that Branwell's behaviour causes continued vexation – & brings debt upon your household. Valiantly his sisters pay those very debts and soldier onwards, ever onwards. Truly I respect and honour your commitment to your wayward brother – I am warmed with anger on your behalf. Nonetheless, I was gratified to be informed of this trouble for I did intuit that this tribulation was being inflicted upon you and daily have I been praying for your deliverance by a change of heart from Branwell.

He, Branwell, could change if he wanted to, as could Joseph have done. Whatsoever occurs in your household I want to know – being like as a sister to Emily and Anne – and you are more to me than ever any sister could be.

I do attempt to laugh at my sister-in-law's attitudes – to find comedy within the circumstances here. I take trouble to procure copies of Punch as you suggest and now choke my kerchief into my mouth or creep to my room whilst reading – for the satire does most cruelly show the 'snobbishness'. What a wonderful new word – I am grateful indeed to Thackeray for its invention and to you for illuminating it for me. This word helps me find laughter in the coldness and to view this time as wings of a theatre. I am a tiny pixie – wrapped into invisibility in the foot of long velvet theatre drapes, peering onto the stage whereon my brother and his wife parade around with their genteel friends. How I wish I were a novelist like Thackeray to capture onto paper their phraseology. Thank you – you have given me a way of getting through, though I should also enjoy more logs or coal on the living room fire.

I have received the French newspaper and have now read it cover to cover, both silently and aloud, for I intend to remain fluent now that my French conversation tutorials are no longer available.

I am invited to south to stay with Mary Gorham and hope to avail myself of that pleasure before returning to Brookroyd. I will write when I have the schedules.

My news else is only about George. His condition worsens at present and he has fears that the family abandons him and consequently plagues himself with thoughts of our hatred of him. What could be further from the truth? He has been always my most beloved brother.

It remains only for me to wish you a bright and blessed New Year – I shall think of you as the church bells chime at midnight. Only a few weeks from now the lanes around Haworth shall brighten with primroses, and green buds shall fatten on the old elm trees. I do so love the 'greening of the year'.

Soon, soon, soon shall the light return, brought by our Redeemer. I pray for happier times for you – and a new pattern of daily life for your brother who must surely love his sisters well enough to want to change.

Give my love to your papa, Emily and Anne. Wish them a happy New Year from me. And much besides for yourself.

Your loving friend,

Nell

Brookroyd, 24 January 1847

My dear Charlotte,

I am home from Oundle – and hope soon to stay for a few days at Woodhouse Lane, with Richard and my dear sister-in-law Elizabeth, a visit postponed since the spring. Oh I can tell you with what relief I depart Joshua's vicarage. With what lightness of heart I say good-bye to the coldness therein, the airs and graces of Mrs. Joshua Nussey! Your letter of 19th January makes me laugh aloud: *'Is she a frog or a fish –? She is certainly a specimen of some kind of cold-blooded animal.'*

Well, I have my freedom now – here there are warm fires and warm-hearted relations, so at last I can become once again happy and contented. When can you come to visit me? Mama extends a kind invitation – as indeed do my sisters, Ann and Mercy.

Warm again by the fireside,

I am sincerely yours,

Your affect. friend

Ellen

My dear Charlotte,

Thank you for your letter of 14th February and your kind enquiries after poor George and Amelia Ringrose. I am in frequent communication with Amelia – who is burdened by the illnesses of her young sisters – in particular Laura has had a dreadful cold – all in the family were worried – but, thankfully, Laura is considerably improved. Nevertheless, Amelia remains low in spirits – her life seems sad at present: she does truly love my brother George – but he cannot respond – his illness so sets him apart. I shall repeat my invitation for you to come to Brookroyd. How is everyone at the parsonage? Why are you so busy therein? Cannot your sisters spare you for even a few days?

Please write to me soon. This is just a short note, because I am hoping that you will visit us.

Your loving and affectionate friend,
Ellen

Haworth, 24 March 1847

Dear Nell

As I am going to send the French Newspaper to-day I will send a line or two with it – just to ask you how you are and to request you to let me have another letter or note, as soon as may be – I am sorry for poor Miss Ringrose – Do you think there is any chance of her father permitting her to visit you at Brookroyd–? I wish he would, both for your sake and hers – she would have a comforter and you a companion – and then you would let me alone a while –I should like you to be occupied pleasantly – till I can ask you to come to Haworth with some prospect of making you decently comfortable – It is at Haworth, if all be well, that we must next see each other again –

... ...

I shall be 31 next birthday – My Youth is gone like a dream – and very little use have I ever made of it – What have I done these last thirty years–? Precious little –

No arguments in the next epistle
Yours faithfully C.B

Brookroyd, 5 April 1847
Easter Monday

Thus do I discover that Charlotte would rather I go to Haworth than that she should leave for Brookroyd – 'twas ever thus! Unhappily I suspect ulterior motives yet know not what they might be. Nevertheless I concur – Letters dash hither and yon as we try to attain my release from home.

Brookroyd, 23 April 1847

Dear Charlotte,

I write in haste – in answer to yours of 21st April.

Amelia Ringrose might have come here for Whitsuntide, but finally, we hear that she cannot. Therefore I am free to go to Haworth, as you suggested, during the week leading up to Whit. Please let me know which day is best for you. May I suggest Thursday 20th May?

Your affectionate friend,

Ellen

Haworth, 14 May 1847

Dear Ellen

Your letter and its contents were most welcome. It will however suit us better if you can come on Wednesday in next week –we fix this day because it is the only one on which there is a carrier who can take charge of your luggage from Keighley Station – You must direct it to Mr. Brontë's Haworth – and we will tell the carrier to inquire for it – The railroad has been opened some time but it only comes as far as Keighley – the remaining distance you will have to walk – there are trains from Leeds – I believe at all hours – if you can arrive at Keighley by about 4 o'clock in the afternoon Emily, Anne & I will all three meet you at the station – we can take tea jovially at the Devonshire Arms and walk home in the cool of the evening – this, with fine weather will I think be a much better arrangement than fagging through four miles in the heat of noon   Write by return of post if you can & say whether this plan suits you and mention the precise hour when you will be at Keighley

Yours

C Brontë

Dearest Charlotte,

Yes, I write by return. We cannot arrange Wednesday but Mama says Friday. I can arrive Keighley at four o'clock. I am trying to decide whether to wear my good blue dress for travelling by train. Is the 'jovial tea' at Devonshire Arms possible on Friday? Or does my change from Wednesday create too much inconvenience to your sisters or yourself?

My warmest greetings to the whole family.

Yours, Ellen

Haworth, 17 May 1847

Dear Nell,

Friday will suit us very well. I <u>do</u> trust nothing will now arise to prevent your coming. I shall be anxious about the weather on that day; if it rains, I shall cry. Don't expect me to meet you; where would be the good of it? I neither like to meet, nor to be met. Unless, indeed, you had a box or a basket for me to carry; then there would be some sense in it. Come in black, blue, pink, white, or scarlet, as you like. Come shabby or smart; neither the colour nor the condition signifies; provided only the dress contain Ellen Nussey all will be right: à bientôt .

C. Brontë.

Journal
Brookroyd, 19 May 1847

All set to go to Haworth on 21st. However, at the last moment, Ann wrecks my arrangements as certainly as any storm might cast branches of old beech trees across the stagecoach highways. Ann takes her chance to rendezvous with the Swaines at Brier Hall and travel on with them to York, where she can see George. Suddenly, I'm required to jettison my schedules, abandon my wishes, and housekeep for Mama. I'm frustrated in the extreme, resentful of my sister, but can hardly let her down in a letter to Haworth. Charlotte will be furious – both with me and Ann – I fear she will not soon regain equilibrium.

Haworth, 20 May 1847

Dear Ellen

Your letter of yesterday did indeed give me a cruel chill of disappointment. I can not blame you – for I know it was not your fault – but I must say I do not altogether exempt your sister Ann from reproach – I do not think she considers it of the least consequence whether little people like us of Haworth are disappointed or not, provided great nobs like the Briar Hall gentry are accommodated – this is bitter, but I feel bitter–

As to going to Brookroyd – it is absurd – I will not go near the place till you have been to Haworth –

My respects to all and sundry accompanied with a large amount of wormwood and gall – from the effusion of which you and your Mother alone are excepted–

CB–

May 20th.

You are quite at liberty to tell your sister Ann what I think if you judge proper – Though it is true I may be somewhat unjust for I am deeply annoyed – I thought I had arranged your visit tolerably comfortably for you this time – I may find it more difficult on another occasion

Haworth, 25 May 1847

Dear Ellen,

I acknowledge I was in fault in my last letter, and that it was as you say quite unreasonable, especially as it regards Ann. After all, I cannot deny that she was in the right to take the chance that offered of going from home. I forgive her, and I hope she will forgive me for my cross words... I have a small present for Mercy. You must fetch it, for I repeat you shall come to Haworth before I go to Brookroyd.

I do not say this from pique or anger, I am not angry now, but because my leaving home at present would from solid reasons be difficult to manage.

... ...

My sincere love to your mother and Mercy. –

Yours,

C.B.

176

Dear Ellen

I return you Miss Ringrose's letter which, like all her former ones, bears with singular clearness the stamp of goodness and candour.

... ...

When can you come to Haworth? another period of fine weather is passing without you – I fear now your visit will be dull indeed –for it is doubtful whether there will even be a Curate to enliven you – Mr. Nicholls is likely to get a district erelong and then papa will be left without assistance for how long I do not know –This rather troubles me – the whole duty is too much for him at his age – he is pretty well but often complains of weakness–

When your Sister Ann returns write again and tell me how soon you are likely to come—

Yours faithfully
C Brontë

Journal
In transit, July 1847

On twentieth of July – after a refreshingly delightful visit to my brother Richard in Woodhouse Lane, Leeds – where my sister-in-law, Elizabeth, makes me so warmly welcome – I take the train from Leeds to Keighley, my portmanteau and hat boxes set for a holiday in the summer sunshine in Haworth.

Journal
Haworth, 4 August 1847.

It's the loveliest August of hot, dry weather. There are delicious days with Emily, Anne and Charlotte on the moors, and by night I read while Charlotte finishes some writing. So, now I understand the hidden circumstance – why Charlotte would not, could not leave home during the months of spring – there is writing happening all around me. Not only am I aware that Charlotte's volume of paper is extensive, some sort of coherent whole, but also that I shall ruin my vacation if I venture to ask questions.

Charlotte will lie directly to me if I intrude. I therefore concur with the pretence, which echoes words from Charlotte's letter last December: '*You say I am to tell you plenty – What would you have me to say – nothing happens at Haworth.*'

I lie to her as well – by omission. Of course, I now understand that 'SOMETHING *happens at Haworth*'. How else – am I to interpret this circumstance – when faced with ink-stained fingers and surreptitious glances between three sisters? They invited me here – they know that I am included within this conspiracy – like ale in a glass – some of it's the layer of froth on top, masquerading as ale, but the real drink is under the surface, deep, refreshing, locally-brewed and very potent.

I am complicit in this conspiracy of silence. I curl each night with Charlotte whose sleep is steady, continuous and undisturbed. I understand – Charlotte needs to write or she cannot sleep. I recall Roe Head and her sound sleep after 'making out' any of her stories. I have no intention of upsetting the equilibrium so hard-won here in the parsonage – there is enough turbulence around the sight, sound and smell of Branwell to fill any household in the land.

Collusion is my middle name. I know the time-honoured saying: 'Ask no questions get told no lies', which I now uphold to the last quotation mark. Therefore, during this long-awaited sojourn with Charlotte, I fully comprehend that there is *literary* activity around me – and no-one says a word about it. Charlotte, Emily and Anne are busy bees – one or other of the sisters is writing, every night, and whenever she can by day. But would I choose to put my hand in a beehive? Surely not – lest I get stung. As far as my visit is concerned, the sisters are 'just scribbling in their diaries' – I'm the only one to call mine a 'journal' – or they are 'just writing letters'.

I have what I want – Charlotte for companion and sleep-sharer. This is enough.

Journal,
Brookroyd, 14 August 1847

Back home after a bizarre but intense holiday at Haworth. I keep my own counsel as to the frenetic literary activity therein. I am hopeful that Amelia's visit here – she rests under a canopy in the garden, as I write – will refresh her spirits. She is a dear soul, very gentle. I am deeply sad on her behalf that George cannot become the longed-for husband of her desires. She would make someone a loyal and loving wife. She reads Mama's garden notebooks with delight. Mama organizes, in our locality, a friendly garden association, to which belong many of her acquaintances. Thus is facilitated an exchange of information pertaining to all forms of horticulture. Seeds and rare plants gathered by explorers, who travel to distant countries in search of new specimens, are likely too expensive, beyond reach of Mama's associates – but currently the enthusiasm is for lobelia seeds, which Mama brings on under glass. Amelia's favourite are everlasting flowers – Mama teaches us the Latin name – Helicrysum mostrosum. Amelia and I are set to harvesting them – Mama instructs us how to bunch and dry them, for winter colour indoors. My preferred flowers are columbines and sweet williams, but especially our York and Lancaster rose, its red and white stripes gleaming with happiness through to October.

'Fortunately for us the Wars-of-the-Roses are long gone, Ellen.'

'You're enjoying a peaceful sojourn here?'

'Your mother is generous of heart. Unused am I to…'

'Is it not harmonious at Tranby?'

'No. In a word. My parents desire Money. Making money is Papa's *sole* aim. He enjoys commerce, Nell, its challenge and its strife.'

'He always wins?'

'So it would seem.'

Journal
Brookroyd, 21 August 1847

Amelia leaves on September 1st and I shall miss her exceedingly. She favours the garden here, so abundant with fruit and flowers. Daily we're busy picking red currants, black currants, raspberries and cultivated blackberries for summer pudding. We are bottling pears and apples, quince and plums. With some nostalgia I recount [to Amelia] Charlotte's first visit to Rydings when Mama gave a grand tour, and reflections winked and glimmered in our still room.

But saddened am I by Amelia's circumstance – I desire a continuance of this friendship. I shall miss her exceedingly although, on September 9th, Charlotte will come. It is a golden summer, filled with the scent of ripe apples and rambler roses small, bright, flamboyant and dancing in deep pink frills. They are underplanted with love-in-a mist, some gone to seed already, and white pom-pom daisies, which shine in the evening light.

As it was in early August, so it is now, in September. Charlotte is here *in my home*, silently studying dozens of proof pages about which she says *nothing*, absolutely nothing. Am I so ignorant that I know not the appearance of printed page-proofs? Charlotte looks up, smiles, returns to her task.

Shall outsiders ask me in the future, 'Did you not feel betrayed by her deceit?' I shall recall this evening, in my dining room, where it's obvious that this is the *work of great significance* to which I have long urged her to attend.

Perhaps, history shall write me out of her life, on the assumption that I should be included – allowed to read her manuscript and share the process of publication. Might she not have turned me to copying, by way of assistance? Yet I *am* included – in the conspiracy – the complicity.

To explain to anyone outside the Quartette – one must talk of Geometry – the Geometry of relationship. This is the trick I serve upon myself, to steady me, to keep me calm, in this close but unequal proximity.

Geometry – my mind returns to school days where myself, Mary Taylor and Charlotte are equals. As a threesome we are very close, united by our similarity in age, notwithstanding the presence of Mary's younger sister, Martha. We are Miss Wooler's young lions. An equilateral triangle, my brothers would call it. Girls, of course, are not expected to understand mathematics, but there are many like me who imbibe from brothers.

Mine enjoy figures – summation and subtraction – a prerequisite for successful business and commerce. However, it's from Joe Taylor that I, in the intervening years, absorb geometry.

Charlotte attends to her manuscript, but my mind flits along mental pathways to Hunsworth, where Joe's table is covered with books and theorems, which are his hobby. He is fascinated, and I become so, for he is willing to discuss them. I think Joe Taylor so enjoys an audience that he minds not what is the topic.

I leave this journal for a moment, open where I am writing, depart the dining room and return with warm, milky drinks for both of us. Charlotte's hand pauses, mid-mark, she drinks thirstily, again a smile, one of trust and complicity – she knows I will not ask what she is marking.

She is completely absorbed, attending to her work – therefore do I quietly absent myself – then upstairs, in my room, I retrieve my box of letters. Tenderly do I untie the ribbons around a bundle: 1846. There it is, her letter from December 13th, '*nothing happens at Haworth*' – except a small incident when a Sheriff's

Officer comes for Branwell. But not a word about three sisters, in the dining room, every evening, writing, '*nothing happens at Haworth.*'

A tear falls onto the 13th, smudging the ink – I realise that I am crying.

Privacy is the normal, the preferred way of being for the entire Brontë family. I cast my mind to autumn '46. Do I not ask Charlotte to come and co-tutor at Brookroyd? I recall my flight from my house – my own voice in my head – *She says No, She says No* – and my refuge under a woodland canopy, on the road to Batley Hall.

Here now, at Brookroyd, I confirm my intuition – new projects at Haworth. Charlotte with Emily and Anne – three sisters at home – three sisters writing – not a quartette but an authorial triangle, the pseudonyms of which are hidden from me.

A shaft of autumn light catches my attention. Beyond my bedroom window, sunlight gilds our trees like Biblical illuminated scripts, scrolled and curled alphabets, embellished capitals in auburn, russet and gold. A magpie stalks across the terrace, below the window. With a flash of dark blue wings he takes me to childhood. One for sorrow, two for joy, three for a girl, four for a boy. Quick as a flash, I am the magpie and I collect bright shiny objects. From my first school, an enamelled brooch, with the Moravian emblem – a small lamb, which holds a flag aloft. I hear again the Moravian motto, which I absorb as a child: *In essentials, unity; In non-essentials, liberty; In all things, love.*

Then I understand that I shall not create disunity, while a triangle of sisters, in unity, endeavour to pay their brother's debts, maintain liberty, and establish love.

Gently therefore I replace the letter in its bundle, with its embedded lie, tie the ribbons, close the box, which hides also the enamelled brooch, and reposition it under my bed.

In the dining room, my journal lies open. Charlotte does not say whether she steals a glance. *In non-essentials, liberty.* We do not refer to her manuscript. By this means, do we contain a momentous event – *nothing ever happens* here.

Journal
Brookroyd, 18 September 1847

We wrap the Quartette and its secrets in a thick wool blanket, as carefully as are wrapped some page-proofs, upon the hall bureau, in readiness for the post. Charlotte writes a label: Messrs Smith, Elder and Co, in London.

I shall occupy myself with preparation of gifts – a most enjoyable task. For her papa, a small face screen – made of cloth on a wooden frame, with a handle – he may hold it between his face and the fire; for Tabby, a hand-embroidered cap; for Emily some apple jelly; and for Anne a small jar with A B upon it filled with Mama's home made crab-apple cheese, efficacious for coughs and colds, on account of the oak geranium leaves it contains.

After Charlotte returns home, on 23rd, I shall turn my attention to George – and shall attempt to provide further comfort for poor Amelia.

Brookroyd, 17 October 1847

Dearest Charlotte,

Thank you for your letter of 15th and your concern for the condition of Amelia Ringrose. She writes frequently, deeply distressed following the break-up of her engagement. She is a dear soul, most affectionate and amiable – I should have wished for no other as a sister-in-law. Her letters reveal an obsession with whether she is loved by God – she spends hours in prayer, meditation and reading her Bible, yet derives but little consolation – she sees no happy way forward in life. As you already acknowledge: her father's very wealthy – he could send her to a spa town but would not think of it. I now enclose a letter from Rosy Ringrose – though I hope it won't make you melancholy – I have chagrin that despite their father's wealth there is no happy environment for the Ringrose family. What good indeed is all his money? I am free to visit Amelia, having satisfied myself as to George's condition in York. He is un-recovered and yet he does recognise me, which is a blessing – but it's shocking to observe his low state of mind. He has no self-esteem – no lightness of heart.

I was surprised to hear of your assessment of poor Mr. Nicholls. Your words were harsh. '*I cannot for my life see those interesting germs of goodness in him you discovered, his narrowness of mind always strikes me chiefly – I fear he is indebted to your imagination for his hidden treasures.*' It seems that on his return from Ireland, Haworth's collective memory of our beloved William Weightman still overshadows *this* unfortunate curate.

We await news from Henry – clearly he is not suited to his vocation. But has he not made a most auspicious marriage? He and Emily intend to travel onwards from Geneva to Nice – their winter destination. No-one knows whether he'll return to Hathersage, or take up his duties as Vicar there or elsewhere.

182

Meanwhile, I trust that you, Emily, Anne, your dear papa and Tabby are all well. I pray every night, always at ten o'clock – most especially that your endeavours will bear fruition.

Your loving and affectionate friend,

Ellen

Tranby Lodge, Heads Lane, Hessle, Hull

20 November 1847

Dearest Charlotte,

This house is a *mansion* – a *very* large house, in wooded grounds. Amelia's father bought it about six years ago. It isn't an ancient dwelling – I understand it was built only at the commencement of this century. The powder rooms and water closets are of the highest, most modern convenience – I am quite taken with the facilities here – there's constant hot water and the bathroom is so luxurious. I may dawdle and pamper until thoroughly spoiled. You may call me Princess Ellen. I share a room with Amelia and I'm sleeping well. We eat wonderful food – though perhaps there would be too much red meat for your liking – always there is wine, which turns me quite pink with heat. We have taken the carriage to town, where fish markets are a sight to behold – such volume or variety – the whole place is alive with trading ships for the continent.

My effusions over and done with – I must now thank you very much for your letter of 2nd December. I am intending to return to Brookroyd on or around 15th December, in time to prepare for Christmas. You are right that Amelia should leave Tranby – I thereby plan to bring her home with me – I hope that in 1848 she will reside for long periods at Brookroyd. There she can meet our friends – & make new ones. Amelia's parents are hospitable but I rejoice in my own family, and yours. These parents are not interested in their children. I do not pretend to understand them. Love for their daughters is a distant country to which these parents do not travel. I believe that Amelia needs *my* mother. With love and cherished care from my family, she will not experience further bereavement – but her broken heart can mend.

My sincere good wishes to you, your Sisters,

your dear papa and Tabby.

I shall see you, ere long.

Your loving and affectionate friend,

Ellen

Dear C.B.,

Were I in a jester's frame of mind I should certainly see the joke in your last letter – but it rings with a different feel – and has made me certainly uneasy. I refer of course to your words concerning Mary Gorham's brother, John. '*But certainly if some kind, sensible man with something competent to live on –would take a fancy to ask you to have him – and you could take a fancy to say "yes" I should be glad to hear of the event.*'

I understand only too well that you're busy at home and that during the continuous imposition by Branwell of his suffering upon the entire household you may be distracted into setting straight *my* future. Nevertheless, it chills me to the pit of my stomach – the exact opposite of high fever to receive this latest epistle which gives all the impression of a dismissal. Nay, I am again fourteen in Miss Wooler's dining room, the evening is completed and she stands for us all to leave. In short, I am dismissed. That you write courteously, nay with chivalry, as if the care is for *my* well-being rather than for *your* peace of mind, does not diminish the rebuttal. In truth I enjoy male company – and that of John Gorham is more agreeable than most. We are riding companions, a great joy to me, since I lost my former one, when my poor George became ill. Of course I hear of John Gorham through Amelia because her family are delighted that he is tutor to her younger brother. Of course I enjoy riding with him when I visit Mary. But I shall not marry John Gorham. In any case, I am sure he has no intention of asking me, or, at least, I have to date no evidence of this being forthcoming. You ask his age – he is Mary's older brother by three years, which makes him six years younger than I. Truly I do not enjoy such dismissal by you. As to Mary's brother, my mind is content, my heart is calm. As to you, and your reasons for so writing, a fair-ground jumble of voices and jangling sounds sets my mind a-whirl. I become a hurdy-gurdy, when least I expected.

Nevertheless, we are all well at home, the more so for having enjoyed most thoroughly the weeks of companionship whilst Amelia Ringrose was staying here. Certainly our agreeable visitor has foreshortened our long winter. Now I miss her easy laughter, for we have become good friends.

From our household to yours, Mama and both my sisters send greetings. Ann visits Brier Hall next week, for they're in mourning for Mrs. Swaine and Caroline Swaine writes to request Ann's comforting presence. Also, I hear from Miss Wooler – that they have none escaped the influenza but are now recovered. She intends presently to write to you.

Eleven o'clock p.m.

I feel now inclined to tear up this silly letter for you will scoff and tell me I practise too often such scolding. But I shall allow it, then perhaps your matrimonial schemes on my behalf will cease for all time.

Write soon and tell me how you fare currently with Branwell. How are Emily and Anne? You do not mention the influenza therefore do I trust with all my heart that you're free from its occurrence.

I am ever your true friend,

E.N.

Brookroyd, Sunday 15 April 1848

Dear Charlotte,

In Birstall Church, this morning, sunshine falls through our stained glass windows, pouring at a new angle, casting rainbows on the faces of the congregation, transforming them – old and young, men and women, yeah one and all – into droplets of coloured light. I sit with Mama and Ann in our usual pew splashed with rubies, emeralds, sapphires. This phenomenon, this trick of springtime light – I have seen before – maybe twice or thrice – I cannot count – but rarely, in all my attendances.

I endeavour to concentrate on the lessons, Exodus 9 and Matthew 26. It's the Sunday before Easter, the start of Holy week, so the sermon is the Passover and our redemption through our Lord Christ Jesus. It's a long sermon but today I don't mind, because of the windows, which gladden my heart. I am filled with colours. Also I attain – in the church, I mean – a quiet sense of peace, due in part to a letter from Amelia, who is happier in spirit – she mentions Joe Taylor and I have reason to hope that they will be good friends.

The service being concluded, I leave with Mama and Ann – we join the congregation who emerge smiling into a sunlit spring morning. Surely this will be a lovely Easter with its promise of resurrection and hope? We linger because we so enjoy 'meeting and greeting' outside afterwards and the warm air is redolent with birdsong. Behind me, a group of local acquaintances are talking animatedly. I don't intend to eavesdrop – but unfortunately, I catch a phase – 'Heroine is't'title, Jane Eyre.'

Swifter than a slide down a rainbow I am with you in Henry's church, Hathersage, July '45, whilst on our visit, preparing for Henry and his bride-to-be. You and I stand in awe of wonderful stained glass windows, with filtered sunlight, polished pews and magnificent Eyre brasses.

Behind me – outside Birstall church, various voices inter-mingle –'In't'said book, Lowood school.' 'Our Janet knows that school – low, damp, miserable place'. 'Author? Unknown, name of Currer Bell.'

Mute, I stand, fixed to the spot. Mama and Ann have not heard.

I remain silent, stock-still, my eyes determinedly fixed on some grey flat slab on the ground. I cannot move but I'm visibly trembling. Heat suffuses my neck and face. Ann sees my discomfort, takes my arm: 'Are you ill, Ellen? T'was a long sermon? Come, Mama, let us go home.' I am led, without undue haste for fear of discourtesy, away from the milling, chattering parishioners. I am put to bed, with warm milk and chamomile, told that I will be alright in the morning.

I say nothing, absolutely nothing, confused perhaps, bewildered certainly, but nevertheless your faithful and silent friend,

Ellen Nussey

Brookroyd, Easter Monday, 25 April 1848

Dear Charlotte,

A friend of Mercy's called yesterday. She asked if I knew Currer Bell. I replied that I did not.

Did you receive mine of 15th?

Yours faithfully,

Ellen Nussey

Haworth, 28 April 1848

Dear Ellen

Write another letter and explain that last note of yours distinctly. If your allusions are to myself, which I suppose they are – understand this – I have given no one a right to gossip about me and am not to be judged by frivolous conjectures emanating from any quarter whatever. Let me know what you heard and from whom you heard it.

You do wrong to feel any pain from any circumstance or to suppose yourself slighted. You can only chagrin me and yourself by such an idea – and not do any good or make any difference in any way

C Brontë.

186

Dear Charlotte,

Another lady called yesterday – this time, a friend of Mama's.

She also asked if I knew Currer Bell.

I replied [again] that I did not. She hinted that she had heard reported that it was you. Do I not reside nowadays in uncomfortable circumstances, in tight corners? Is it not well known that you and I have been very close friends for many years?

Yours faithfully,

Ellen Nussey

Haworth, 3 May 1848

Dear Ellen,

All I can say to you about a certain matter is this : the report – if report there be – and if the lady, who seems to have been rather mystified, had not dreamt what she fancied had been told to her – must have had its origin in some absurd misunderstanding. I have given <u>no</u> <u>one</u> *a right either to affirm, or hint, in the most distant manner, that I am "publishing" – (humbug!) Whoever has said it –if anyone has, which I doubt – is no friend of mine. Though twenty books were ascribed to me, I should own none. I scout the idea utterly. Whoever, after I have distinctly rejected the charge, urges it upon me, will do an unkind and an ill-bred thing. The most profound obscurity is infinitely preferable to vulgar notoriety; and that notoriety I neither seek nor will have. If then any Birstalian or Gomersalian, should presume to bore you on the subject, — to ask you what "novel" Miss Brontë has been "publishing," — you can just say, with the distinct firmness of which you are prefect mistress, when you choose, that you are authorised by Miss Brontë to say, that she repels and disowns every accusation of the kind. You may add, if you please, that if anyone has her confidence, you believe you have, and she has made no drivelling confessions to you on the subject ... ...*

... ... Laugh or scold Ann out of the publishing notion; and believe me through all chances and changes, whether calumniated or let alone.

Yours faithfully,

C Brontë.

Dear Charlotte,

Now I enter my darkest time. I fear that you speak untruth upon paper as directly as looking me in the eye and disclaiming your authorship under the name of Currer Bell. Calumny – do you accuse *me* of perpetuating false rumour, uncorroborated news? The author Currer Bell is news upon the wings of time. One could stand in an open field and hear this name in the green, waving corn, one could see it as lexicon spreading within folds of grass around the hills in a summer wind; one hears from London that everyone is reading a book called *Jane Eyre*, and one hears identification of a school known as *Lowood*, situated at Cowan Bridge. The book itself is unknown to me, but I take the risk and present this name to you, my longest, dearest friend, and you rap my fingers with a willow switch, leaving red swollen wheals upon my skin. You find in my very question a sense of betrayal of your privacy.

Do I not deserve such a scolding? In truth I am myself to blame for breaking my own rule of silence. I vow I will never ask you – indeed I promise aloud to your very self that I will never approach the moat around your motte-and-bailey castle on Haworth hill. Did I not expect such a rebuttal? Were my instincts not true? I break my silence and you break my heart. I am not wanted in that castle where you write, this being indication, nay invocation, of the intimate triangle of the Brontë sisters. Is not the name Bell chosen, concurrently with new bells in Haworth? Is that not clever, witty and timely? Do not the initials tally par exactement? C for Charlotte? E for Emily? A for Anne?

In the last resort the Quartette is not of four equal sides. There is neither quartet nor quartette. There is only the triangle, from which I am excluded. This pain is of most awesome magnitude. The more so in that it must be contained. I can confide in no-one, communicate with no-one. Thus is my isolation extreme, nay total. The triangle of sisters seeks privacy, as always. Did I not already know this? How foolish was I, to suppose I could make such a challenge, pose my request for truth, approach the portcullis, pound my fist upon an oak-studded oak door? Moreover, there is a further aspect of betrayal which strikes me now with its full force. Birstallian? Gomersalian? Is it that my residence in this neighbourhood is of the utmost significance? Am I too close? Suppose, let us say, that I were to emigrate to New Zealand? Would then my distance make my knowledge of the identity of Currer Bell, author of *Jane Eyre*, the more possible, the more appropriate? In my anguish I ask: does Mary Taylor know? Is she in receipt of the knowledge denied to me?

I examine the title, *Jane Eyre*, which turns in my mind like a leaf in the wind, blowing hither and yon. The Eyre brasses *are* in Hathersage. I cast my mind back to your wonderful visit there, at my invitation. I recall your excitement at the sight of those magnificent brasses. I can only hope and pray that one day this conundrum will be resolved; one day this labyrinth will be traversed.

In the meantime there is seepage in the foundation of the building which is my love for Charlotte Brontë, my love for Currer Bell. The decay has a deep, rotten stench. It swirls beneath the pattens which we wear to protect our shoes in Haworth church where we listen to your papa, during my visits. It is putrefaction, carried in rain which runs from the cemetery into the stone flags of the church in Haworth. It is the decomposition which arises from death.

The death about which I speak is your love for me. In your denial, my love for Cee Bee is tested to and beyond its limit. Am I not being taken for a fool – on the outside. My feelings are unrequited. There is no doubt in me of this chance and change. Though my friend signs *Yours faithfully,* she is not faithful to this heart. Her sisters come first. I reach not even second place. Indeed in these my darkest moments as the zenith of summer approaches, I doubt even that I come before Polly in New Zealand.

Did I not encourage you to write, to write, to write? Did I not place the manuscript in the post bag here in my own home? Does not your denial reveal my most unwelcome truth? I am utterly alone.

The moon mocks me tonight from a clear, starry, forlorn sky. It shines so coldly, upon all unloved creatures. Henceforth, detachment?

So be it. So be it.

Nell.

Cakeham, Chichester, Sussex
2 August 1848

Dear Charlotte,

My friends here exhibit natural generosity and kindness. I write with a less lonely heart than of late. I have kept counsel over the matter of *Jane Eyre*, although my London sojourn fair threw the name into my every waking moment. Currer Bell, whose identity is still unknown, is famous throughout the world of literature. Upon that subject I shall be now silent for the remainder of this letter.

On 28th July you say, *'There were passages in your last letter which touched me, but I shall not dwell on them.'* So my friend, shall we resume a regular correspondence, pertaining to everything else but the most important part of your daily life? This would be my choice also. The alternative is nay unthinkable, for have we not been too long in close communication to decide upon the totality of loss?

For my part, the summer in this household is both a pleasure and a necessity. It is God's gift to me. Mary is a dear friend, notwithstanding our difference in age. I'm accepted as one of the family, part of the furniture, which is an honour as much as a delight. My sleep comes more easily now and I am grown plump from good food and fresh air. I take regular walks with Mary and the dogs, and we ride together frequently. The countryside hereabouts is of a softer greener variety than our native Yorkshire. The hills are rolling, the fields abundant.

Bye the bye, you have not mentioned yet the arrival of a parcel containing the *Life of Simeon*, which my sister Ann has posted to Haworth. I am curious for I had thought you would much enjoy its contents. It is sent via Bradford, should you wish to make enquiries. In particular it includes the Rev. John Venn, one of the founders of the Church Missionary Society in 1799, and the Rev. Henry Martyn who was Simeon's curate and was a missionary in India from 1805. I recall that he was one of your papa's benefactors, n'est-ce pas? Also, there is mention of the great William Wilberforce. I am most happy to lend this Life to your papa, and I pray that eventually it will safely arrive. Please let me know.

My visit here will continue through to autumn – there are plans to visit friends by the sea, in both Hastings and Rye, for which we're pleasantly delighted. I recall with such pleasure the sea at Burlington, although the years do fade into the distant horizon, so long ago does it seem. Mary calls up the stairs because we're off to visit within the parish. I must hurry for the post.

That we are once again in correspondence is, I am sure, God's will for our friendship. Remember me to your sisters and papa.

Your – life-long – friend,
Ellen

From Ann Nussey,
Brookroyd, 3 October 1848

My dear Miss Brontë,

I write with sincere condolence from the Nussey household to your dear papa, yourself and your sisters upon the death of your brother Branwell on 24th September.

190

In our family as in yours the close connection between all the brothers and sisters has been of the utmost significance during our God-given years upon this earth. Upon your tragic bereavement and on behalf of my mother and our family I offer our prayers and heartfelt sympathy at this sad and difficult time. I have written to convey these sad tidings to Ellen who resides at present with family friends in Rye but will travel to Dr. John's house in London on 14th of this month. Thereafter it is our intention that she shall rest temporarily in Dr. John's country residence, Ivy House, in Chiselhurst. However, it falls to me also to tell you that Ellen is not presently in the most robust of health. Whilst enjoying the summer with Mary Gorham's family Ellen has received kindness, care and attention unsurpassed even by that which we would offer at home. For this we are truly in their debt. However, we are disappointed that the country air in Sussex has not been of greater benefit to Ellen's constitution. It is indeed Mrs. Gorham who has recommended this change of scene for Ellen, because whilst staying with our brother she is afforded both the opportunity of his medical scrutiny of her condition and his professional advice as to her more rapid recovery. My dear Miss Brontë, please accept our warmest wishes, and our prayers for all your family.

Yours most sincerely,

Ann Nussey.

4 Cleveland Row, London

15 October 1848

Dearest Charlotte,

Thank you for your kind letter of October 9th which follows closely upon a letter from my sister, Ann, with news of Branwell. I am so very sorry indeed for the poor man, for his suffering right to the end and for yours.

Now he is at peace and as you rightly assert, it is the woes we shall remember not the *'erring, suffering, feverish life'*. How similar did I feel after the death of Joseph, from similar causes. As time passes, I miss the 'old' Joe most dreadfully. Nostalgia calls one to play again the memories, with pictures of happier times.

God's will is His to perform, ours not to fathom. How can we, who are mere mortals? Turn again to your Bible, open it at random, and read, absorb, for it falls open always at a most comforting fold, bringing close the love and redemption of the Almighty. Remember also, in this time of sorrow, the Moravian doctrine that all can be saved, and Branwell before his death changed once again into the old amiable self, the one we simply adored to be near.

I thank God on your behalf, and on behalf of all your friends that your bilious fever is now quite gone – I plead that you shall obey the instructions to attend carefully all aspects of your diet &c. As to Anne, who is in frail health, and Emily, who has a cold and cough, I trust that my arrival of this letter coincides their full recovery. For myself, I am gaining in strength. Dr. John (as we insist upon calling him even though he's my brother!) prescribes an unctuous brew by way of medication, which I take dutifully – and my household tasks are light, in extreme. Time I have, and plenty, for letters. I amuse myself with such and some bread making, which is pure enjoyment and reminds me always of Emily. Even the smell can conjure her presence, speaking French, while your Anne quietly looks on! You think me fanciful, blame the concoction!

Truly I send my warmest condolence,

You are – all of you – in my heart and my prayers

Good-bye dear Charlotte

Ellen

4 Cleveland Row, 8 November 1848

Dear Charlotte,

In haste do I scribble the shortest of notes. I am packed and ready for home. I travel on 10th, preceded by this letter. How is Emily? Have her cold and cough, which you describe as obstinate, now left her? Is she fully recovered? You mention again Anne's great delicacy of constitution. How is she? Remember me most kindly to Emily and to Anne.

Give my love to them both, likewise to your papa.

Believe me, always your friend,

Ellen

Brookroyd, 21 November 1848

Dear Charlotte,

News travels fast via the Taylors. Therefore am I cognizant of the terrible suffering in your household, and Emily's rapid deterioration. I am aghast at the news and the recognition of its meaning. If there is anything I can do to help you, in any way, my dear friend, call upon me. Whatever it takes, I will do it. Whatever you need, I will try to obtain it. I will beg, borrow, nay steal the money for medication – though knowing Emily as I do, I doubt she gives anyone around the satisfaction of succumbing to medical treatment. Would that there were some. I know of none for this scourge.

We need a miracle.

Emily is so strong-minded I have no doubt she trusts in God and will take no remedy, whatsoever. Has anyone made suggestion of homeopathy? I have heard it efficacious. What ever I can do, just ask me.

Nell

P.S. There is rumour floating around – that from an unidentified source Miss Brontë obtains a large fortune. I heard it in connection with the Miss Woolers. Do you know anything about this? To what does this rumour refer, if anything? Part of the rumour is that someone has left Miss Brontë a large legacy – I should be glad for your family, were it to be true. Nell

Haworth, 27 November 1848

My dear Ellen

I mentioned your coming here to Emily as a mere suggestion – with the faint hope that the prospect might cheer her – as she really esteems you perhaps more than any other person out of this house – I found however it would not do; any – the slightest excitement or putting out of the way is not to be thought of, and indeed I do not think the journey in this unsettled weather with the walk from Keighley & back at all advisable for yourself. Yet I should have liked to see you – and so would Anne. Emily continues much the same: yesterday I thought her a little better – but to-day she is not so well. I hope still – for I must hope – she is dear to me as life – if I let the faintness of despair reach my heart I shall become worthless.

The attack was I believe in the first place – inflammation of the lungs – it ought to have been met promptly in time – but she would take no care – use no means – she is too intractable. I do wish I knew her state & feelings more clearly. The fever is not so high as it was – but the pain in the side, the cough, the emaciation are there still.

Take care of yourself dear Ellen, for the sake of all who have any affection for you. I believe these influenza colds are most insidious things.

I think I scarcely need make a reference to the absurd rumour about the for-
tune &c. In what it had its rise I do not know – I am not aware that we have a
relation in the world in a position to leave a handsome fortune to anybody. I
think you must have been mistaken in saying that the Miss Woolers spread so
groundless a report – they are not such gossips.
  Remember me kindly to all at Brookroyd and believe me
  Yours faithfully
  C Brontë

Brookroyd, 12 December 1848

My dear Charlotte,

I have here on my desk your latest letter, of 10th, and the previous, of November 27th. I have also a copy of Graham's Domestic Medicine, and my notes from Dr. John to whom I wrote, last week. He says that Graham may be relied upon for the symptoms, you may trust the evidence, which therefore is of little consolation in this critical time. To check the diarrhoea of the last stage the patient my resort to 'extract of catechu with tincture of opium, or to an astringent powder of mixed tormentil root and pecacuan'. He trusts that you may obtain these from an apothecary in Haworth.

It is worrying for all of us that Anne has a pain in her side. And I note that your papa is very anxious as to Emily's state of being.

Believe me, there is not much news from Brookroyd at present except that Mary's cousin Ellen Taylor shall indeed set sail with their Henry next February. News from Mary is not forthcoming as yet although I have been to Hunsworth Mill to take tea with the brothers, and found them in excellent high spirits, though much subdued when I relayed the state of health at the parsonage. They send their sincere wishes to you all.

Write to me soon with any word of hope.

I await your reply anxiously and I pray for Emily's return to health.

Sincerest warm wishes to you, my dear friend

Ellen

Haworth, 19 December 1848

Dear Ellen

I should have written to you before if I had had one word of hope to say – but I have not – She grows daily weaker. The physician's opinion was expressed too obscurely to be of use – he sent some medicine which she would not take. Moments so dark as these I have never known – I pray for God's support to us all. Hitherto he has granted it

Yours faithfully

C Brontë

Haworth, 23 December 1848

Dear Ellen

Emily suffers no more either from pain or weakness now. She never will suffer more in this world – she is gone after a hard, short conflict. She died on Tuesday, the very day I wrote to you. I thought it very possible then she might be with us still for weeks and a few hours afterwards she was in Eternity – Yes –there is no Emily in Time or on Earth now – yesterday, we put her poor, wasted mortal frame quietly under the Church pavement. We are very calm at present, why should we be otherwise? –the anguish of seeing her suffer is over – the spectacle of the pains of Death is gone by –the funeral day is past – we feel she is at peace – no need now to tremble for the hard frost and keen wind – Emily does not feel them. She has died in a time of promise– we saw her torn from life in its prime –but it is God's will –and the place where she is gone is better than that she has left.

God has sustained me in a way I marvel at through such agony as I had not conceived. I now look at Anne and wish she were well and strong– but she is neither, nor is papa – Could you now come to us for a few days? I would not ask you to stay long. Write and tell me if you could come next week and what day and by what train – I would try to send a gig for you to Keighley – You will I trust find us tranquil

C Brontë

Try to come – I never so much needed the consolation of a friend's presence Pleasure, of course, there would be none for you in the visit, except what your kind heart would teach you to find in doing good to others.

Dear Charlotte,

Richard is happy to pay for my travel, for which I owe him a debt of gratitude. You shall have no need to send the gig – he offers to provide a gig from my home to yours. Expect me on 28th. I open my arms and gather you into them. I hold you and Anne, most dearly.

From my household to yours, sincerest prayers.

I will arrive by noon.

Ellen

Journal
Where the Waters Meet, 20 April 1849

Here in the valley, sunlight falls through the air, shimmering onto the moving water's surface. Leaves shift in a benign breeze on the nearby hazel trees. Gnarled are they, leaning over, wind-pruned by a funnel of air that rushes down from the moors whose wild beauty lives on in *Wuthering Heights*.

All around me today is the spirit of Emily, my lost friend, who upon her death bed insists I shall be given copies of all the books written by Currer, Ellis and Acton Bell. Emily's death breaks through the lies.

Freely do I now read whatsoever I choose from the words of three sisters – but I am no more free than ever I was, to live side by side with Charlotte at the parsonage.

It's my birthday – thirty two years of age but I know not what age to feel. Sometimes grief over Emily's death, the nineteenth of December, four months yesterday, weighs so heavily that I appear very old, grumpy, gnarled, withered and lined like the wind-blown trees that scatter the moor's horizon.

I see her again here – she dances in this place, lies upon the earth, spread like a starfish, ear down to the ground. She says she's 'just listening'. She is elemental.

This week, in preparation for this day, I begin to sort out my letters, and I think of her, how she loves all the elements and talks with me about them: they're the true source of all passion she says: Fire, Water, Earth and Air. At home, my bundles of letters are in disarray, for I have been reading them over and again since Emily died.

I'm a tidy person – not like Emily although she was a wonderful housekeeper. Unlike Emily I daily rely upon more order and neatness than she would. But

I see her footprints in each blade of grass. I hear her laughter in this sparkling stream. I feel her spirit in that skein of geese. I hear her voice upon the wind.

Fire : Water : Earth : Air

When sunlight falls upon the waters like **Fire**, I think of Charlotte.

When **Water** tumbles under the small stone bridge, I pray that pain will be washed from the body of Anne, who is terminally ill.

When **Earth** is all around me, as it is this day, I balance my journal upon my knee as I write : E is for Earth, Emily and Ellen.

When **Air** is calm, as it is today, it carries my grief so gently.

I grieve for one lost Brontë-sister, and fear, with keen pain, the future of another, who walks through the valley of the shadow.

I cannot write anymore.

Heaven help us all.

EARTH (Two)

Ellen's Journal and Letters
June 1849 to March 1855

Dear Polly,

We travel here after the funeral, my dearest Charlotte & myself.

With considerable endeavour do I present myself calmly but a disturbing question vexes my heart. How best may I provide comfort for one who suffers deep, sustained shock? Answers, I don't have – yet am I conscious of this question every minute of every mile. Is not Charlotte in utter devastation, unwilling to be smothered or fussed around? May I, perhaps, find unobtrusive ways to offer consolation? No stranger am I to loss – yet have I inadequate preparation for such as this.

Rational thought nigh escapes me. I am the lantern bearer, but so dim is the light, so unsteady the terrain. I desire to be available – to learn quickly or slowly, as appropriate. I'm no saintly companion, just an ordinary mortal, but I pray hard for truth & wisdom, for both our sakes.

Charlotte orders the stone before we leave. It will read: *Here lie the remains of Anne Brontë, daughter of the Revd. P. Brontë, incumbent of Haworth, Yorkshire. She died aged 28, May 28th 1849.*

Let me pause a while in the narration of this anguish. Let me press fingertips into my closed eyelids & gather my thoughts like floating feathers. Remembrance is as raw as yesterday. If I move these fingertips – place cupped palms over my closed eyes – search therein dark caves – these pictures are clear, without the dimming of time to render them vague, nor the loss less searing.

Now then – most urgently and with intense immediacy – must I take you to a room in Scarborough, where silently do we flow with that same fluidity as the warm water with which we prepare Anne's body. This is Anne, our dear gentle Anne. Despite the shock, we know she has gone – her body tells us. We're breathing but she no longer breathes. We're warm but no longer is she warm under our loving hands. It is necessary to wash & clothe her body – comb her hair – manicure her nails – place flowers & shawls gently about her – a pillow under her head. We desire for her a soft resting-place – with her books and pens, the things she loves.

En route to Filey, we pass by green wheat fields, which in their true season shall become waving cornfields, resplendent with red poppies at their margins. Our route is fringed by hedgerows entwined with wild roses, honeysuckle and brambles, foretelling rich bounty. But shall there be harvest gladness in Haworth? I think not – has not The Reaper claimed already his grim untimely tithe?

Through our carriage windows, we observe green canopies under summer skies – in other circumstances would it not be joyful? It cannot be – we are so sad & find no justice in this untimely dispensation.

Providence is inscrutable – I struggle to comprehend – for where once there was laughter *en plein air*, our hills must ring silent with loss. There is no Quartette. I recollect our wild Pennines, where cotton grass blows – and trees bend like old women carrying baskets on their backs. Clouds gather like scoops from a sky sculptor's hands – then hurtle themselves across the heavens & cast upon the heather their shadows. I recall lightning, as it streaks to earth in summer storms – when horses huddle by dock leaves, backs to the wind. I recollect cottage gardens – abundant with blossom – But how long till flowers bloom on bare earth raked barren in our souls?

In our mutual silence, as we travel along, I am transported to the parsonage, which will henceforth be silent. Oh Polly, it's with deep compassion that I fear Charlotte's home-coming. Of Scarborough, now behind us, must I pen & ink the tableaux herein, but of Haworth ahead of us, with dreadful foreboding, must I *listen.*

Sounds there were which shall be forever absent. No scratching of several pen nibs in the evenings – but one lonely pen, its sound enormous when echoing through stillness. At Charlotte's dark wood dining table, no other chairs scrape as a sister rises. No sisterly hug accompanies that absent sound. No rustle of garments as one glides past, no catching of another's sleeve at the turn of the stairs. No crackle of the pages of German prose accompanying the thump of bread dough while one is baking. No sister leans forward to stroke the dog – or rattle the fire irons, while placing a new piece of coal. No sister creaks open a glass-fronted book-case, tidily tugging book spines till, side-by-side they sit, arranged & treasured therein. No sister reads poetry by oil lamp. No click of teeth as a nimble-fingered one bites the thread from a darning needle. No snap-shut of a writing-box-lid by another as the evening's words are done. No feet but

Charlotte's rising the stair treads. No sounds of sisters kissing goodnight. No sister snuffs a night candle.

Our carriage rolls along – I listen to the wheels on rough roads, holding Charlie's hand. She turns, smiles, and presses my hand as we trundle towards Filey. She says, 'Listen, Nell, how the movement of the carriage is a reflection of the movement of life. Its motion takes an unexpected route upon which we know not what's ahead, what we should do, how we should feel in these new circumstances.'

'Bumped about by the momentum?' I venture. 'We are shaken sometimes, jolted if there's a rut, if a cart has gouged the track – our carriage wheels catch in it – we're thrown together, violently.'

'I see that you comprehend me, Nell. Nevertheless, we must endeavour to stay steady through all changes. Though, sometimes I'm so exhausted, Nell, I can barely breathe.'

'We shall curl up and sleep. Tomorrow, we'll walk the beach?'

'Yes, we shall. You recollect Scarborough, standing by the harbour?'

'That you're a ship – on a wide ocean – cast adrift – on a journey – without any moorings?'

'Yes. I am far, far away. Forgive me, in truth I am distant from all human life. Navigating, it seems, by some far distant star.'

At other times – Charlotte is of the earth, real and present, connected as if to a deep well – a well of grief that cannot run dry, replenished with living waters from some subterranean lake. Those are wordless waters – which swell up into her brown eyes, and flow, as if for eternity.

My dearest Polly, such comfort do I derive from your friendship and our correspondence. I trust that Charlotte shall find words for her experiences, or she too will die. To write – is C.B.'s survival, her true self.

She shall blend C.B. with C.B., because she says, *'Labour must be the cure, not sympathy – Labour is the only radical cure for rooted Sorrow.'*

Inevitable separation must follow our shared sojourn – for freedom to reside is not forthcoming despite Charlotte's publication, which now provides a competency. I must return to Brookroyd; C.B. to Haworth. Yet does my heart believe that we belong together [but dearest Polly, of this durst I tell only to you].

To love her is to comprehend her whole self – not only her grief, but also her employment, through all chances and changes. She will write for many hours, by day and night – Charlotte will make something significant out of every tragedy, every disastrous circumstance. She will write brilliant words for other people to read. I love her for that genius.

We shall sojourn at Filey until the 14th, when we depart for Easton, to the Hudsons. I mentioned to you their kindness when we were on holiday in Burlington. They have a most beautiful garden: so, Polly, to my future – I shall stay sane though all changes, Polly. I shall create a new flower garden, in a corner of one of Mama's lawns. I shall tend & nurture it – through all seasons – shall name it for Anne & Emily – and I pray that somehow shall I endure this dark time. I shall entrust my survival to my own hands & to God's living things – that grow from the dark earth.

I pray to the Lord my Shepherd for his guidance. He is always my friend. In the midst of darkness he brings forth light – great joy in the forthcoming marriage of my Sister Ann to Robert Clapham – and with this marriage comes therefore some financial security at last for Brookroyd. Write to me soon, Polly, my cherished friend, whose steady approbation surrounds me with loving warmth. Charlotte sends greetings to all your family.

Your affect, friend,

Ellen Nussey

Brookroyd, 16 July 1849

Dearest Charlotte,

I acknowledge that I '*will hear you with moderation*'. In truth I am not alarmed – your depth of grief is not unexpected after sustained and untimely bereavement. You describe the clock ticking on the stairs and the long lonely hours with raw honesty and my heart cries for you. I know only too well that '*Solitude, Remembrance and Longing*' are your '*sole companions all day through.*' Be unafraid to weep. Weep but do not despair – God is your companion and your guide. I am but a penned conversation away. Write to me often, as if I'm in the same room. Speak to me by paper – I will reply immediately as indeed have I done this day. Since our return from Filey, but especially this past two weeks, I have again read *Jane Eyre*. I have always loved you, my dear, dear friend and I hasten to affirm *again* that *Jane Eyre* by Currer Bell is a wondrous construction. I can taste the burnt porridge, smell the wild heather, touch the wet earth, feel the heat of fire as it rampages through the galleries. I'm in church in Hathersage, watching you trace the Eyre brasses with your fingertips.

I have good news from home – Ann is to be married *soon* to Robert Clapham – 26th September. This will alleviate some of our financial insecurities – we refuse Dr. John's preposterous plans that we leave our fortunes to his offspring if he pays off all our debts. Much as I love him this is in his favour not ours. I have no doubt you will continue to jest about my solutions to my problems being marriage – but we both know it's no solution save superficially.

12 noon

I am just this very minute in receipt of *The Tenant of Wildfell Hall*. I am in a dither of excitement – also it sets me to terrible trembling of grief. Surely its publication must bring to you, likewise, excitement and anguish in equal measure. Thank you also for the note it contains. I am sorry to hear that you so wanted it published by your own Smith, Elder & Co – rather than Thomas Newby – Nevertheless, I send deepest gratitude that you continue to honour Anne, by forwarding The Tenant to me – and in so doing you pay homage to Emily's last wishes, that I shall receive copies of all the books by all the sisters. I shall begin to read next week, when it shall be possible and enjoyable to set aside time here at Brookroyd.

It continues a great source of pleasure to own the published works of Currer, Ellis and Acton Bell. You and I may now refer openly to your labours – which I hope shall sustain you through the months ahead. I am so very proud of you and your sisters – over *all* the said works have I wept copiously. It's not that I treasure one book above others, one author beyond her sisters. I take them together – the fruits of the harvest of three brilliant women. It's my great honour and privilege to own these books: I predict that for generations to come they will be beloved by women, and by some men. Their images enter deep into my soul, the strength of 'the rage of the Brontë sisters', the powerful challenge of the truths contained therein. In remembrance of Emily and Anne, I continue to re-read both WH and AG. In truth do I admire the works of both sisters: Emily's passion sings throughout WH; Anne's honesty underlies AG. But oh how I weep again at Anne's description of the sea. Oh how I long for her to reside with her Celia Amelia not in heaven but somewhere such as – Scarborough – or maybe Filey.

Forgive me – cannot continue.

Eleven o'clock

I pray every night, as usual at ten o'clock, which calms my soul. Therefore do I hastily return to complete this. I'll post it first thing. You must not think that for one moment do I deny or belittle your grief, when I declare that your sisters are alive, for me, everyday, through their words. So be it.

Write to me very soon.

I love you C.B. and C.B.,

Nell

To Mary Gorham
Brookroyd, 28 September 1849

My dear Mary,

Thank you very much for your letter which awaited me at home. My sister
Ann and Robert Clapham are now married – their wedding took place on 26th
from my brother Richard's home in Woodhouse, from which I am today just
returned. I hasten to reply to yours, because I'm so very sorry to hear of your father's death on 24th. In this time of sadness, dear Polly, I assure you of my deep
friendship and sympathy in your loss. I received always gentleness and generosity from this lovely man– truly a good man who has been a devoted father to
you and a source of strength and kindness in his family. Now he rests with Our
Heavenly Father, where he suffers neither pain nor illness.

Mama and Mercy send their deepest condolences to you and your friends.
My kindest good wishes to you – I enclose with this letter a short note for your
mother.

All is in disturbance, hurry and bustle now at Brookroyd because Mama,
Mercy and I are removing ourselves to a separate part of the house – so that our
'older newly-weds' may have their own arrangements here. Mercy has been in
Redcar – C.B. observes – I believe not-unjustly – that Mercy has taken umbrage
because she's not also to be married! Anyway, we're amidst re-location within
the house – our new rooms are to be decorated – I'm to choose my own preference but Robert and Ann will pay. Is that not a fine circumstance?

Be assured, dearest Polly, that a warm welcome awaits you
always, at Brookroyd.
Your affectionate friend,
Ellen

Journal
Brookroyd, 22 October 1849

Amelia is here and tomorrow I go to Leeds to meet Charlotte! Poor lamb she
hates the dentist but she hopes some remedy for her terrible teeth.

I hope for this glorious weather to continue throughout her sojourn here. I
shall hold her again. We shall put our feet up, catch up, and share calm, un-
troubled sleep. I thank God for this visit.

Two pieces of news today – the smaller [as far as the world beyond Birstall is concerned] is a visit from Joe Taylor who has of course known Charlotte for hundreds of years. The larger is that – today– Charlotte's novel *Shirley* is published, while she stays with *us*. Mama bakes autumn apple pie as celebration. Charlotte reads to us – Amelia, Joe, Mama &c – the first chapter amidst excitement, interest and laughter at C.B.'s satire upon the antics and voices of the curates.

To Mary Gorham
Brookroyd, 8 November 1849

Dear Mary,

Charlotte is now back home but my copy of *Shirley* arrives – Robert Clapham travels to Bradford and kindly collects it – today – from the Commercial Inn in Tyrrel St. Here is a copy also for you, dear Polly, from Charlotte. Is that not a wonderful surprise? I shall write immediately to thank her on your behalf.

Urgently do I skim the book. Herein are the voices, anecdotes, history, of folk who inhabit our West Riding. I am entranced. My friends at home are as excited as I, finding in Caroline Helstone a voice they recognise, albeit changed into this so-called fiction. Gossip is buzzing hereabouts, when folks believe they recognize characters in local dignitaries.

However with deep poignancy do I long for Emily and Anne. To read *with them* would be my heart's desire.

Nevertheless, for myself I have immense joy in despatch of this parcel, because I'm at liberty *now* to add my voice to the chorus. Such freedom takes me to high moor-lands, where winter winds send wild clouds scudding & March winds bring wild geese winging.

Ever your affect. friend,
Ellen Nussey

We continue to enjoy Amelia's presence here – and I must record in this journal that Joe Taylor makes now frequent appearances. Mama always extends an invitation to dine with us. Mama takes me aside and whispers, 'What do you observe, Ellen? Are they not delighted to be together?' We, Mama and I, open our arms and stand many minutes holding warmly to one another. Then, she wipes away a tear. The Taylors are long-term friends of our household and we all love Amelia. Mama says, 'She would have been my daughter-in-law, Nellie. It was not God's will – My poor George – but look at her – Joe's making her laugh again.'

To Mary Gorham,
Haworth, 28 December 1849

Dear Mary,

It is bitterly cold on the hill. Charlotte has a slight cough, which makes her papa visibly anxious. Poor man, five out of six children and a wife and sister-in-law all gone.

Calm, peaceful sleep and open honesty between us – these are ingredients for a recipe of harmony and, perhaps, renewal. As I lie in bed, before sleep, I recall an image from summertime near Cakeham. I must write this – because you're the only friend who knows how I *really* feel towards C.B.

Let me paint the picture – a beautiful field, where two hedgerows meet. There are wild flowers, blackberries, old man's beard, hazel and elder. It's a sloping field where you and I collect blackberries and share a picnic. However, in the corner there are discarded a couple of old ploughshares stacked, away from harm. The brambles are already growing though – the ploughshares span a gap. The method by which they're stacked makes you giggle. You laugh, pointing: 'They look like two spoons in a drawer.' So permit me to extend the metaphor with 'A tale of two women' –

Passion is long gone – two grown women endure tragedy and they are worn out. They are, both of them, rendered numb by hard work and an onslaught of the heart. Two years pass during which they undergo every conceivable emotion in every newspaper, book, or magazine. They sleep together now for comfort, curved like parallel ploughshares. They resemble old farm machinery, in the corner of their own beautiful field – they are not a little rusted, somewhat blunted, their wooden handles are worn, but they are still useful, in a different manner. They are still beautiful – woven now with brambles, honeysuckle, hawthorn and myrtle – by their own hedgerow through all seasons.

That's my story, Polly. I surmise that C.B. will continue to work very hard – she drives herself onwards fiercely – she desires to travel. Bye the bye, I look forward to hearing how you and your friends experience *Shirley*.

I wish you a very happy new decade.

Your affec. friend

Ellen Nussey.

Journal, Fragments
1850 and 1851

Weeks and months spin by, whirling forwards, threads circling around the dropping spindle. Charlotte travels widely. Her friends in the north are the Kay-Shuttleworths of Gawthorpe Hall and the Gaskells of Manchester.

Charlotte is absorbed in continuous correspondence. Ours concerns our mutual friends, as indeed always it has done.

When Charlotte is home, I stay in Haworth. Always we talk, often into the night. Intermittently my mother is ill and needs my attentions. Charlotte's papa requires hers.

Martha Brown now lives in the parsonage. Mr. Nicholls renders himself indispensable to Charlotte's papa.

In London, Charlotte meets Dr. John's family – and brings books and gifts home to Brookroyd for me.

My life changes very little whereas Charlotte is now famous. Martha Brown has recognised that Charlotte's the author of *Shirley* – Charlotte's place in Society here in Yorkshire is changed, perhaps for ever.

Brookroyd, 16 January 1852

My Dear Charlotte,

That I should not be alarmed or uneasy when I hear how the mercury pills affect you, is a possibility I cannot sustain. Of course I am uneasy. Mr. Ruddock certainly should take care when prescribing for his patients. I'd like to smack him – should I see him face to face I should berate him most soundly. Mama says please come, stay with us – put yourself in my hands – I will nourish you and administer your every need, my dearest. Tell us when to expect you – all is ready and waiting for your person.

Write to me soon,

Nell.

Brookroyd, 25 January 1852

My dear Charlotte,

We are pleased to receive your letter with descriptions of the food you must have – all is in order and we await your arrival – A change of location will suit you – I am sure you are right to avoid butter, also tea – just milk and water with a little sugar. My dearest, do not fear that we would advocate anything you might choose to avoid. The choice must be entirely yours – you shall have a little mutton, as you fancy. Now, I'll tell you something of delight – the first snowdrops are peeping – joyfully do they predict your return to health.

So, we anticipate your arrival with quiet pleasure.

Soon, soon.

Nell

Brookroyd, 20 February 1852

My dear Charlotte,

How unfortunate that Mr. Ruddock should hear so soon of your home-coming. I doubt not that he hopefully continues to affirm you're his patient. He durst not admit that his 'skills' brought you to a state of fatigue and debility! The sooner you dismiss him from service the better. I'm thankful to the Almighty for your increasing good health, especially do I pray for your improved physical strength – which would henceforth permit your return to writing. Therefore do I hope most fervently to hear of the re-establishment of your work – which would provide a source of satisfaction & fulfilment to you. I hear from Miss Wooler this week – she hopes that you shall visit her when you're fully recovered. But still no news from Polly Taylor – they're expressing some concern at Hunsworth Mill – let me know immediately if a letter arrives. I should like to set their minds at rest.

All here send their love & etc

Nell

Brookroyd, 6 May 1852

Dearest Charlotte,

I am so sorry to hear of E. Taylor's death and I thank you for forwarding Polly's letter. You were right only to read it once. In three minutes it took me back years to a desolate room by the sea– I know, dearest one, that you had decided not to leave home until your manuscript is finished but I venture to suggest that you might benefit from a change of air. Would that I could journey hence forth with you – indeed would that I could accompany you on all our journeys. Did we not discuss in February that perhaps we might make pilgrimage to Scarborough and Filey – on the appropriate date? However I am unable to be on the East Coast at the end of this month, for which restriction of our shared time most sincerely do I beg indulgence. I am requested to stay with Mary Gorham in Sussex for a prolonged period prior to her becoming Mrs. Hewitt.

You are invited most warmly to accompany me. Will you let me know in good time? I should dearly love to have you visit with me – in Sussex – I miss you – but I could well imagine the sociability of the Gorham residence to be at variance with your heart's wishes – it's far from the East Coast and would allow neither peaceful contemplation of the *anniversary*, nor solitary quietude for your completion of *Villette*.

I hope you will not be angry at my forthcoming itinerary – you know my true feelings? Please write to me c/o the Gorhams at Cakeham.

I am your most affectionate friend,

Nell

P.S. Charlie, don't mind me, don't forget…my promise.

Cliff-House, Filey, 6 June 1852

Dear Ellen

I am at Filey utterly alone. Do not be angry. The step is right. I considered it and resolved on it with due deliberation. Change of air was necessary; there were reasons why I should <u>not</u> go to the South and why I should come here. On Friday I went to Scarbro', visited the church-yard and stone – it must be refaced and re-lettered – there are 5 errors. I gave the necessary directions – <u>that</u> duty then is done –long has it lain heavy on my mind – and that was a pilgrimage I felt I could only make alone.

I am in our old lodgings at Mrs. Smith's – not however in the same rooms – but in less expensive apartments –They seemed glad to see me –remembered you and me very well and seemingly with great good will. The daughter who used to wait on us is just married. Filey seems to me much altered – more lodging-houses – some of them very handsome —have been built – the sea has all its old grandeur–I walk on the sands a good deal and try <u>not</u> to feel desolate and melancholy. How sorely my heart longs for you I need not say. I have bathed once: it seemed to do me good –I may perhaps a stay here a fortnight.

... ...

Believe me—dearest Nell
Yours faithfully
C Brontë

Brookroyd, 30 August 1852

Dearest Charlotte,

It grieves me to hear of your loneliness. I tried to write with reserve for I was anxious not to reveal myself in letters to you, but on receiving your letter, written on 25th, my heart wept. Forthwith I shall be more affectionate, wear my heart on my sleeve, whatever you will. Sometimes, I have foreboding – a dread that in your loneliness you might search for friendship and affection elsewhere. Perhaps I was reticent for that reason. It is not my intention to cause dismay – nor increase your sense of isolation. I will write often, if correspondence is a life-line in your silent times. Don't berate yourself for the slow development of *Villette*. Your publishers are, from your own words, good men, God fearing and sensible of your predicament over these past years. Since they are also your friends, is it not likely that they'll accept completion and delivery in due course? Meanwhile, I am glad your papa's eyesight improves & you *must* rest assured

I'm *never* wearied by detail of your circumstance, for through such details I conceive your daily life, the minutes which compose your hours.

As to your loneliness, I wish fervently that I could be your companion. I'd like to curl around you every night, seal close your eyes with my lips until you sleep, treasured, cherished and safe. If Mama were not in need of my attention I would come often – but also, I'm nobody's fool, Charlie – You're fiercely independent & would soon send me away, in order to complete 'the work'. When you look in your mirror, Charlotte Brontë, you meet Currer Bell – anyone who truly loves you, must love you *both*. I'll come when you call – till then I pray your manuscript will complete itself while you're asleep.

My arms are warmly around you.

Always, Nell

Haworth, 24 September 1852

... ... But oh Nell! I don't get on – I feel fettered –incapable – sometimes very low– However – at present the subject must not be dwelt upon – it presses me too hardly – nearly and painfully. Less than ever can I taste or know pleasure till this work is wound up. And yet — I often sit up in bed at night – thinking of and wishing for you. ... ...

Haworth, 9 October 1852

Dear Nell

Papa expresses so strong a wish that I should ask you to come and I feel some little refreshment so absolutely necessary myself that I really must beg you to come to Haworth for one single week. I thought I would persist in denying myself till I had done my work – but I find it won't do – the matter refuses to progress – and this excessive solitude presses too heavily –So let me see your dear face Nell just for one reviving week

Could you come on Wednesday? Write tomorrow and let me know by what train you would reach Keighley– that I may send for you.

... ... We will leave all other matters to talk about.

Yours faithfully

C. Brontë

If you write a line tomorrow –I shall get it on Monday

Haworth, [?] 11 October 1852
Monday morning

Dear Ellen

I find I cannot have the gig till Friday – On that day (D.V.) it shall be at the Station at the hour you mention viz. 43m past 3 o'clock –and then I hope it will bring you safe to me. The prospect of seeing you already cheers. One reason which I may tell you when you come partly reconciles me to this temporary delay. If I do not hear anything from you to the contrary–I shall consider the matter settled. May no other hindrance arise either here or at Brookroyd – kind regards to all –

dear Nell Yours faithfully

Brookroyd, 22 October 1852

Dearest Charlotte,

I arrived home safely, but delayed by two hours as the train was shunting in the station. How wonderful it has been to share this past week with you. I miss you already. When I called in on Joe and Amelia there seemed much unhappiness in the house but Tim was bubbly & chattering away as usual – I will write longer when there is any news. Please thank your dear papa – and Martha & Tabby – for all their kindness & generosity during my visit. Tell Tabby her apple pudding is the best in the world. All at home send warm wishes for yours and your papa's health.

Love to you, always, Nell

Haworth,   ?26 October 1852

Dear Nell,

Your note came only this morning, I had expected it yesterday and was beginning actually to feel uneasy, like you. This won't do, I am afraid of caring for you too much.

You must have come upon Hunsworth at an unfavourable moment; seen it under a cloud. Surely they are not always or often thus, or else married life is indeed but a slipshod paradise. I am glad, however, that the child is, as we conjectured, pretty well. ... ...

214

On Saturday I fell to business, and as the welcome mood is still decently existent, and my eyes consequently excessively tired with scribbling, you must excuse a mere scrawl. You left your smart shoes. Papa was glad to hear you had got home well, as well as myself. Regards to all. Good-bye. –
Yours faithfully,
C. Brontë
I do miss my dear bed-fellow. No more of that calm sleep.

Journal
Brookroyd, 24 November 1852

Charlotte has finished *Villette* & posted her parcel to Cornhill. Now she is here. Thanks be to God. She brings *Esmond*, Thackeray's novel. We shall read aloud, in the evenings. Now she may rest & wake refreshed from calm sleep.

Brookroyd, 16 December 1852

Dear Charlotte,

There are dragons, in the Book of Revelations, threatening an uncertain terrain, which now we must traverse. Turmoil & terror descend upon me, in equal measure. I receive, this morning, your letter & the note to you from Mr. Nicholls.

How may I scribe, upon papyrus from the Nile delta, where never have I travelled, my most trustworthy response to your epistle?

Sometimes (you say) that my perception is generally quick enough, my intuition trustworthy – not in this instance. During your visit here we were unfettered by this occurrence. Yet does your happy return home, fully rested & content, seem so long ago, due to this turbulent change of climate.

Of course it is not for my benefit that Mr. Nicholls allows himself *'constant looks – and strange, feverish restraint'*. It isn't difficult to imagine his words – as you rightly conjecture, I can guess. As to his manner, you say, *'Shaking from head to foot, looking deadly pale, speaking low, vehemently yet with difficulty'*.

Thankfully, your letter affirms that *never* have you entertained attachment to Mr. Nicholls – I know that to be true, but now, Charlotte, we enter a dangerous land, do we not? The beasts have many horns & strange feet. I know not what provisions shall suffice, to bring *me* safely to my ultimate destination, nor what or where that may be. I may be scorched by the glare of unwelcome words from unexpected scrolls; parched by drought mid-day; frozen by the chill of night. I'm without shoes in stony desert, without fire & weapons, should I require them. Now because your papa has responded with *'Agitation and Anger disproportionate to the occasion'* you are boiling with a sense of injustice.

Here be dragons. I know you well, dear and beloved woman. Nothing does penetrate your heart so fast, deeply & surely, as injustice. This, above all, is my cognisance of Currer Bell, the author I admire, whose soul touches readers by simple means: the placement of a child unjustly upon a classroom stool, the ranting of a clergyman against the flamboyant curls of a young girl, born with ringlets & cannot help it.

You are consumed by a sense of injustice. So now *I* must be afraid. Your reaction instils in me the deepest apprehension, in this sudden change of circumstance.

Anger at injustice is a variety of passion, is it not? Therefore, take note, my dear. Love; anger; pity; compassion for those who suffer injustice – all are passionate responses – fed from the same subterranean waters – all may be reached by piercing the previously impenetrable topography.

Moreover, it is easy for me to imagine persons loving you. Why should they not? How could they not? Your letter – this morning – makes mention that you have long suspected that Mr. N. cares for you. He wants you to care for him.

You are wilful and strong-minded – for which I love you. You will do your utmost to safeguard your future & that of your papa. I know not whether it's worse to marry with or without love. I think not clearly, when faced with a proposal of marriage from Mr. N. to you, even though you refuse him.

It is but nine days to Christmas. Yet terrible darkness is upon me. Surely – if my Saviour is The Light of the World – if Christ's birth heralds return of the light – should I not anticipate with pleasure the coming season?

Not this year. Not now, my dear. Your revelation re-shapes the landscape & changes the climate. Since this morning, I anticipate with no inner joyfulness the forthcoming year. I dread it. How *should* I feel? Your papa is selfish – he believes no one worthy of you. I am selfish for longing that you remain unmarried. So two beings, who probably love you best in the world, are unworthy of you.

In this cold desert – there are stones of nightmare proportions, hard, rocky outcrops, barren tracks leading no-where, dark caves without comfort, fearsome obstacles, hidden corners, beset by unfamiliar creatures.

On the domestic prospect, how is your papa's behaviour now? Is he demeaning himself in an uncharitable manner to Mr. N? If so, I should think the air

216

in your home nigh impassable as a cold-crusted turnip on Tabby's table with a blunt knife in midwinter.

Would that I could move into the parsonage, take the Sunday Services, preach to the congregation, minister to the sick, bless the poor.

Marry you.

I am yours, in anguish,

Nell

Brookroyd, 8 January 1853

Dear Charlotte,

How wise you are to leave for London – this being a perfect solution for your troubles at this time. Thank you for your kindness in your reply to mine, written in anguish. Peace and calm are re-instated at my table. I almost attain serenity, being assured again of your refusal of marriage – and that Mr. Nicholls resigns his position in Haworth.

Your words have a very definite ring, which bells I need to hear because they peal a round of truth. '*I feel persuaded the termination will be –his departure for Australia. Dear Nell – without loving him I don't like to think of him, suffering in solitude, and wish him anywhere so that he were happier. He and Papa have never met or spoken yet.*' In truth I applaud your compassion. It is the bridge between Charlotte Brontë and Currer Bell. Nightly do I continue to pray, and have spoken psalm Twenty-Three most often, with my spirit nesting in high places, where David plays his shepherd's flute. His haunting lyrics bring comfort to my darkest hours. The psalms of David inspire me – I recall from school days the story of David and Goliath – so I am reading again Samuel 1 &2. If David can… anyway I shall resist all dragons single-handedly and successfully – in one fell swoop shall I conquer. The dragons shall flee to their distant mountain lairs and trouble me no further. I hope you are proud of me – I pray that you enjoy your visit and may this time choose sights for yourself. Let me know how you fare.

Wait on the Lord, be of good courage;

And he shall strengthen your heart. Psalm 27.14

My friends send love to you.

Your loving and affectionate friend,

Nell

Dear Charlotte,

So, your art gallery is extended! I'm pleased to hear that the portrait of Thackeray hangs next to Wellington; and Richmond's portrait of you… They are in good company & should be proud of she who graces them with her presence.

I finish reading my copy of *Villette* with great interest and pleasure. I find it remarkable how your images & experiences of your sojourn in Brussels are woven so skilfully into a tapestry. As an experienced needle-woman, I know how difficult is the reverse side of fine work. People see only the front of a completed canvas, the colours and themes illustrated in wool or silk, with threads so closely needled that shifts in colour and tone are almost imperceptible. But imagine our Church bazaar of women's work when each visitor turns over every tapestry, to examine the reverse. There must be no frayed ends, no slipped stitches, no joins apparent & no knots. Indeed the *test* is whether or not the reverse might stand for the front. The women's eager eyes search more minutely than a night owl seeking a field mouse from a great height – their examination is extensive – nothing escapes their awesome scrutiny. Were *Villette* to be a tapestry under their intent gaze, they could find no fault – so seamless it is and finely wrought. All your hours of re-writing last summer & autumn, all those days of proof-reading in London, all have brought this to a conclusion for which reviewers should be approving. Therefore more's-the-pity that your erstwhile friend and acquaintance, Harriet Martineau – in the Daily News – sees fit to express disapprobation. I'm so sorry – I know that such a review does wound. She is wrong, simply wrong, and I wish that in public she would rescind.

As to the location – I recall Mary and Martha Taylor's letters from Brussels, with some deep nostalgia. As to 'school days'– I'm again in Roe Head, you're making out & we're stifling gasps and giggles. But now we're no longer young girls, naïve and ingenuous, are we? You're a mature woman, a talented author, and if I were Thackeray –or indeed H. M. – I'd be honoured to have my portrait on the wall beside you. Charlotte Brontë and Currer Bell, *both*, are worthy of approbation, love and respect.

Your loving and affectionate friend,

Ellen

Dear Ellen

... ...

You ask about Mr. Nicholls. I hear he has got a curacy – but do not yet know where – I trust the news is true. He & Papa never speak. He seems to pass a desolate life. He has allowed late circumstances so to act on him as to freeze up his manner and overcast his countenance not only to those immediately concerned but to everyone. He sits drearily in his rooms – If Mr. Cartman or Mr. Grant or any other clergyman calls to see and as they think to cheer him – he scarcely speaks – I find he tells them nothing – seeks no confidant –rebuffs all attempts to penetrate his mind – I own I respect him for this –He still lets Flossy go to his rooms and takes him to walk – He still goes over to see Mr. Sowden sometimes – and poor fellow –that is all. He looks ill and miserable. I think and trust in Heaven he will be better as soon as he fairly gets away from Haworth. I pity him inexpressibly. We never meet or speak – nor dare I look at him – silent pity is just all I can give him – and as he knows nothing about that – it does not comfort. He is now grown so gloomy and reserved — that nobody seems to like him – his fellow-curates shun trouble in that shape — the lower orders dislike it – Papa has a perfect antipathy to him – and he – I fear – to papa – Martha hates him – I think he might almost be <u>dying</u> and they would not speak a friendly word to or of him. How much of all this he deserves I can't tell – certainly he never was agreeable or amiable – and is less so now than ever – and alas! I do not know him well enough to be sure that there is truth and true affection – or only rancour and corroding disappointment at the bottom of his chagrin. In this state of things I must be and I am –<u>entirely</u> passive. I may be losing the purest gem – and to me far the most precious – life can give – genuine attachment – or I may be escaping the yoke of a morose temper – In this doubt conscience will not suffer me to take one step in opposition to Papas will –blended as that will is with the most bitter and unreasonable prejudices. So I just leave the matter where we must leave all important matters ... ...

Dear Charlotte,

I pray for you in this and all other matters – that you will make the right decision, and be guided by conscience. I write in response to your phrase '*entirely passive*'. I have expressed no wish that you should act in connection with Mr. N., indeed quite the opposite, but passive is not a word I would in most circumstances associate with your demeanour or your lively, interested mind. For long hours since my receipt of your letter have I thought about this – rightly or wrongly, I choose the following interpretation: That you wish the love of God & the truth of his word to flow through you without interference from raw emotions and fevered thoughts; that you read your Bible & absorb yourself in wisdom contained therein; that you are a stream on its way to the ocean, and all that you read and pray must move unhindered to its natural conclusion. If this is indeed what you infer by *'passive'* then do I concur with your method. D'accord. Perhaps we're intended to follow a recipe – do we not gather our ingredients before we begin & utilise in prescribed order, without too much change or adaptation? However I have some disquiet when I think too deeply about your papa, because his *'most bitter and unreasonable prejudices'* have made you very angry, costing your peace of mind & calm sleep. The prolonged leave-taking which falls to any curate departing any parish is a recurrent source of disquiet for many a congregation across the ridings. Would that I could come & see you, fold you into my arms & bring again serenity – meantime must I wait. I trust you shall enjoy your forthcoming visit to Mrs. Gaskell. En route home from Manchester, you may of course break your journey here at Brookroyd – overnight or if possible several days here. 'As you like it'. Shall you write from Manchester to inform me of your plans? I shall look forward so much to tales from your visit.

Take care of yourself, my dear friend,

Yours, always,

Nell

Brookroyd, 10 May 1853

Dear Charlotte,

We found here your sewing case & small portmanteau – they are not lost. Our carrier has to go to Bradford next week – I shall send them with him for collection from the Inn as usual. The Upjohns are still undecided as to when I'm to visit but it's now set for the end of May.

In haste.

Nell

Dear Ellen

... ...

I cannot help feeling a certain satisfaction in finding that the people here are getting up a subscription to offer a testimonial of respect to Mr. Nicholls on his leaving the place. Many are expressing both their commiseration and esteem for him. The Churchwardens recently put the question to him plainly Why was he going? Was it Mr. Brontë's fault or his own? His own – he answered. Did he blame Mr. Brontë? "No: he did not: if anybody was wrong it was himself." Was he willing to go? "No : it gave him great pain."

Yet he is not always right. I must be just. He shews a curious mixture of honour and obstinacy; feeling and sullenness. Papa addressed him at the school tea-drinking – with <u>constrained</u> civility, but still with <u>civility</u>. He did not reply civilly: he cut short further words. This sort of treatment offered in public is what Papa never will forget or forgive –it inspires him with a silent bitterness not to be expressed. I am afraid both are unchristian in their mutual feelings: Nor do I know which of them is least accessible to reason or least likely to forgive. It is a dismal state of things. ... ...

I am yours sincerely

C. Brontë

Gorleston, Yarmouth, 8 June 1853

My Dear Charlotte,

I have received your letter written on May 27th. Before I answer it, let me thank you with all my heart for something very dear to me – For the intimacy with which you share details in your letters these past weeks, I am deeply grateful. Such inclusion brings me so close you in the chances and changes of the sad & difficult matter of A.B.N.'s leaving Haworth. You say I'll want to know about the leave-taking. I do and I don't. I do because it keeps me close to you. I don't because of all the hurt that Mr. N. causes you, & the disquiet his actions are creating in your Papa. So it is now finished. A.B. N.'s suffering and your pity, which together have strung through these weeks of his leaving – through times when he falters at the altar & cannot continue – to the women sobbing at the piteous sight of him. I agree that Mr. N. ought not to have had to take Sunday duty. It constitutes an ignominious ordeal. In your latest letter, regarding his leaving, you say you find him '*leaning against the garden-door in a paroxysm of anguish –sobbing as women never sob*'. Rarely are we witness to the sight of any man sobbing – sometimes, my brother George would indulge, Bless him. Usually they are taught from children never to allow such emotion, much less to *reveal* it. Have not you and I spoken often at the raw courage with which Anne, in *The Tenant*, describes so vividly the attempts by the men-folk to school young Arthur into hard, callous worldliness?

I believe you are right that A.B.N. must know you are '*not indifferent to his constancy and grief*'. I applaud your words of pity and compassion – '*they all think in Haworth that I have disdainfully refused him &c. if pity would do Mr. N— any good – he ought to have and I believe has it.*' For my part I believe you have acted with truth, honour & integrity, which is no more than I would expect from you, my dearest Charlotte.

You are in my thoughts – I pray for you every night, as usual ten o'clock. We can ask for guidance from Heaven, in this and all other matters. Open your Bible, let it fall as it will & be assured of The Good Shepherd's presence in all your actions.

Your loving and affectionate friend,
Ellen

Gorleston, Gt. Yarmouth, 10 June 1853

Dear Charlotte,

Herein lies 'The strange tale of the unmitigated disaster of Ellen Nussey in the remote village of G—', as told in her own words. Nay, not all is revealed – I will tell you more of my sojourn with the dreaded Upjohns when I return to Brookroyd. Suffice it to say that this is an unhappy place, inhabited by inconsiderate, disagreeable people – a very bleak, brittle environment, isolated from everyone and everything I hold dear.

Consider, if you will, my arrival here – I discover that Mrs. Upjohn is not yet home, although at her request have I postponed my visit, a change which is not only inconvenient to me but also the cause of a prolonged separation from you. I feel thoroughly put about by this circumstance. For almost a year my family has been contemplating the Upjohns' absurd suggestion – that I become a companion & general housekeeper, in return for some uncertain financial settlement in their wills. I suspect they're the sort of people who live to be a hundred & ninety. I'm treated like an out-dated shopping list, back of the kitchen door: curled around the edges, its ink faded in poor sunlight, but no one thinks to remove it, just in case there might be something on it that is wanting. Au contraire, you may imagine me at Brookroyd, just prior to this experience – an inexpensive vase, no longer fashionable, but useful for flower arrangements – easily moved from shelf to shelf. Since at the Upjohns I feel I have neither use nor purpose, I've taken matters into my own hands & arranged to move to Oundle. My brother Joshua assures me of a warm welcome – I shall stay a short while before returning to Brookroyd.

I trust that your sore throat & influenza, about which your papa wrote me, are now cured, & this letter finds you well & happy. Enclosed herein is a short note thanking him for his kindness in so writing. As to meeting you, I should like to offer a holiday by the sea in Burlington, or to accompany you with Joe, Amelia and the baby to Scotland, but neither opportunity would procure Mama's approbation. In Mama's mind, *Oundle* shall doubtless be my holiday. I nearly forgot, when shall Mrs. Gaskell come and see you? Do you plan for the autumn now? Write to me, at Oundle Vicarage, but if and only if, you be well enough,

Your faithful and affectionate friend,

Ellen

Brookroyd, 24 June 1853

Dearest Charlotte,

I will be arriving in Keighley about half past two on Thursday 30th. It's been so long! Can hardly wait. Oh to be with you at home, again!

Soon, soon

Ellen

Journal
Haworth, Tuesday, 5 July 1853
Morning

A letter arrives, which Charlotte takes hastily upstairs. In our newfound openness I recognise the handwriting. I cast my mind back to springtime – when notes in this *same* handwriting are sent to me, enclosed in letters from Charlotte. This letter *today* she doesn't want to share. She doesn't return to the dining room, where I am reading Mr. Dickens' latest work.

Sunlight streams through long windows onto polished surfaces– always Charlotte's home is spotlessly clean. In the grate stands a huge China jug with wild flowers & hedgerow leaves from yesterday's walk. She is upstairs reading her letter. I hear the tock-tock-tock of the clock on the turn of the stairs. I feel a cold shiver, with a premonition of trouble. I sense a shadow, as if clouds are passing across the sun.

Later

This afternoon continues warm & sunny. We don our cloaks & boots, then set off uphill from the parsonage en route to the moors. She is quieter today, neither so chatty nor so full of smiles as when first I arrive for this visit. I sense a reserve & when we pause atop the first incline, looking towards the open moors with a robin's egg sky providing a wide dome all around us, I venture to broach the subject.

'There is something on your mind, Charlie. You're not feared for your papa's frailty, this summer? Does he not seem very well at present?'

'He does, thank you, Nell.'

She takes hold of my hand so we walk on companionably, noticing tiny yellow tormentils underfoot & fat buds on the heather. Presently, almost so quietly that I tilt my head to her, she says, 'Papa's more than three score years and ten. He was seventy-six last March. I am *everyday* aware of the passing of time. He's too old for his duties here.'

Looking west, I observe a new bank of clouds on the horizon. They move now quite quickly, backed by a strong breeze.

'Stand with me, Charlie, let us watch that sky awhile.' I drop her hand, touching her arm. 'Pull your cloak around you. There's a wind getting up.'

'You're stern, Nell. You frighten me, somewhat.'

'I'm sorry, Charlie. I don't mean to. 'Tis myself who has reason…I …I feel a certain chill.'

All around us the moor has short tussocks of rough grass, and I pause, trying to stay calm, taking in the view, but not everywhere is the grass so short, nor the turf so clumped as where we stand together. We know these beloved tracks so well, and as the wind now strengthens, Emily and Anne seem very near to me. I sense Emily's presence in the wind upon these moors, as the wind gathers passing over the turf, like a housekeeper's hand passing upon un-ironed cloth, as she smoothes the rarer, taller grasses, those with soft long silken fronds, into green fabric folds around the hills.

Beside me, Charlotte stands looking towards our pathway to the waterfall, but it's way distant, as we're only just above the parsonage. Her eyes, ever short-sighted, absorb a blurred sweep of moors, hills, sky and driven cloud.

I begin again: 'Today, another letter from A.B. N?'

She nods slowly, considering her reply. 'Of course you know Mr. N.'s hand-writing, Nell. Did I not send you his notes in the spring?'

She turns her head towards me. I pull my summer cloak around me.

I hug myself, my arms around my body, as I look into her face.

Journal
Brookroyd, 11 July 1853

Sometimes I may regain my equilibrium only by confiding in this journal. But unlike my perfect recall of delight for my dance of snow with Emily in 1838, our recent discourse – that of myself & Charlotte during our walk from the parson-age – arrives with only deep disquiet, accompanied by angry, despairing clarity, so that I'm haunted by this our most dreadful confrontation:

'You have been lying to me again, haven't you?'

'We can – all of us – be accomplished liars when protection of those nearest to us is at stake.'

'Nearest? I hoped, foolish female that I am, that I was your nearest, or have you forgotten our intimate letters throughout last springtime? You even sent me the notes he'd written to you. You didn't even like him originally. So be it. Anyway, after my experience of being lied to over *Jane Eyre*, I feel justified now in my assumption that you & he continue to write – behind your papa's back, nay, behind my back.' She looks away, neither affirming nor denying, as I rush on: 'Why would you…I mean how could you, I mean the only reason to … would be…would be…that he wishes a courtship. That you might consider an encouragement?

'I feel not unkindly towards the idea, Nell.'

'You feel not unkindly? Not unkindly?'

'I feel towards the *idea* not unkindly.'

'Let me be clear in my mind. Courtship is a pathway. Like our pathway to the waterfall. Courtship is a pathway, Charlotte.'

She replies with a slow steady tone, as if I were a child, unable to compre-hend rapid, adult discourse. 'The idea…usually…is that it has a direction…yes.'

'How could you consider, even consider, taking A.B. N. to your spouse?'

'I cannot go on any longer, Nell, here on my own. If your mother were not alive things might be very different.'

'But she is alive. And it was *you*, *you*, who persuaded me that duty comes first. That our ageing parents must be our prime concern.'

'As indeed is my father now.'

'Then you have a house companion just as I have my mother. Why cannot you be content with that?'

'My father is a recluse these days. He has been for years and years. Even when Anne and Emily were here, Papa was brought his meals on trays to his room. He stayed in his room, prayed in his room. He barely bothered to leave it, except for his ablutions.'

'I know, I know. But there are friends calling in from the parish are there not? And friends will be visiting, such as Mrs. Gaskell?'

'The house is like a grave, as well you know. Friends are but moments of punctuation in the long passage of enforced solitude. There is no sound but for the movement of my own body. No voices in the air, be it reading, writing, thinking. Unless it is that I read my own written words aloud, which indeed I do. Nell, listen to me – my own heart-beat is poor company. I shall go cabin crazy if I have to endure many more winters sailing this silent ship by myself.'

'I cannot bear the thought of you marrying A. B. N. I cannot bear it. You told me years and years ago, when Mr. Vincent proposed to me, you would cut me if I accepted him. You were jealous. Admit it.'

'I do admit it. But we still had hope in those days. Hope of a shared future somehow – but I have no hope left. I have changed irretrievably since Anne died. I am alone in the world except for a silent, ageing parent and I cannot endure the empty parsonage, which once was so filled with real people laughing, writing and talking. The ghosts of my sisters are not enough for me while I remain alive and breathing. Can you understand that, Nell?'

'Yes, of course I can. I still have two sisters alive and well.' When there's no reply, I change tack. 'If anything were to befall my mother, I could most easily move in with you. We could grow old together in the knowledge that our best years were ahead. But if you marry A.B. N., he will not let me see you. I foresee an unendurable loneliness for me in the midst of my family. I shall be entrapped with them, with you married and me at Brookroyd, unable to write openly to you, unable to visit you.'

'Arthur would never do such a thing. He would never separate us like that. He knows what you mean to me.'

'Precisely. Do not underestimate his anger if he reads the content of my letters. If they were simply about shopping and bonnets, A.B.N. would have no reason to be wary. But they are not, are they?'

'I accept that. But there is more, far more, to say about this before I resolve in my mind what my course of action should and must be.'

'Indeed there is more. You called him Arthur just now. You have continued to correspond with him. He takes encouragement. You allow a pathway. Courtship? Spouse? Indeed there is more. I have waited and been your faithful friend & sleep-sharer for all these years. Indeed there is more.'

'Your rage silences me, Ellen.'

'Maybe so, my darling girl, but it is insufficient to change your proposed course of action, nevertheless!'

'I don't know.'

'So what more do you wish to reveal to me?'

'That my father cannot work this parish as the active incumbent. He must have help with daily duties & Sunday requirements if we're to stay safely housed here until he dies. There is nowhere else to go for him and me. He is not a wealthy member of the Church of England. There is no family fund waiting to bale him out. We live in tied accommodation, and unless I can find someone to work for him, nay, for us, we are doomed. I cannot envisage my father settling happily into the workhouse in Keighley, can you?'

'Don't be cruel, Charlie, it doesn't become you.'

'Nell, I'm sorry. I'm sorry. You did not deserve that.'

'No I did not. That was beneath you.'

'I said I am sorry.'

'So, you intend to allow courtship with A.B.N., Mr. Nicholls, Arthur, because he will work for you?'

'Crudely put. But accurate, my dearest.'

'This is awful.'

'He cares about me. He will be kind.'

'But what about…the physical…everything?'

'He is kind. He is a good man. It will be all right.'

'Charlie, listen to me, I beg you, don't dismiss the risk…the physical,' I stutter. 'This is hard for me but I must speak. You could get pregnant. You have two sisters who have died of T.B…'

'Four. Four sisters who died of T.B…'

'May God in his mercy protect you…'

'Arthur will not give me T.B.'

'Don't speak as if I am a fool. I don't mean T.B. itself … I mean your whole system… your vitality… your life force. You'll put yourself in danger if you risk pregnancy at this age – you know you will.'

'Not necessarily…'

I am desperate, therefore I again change themes. 'What about your writing?'

'Arthur won't stop me from writing.'

'Marriage will. He is not like Rev. Gaskell and you're not Mrs. G., with her stamina, her very vigorous persona. You couldn't sustain a life of writing all night like she does while the rest of the family sleeps. Moreover, your beloved A.B. N. would not let you leave his bed for such a thing. And by day – he will soak up your time just like any other boring husband. He'll demand your attention and your companionship. Let us just do this, Charlotte, let us go to this place, Charlotte, let us go to that place, Charlotte.'

'There is no more to be gained from this fury of yours, Ellen. I want you to go now. I need to have time to think.'

'Thinking is not what I need. I need you… Oh don't look at me like that. I'm taking my leave, as requested.'

To Mary Hewitt née Gorham
Brookroyd, 23 September 1853

Dear Mary,

I thank you for your latest & I'm relieved to hear that the influenza, so troublesome in the north, does not extend to your part of the country. I think of you often. Life continues much the same at Brookroyd – I am kept busy by teaching in the Sunday School & am encouraging the older children with their Bible reading. My sister, Mercy, has for these many years excelled in all forms of teaching & I'm thankful to her for guidance into this occupation. Our schools provide an essential education for the poorest children of this parish. Sometimes there will be a 'bright spark' – a lad or lass whose eyes light up when I enter the schoolroom – or who drinks up my teaching as if a kitten starved of milk. It's a rewarding task, which fills up many hours nowadays. You ask me about Charlotte – but as I hear nothing from her, I feel there is little I can report – I try each day not to anticipate the post. Mrs. Gaskell is currently staying at the parsonage, so I should expect that Charlotte is kept busy with her guest. I can't help but feel excluded, for was I not accustomed to her frequent letters both before & since the departure of A.B.N.? At present, I have disturbed nights on account of the terrible gentleman – I have strange dreams about him, & my intuition informs me that there's something wrong. In my worst nightmares they continue to communicate. I have no means of discovering whether there's justification for my fears.

One person has that information but she is the last on earth to whom I may apply for verification. Write to me if you can give me any advice about nightmares, dear Mary. The mornings find me bleak as the winds that swept over the coast by Gorleston, during my bizarre visit with the Upjohns. I would most appreciate your earliest reply. Silence from Charlotte does make the days long indeed.

Your affectionate friend,
Ellen

To Miss Margaret Wooler
Brookroyd, 20 October 1853

Dear Miss Margaret,

I cannot ask you to betray the confidence of one so close to us, our beloved Charlotte, & indeed this is not the purpose of my letter to you. Instead I'm writing to ask your advice about women of my age – I shall be thirty-seven come next April. I appear anxious, suffering as from shock; my skin is coarser, its general effect being one of ageing. If I were married I would fear each month the patter of tiny feet – because my woman-time is now unpredictable, though not yet ceased. None of my sisters has entered this phase so early, but I cannot ask them, so I turn to you.

The most difficult of my current symptoms is that of insomnia. I wake in the early hours – each morning about one-thirty – from vivid images of Charlotte in extreme danger. These nightmares are insistent & regular, perhaps aggravated by the current silence from my erstwhile friend. Indeed, when I wrote her recently that I had become rather ill, only the briefest of somewhat curt replies was evoked. Never before have I been afraid of lying awake in the dark – not even after my father's death, when I was nine, nor William's suicide when I was adult. Nor even after my bedside vigil with Anne in Scarborough. Indeed it was I, curled around Charlotte, who provided her with calm, refreshing sleep.

I turn to you because of your knowledge & wisdom, gained from years of friendship with many different girls and women – some of whom were former pupils like Charlotte and myself. Always, since first I attended Roe Head, you have been my mentor, my trusted, respected, older friend. I do not know where else to turn.

Charlotte does not answer my letters – there were some inconsistencies in the past, but nothing like this rift ever happened between us until now. Earlier this year, I received intimate accounts from her of A.B.N. – Mr. Nicholls. I mean of Mr. N's letters or actions & of her own responses. Surprised and pleased was I, to be so included & I took this as evidence of our continued love & enduring care for one another. I felt cherished. Now there is nothing.

My nights without sleep create difficulties – I have commitments – household duties to attend to. So, how may this situation be resolved? How shall I overcome this exhaustion & attain some peace of mind? I desire to move my life forward – to anticipate bright mornings once again.

I send you my warmest wishes for your own continued good health.

I am yours most sincerely,

Ellen Nussey

East Marden, 21 February 1854

My dear Ellen,

I was glad to receive your second letter telling me you had heard from Miss Brontë – glad for her as well as you – for it seemed unnatural that she could so throw off all her old friendship that she did not evince some little return of it when you were ill – I was very glad she did – it must have comforted you very much and you had suffered so much pain about her evidently. Now you are ready to forget all I can see – and that is kind and right – but she will not quite forget I hope – but will remember enough to see how your true friendship was shown in it – and be guided by you – her thoughts – and affections must really need control. It is an example of the dangerous gift such a mind as hers must be, and I trust it <u>will</u> overcome temptations, and shine out brightly at last – That will be a happiness to you indeed.

Your third note too I must thank you for, I am glad of any thing that gives you occasion to write – but sorry to hear of Mrs Richard Nussey's serious illness. They have lived together but a few years – ... ... I trust however she may yet recover for a longer time than you anticipate....

I hope Miss Mercy's foot is well again and herself recovered from the jar. I shall be glad to hear Mrs Clapham is better, it is very satisfactory to have a competent opinion in a case like hers – she has been an invalid a long long time.

Mama unites with me in very kind love to Mrs Nussey of whom we are very glad to hear so well – and with best love and regards from us all to you all – dear Ellen, – believe me ever Your most affec. friend,

Mary Hewitt.

This is a most shabby letter, the most so I have ever sent you I think.

Journal
Brookroyd, 14 March 1854

Letters again flow between Charlotte and me. Through Miss Wooler, we are re-connected. Thanks be to God. The rift from July until Charlotte's first letter this February – so long, long a winter's rift – did plummet my soul to bereavement, my body to illness.

Never can there be comprehension of my resistance to 'the idea' of Charlotte's marriage. In Charlotte's world, beyond Brookroyd & beyond Haworth, I am nothing but a friend, a school friend, over-indulged by my family, silly, flighty, interested in only shawls and shopping. What right would I have to comment on this marriage?

Ironically, had I been so insubstantial a being, so flimsy or self-pitying, would I have been welcomed into the Quartette? I think not.

Emily? She had no desire for friends beyond home & no tolerance for fools. Did we not love one another? Anne? Loving, gentle Anne, likewise expressed no needs beyond her sisters, yet called me to Scarborough. Did we not love one another? Charlotte? Would a woman like Charlotte Brontë, who is also Currer Bell, have been interested in me? Would our friendship have been sustained these long years?

I am thankful to God that Charlotte and I choose again to inhabit one another's lives.

But Mary Taylor? Surely I was mistaken to open my heart, across the oceans – so many miles. Letters take months from New Zealand – as likely as not it will be August before a reply arrives. Perhaps Mary will rant – perhaps judge me – therefore in the mirror of her reply shall I see Ellen as others see me – selfish, silly & self-pitying. Shall I find a mirror to reflect me with *kindness*? No. There's no reflection for a woman like me.

In my prayers nightly, I pray for the souls of my departed friends. I pray for continuance with those still alive; I pray also for my brother Richard's wife, Elizabeth, for whom medical opinions are being sought throughout the West Riding.

My dear Ellen

I am very glad to hear that Mrs. Richard is pronounced out of danger for I think her loss would probably be severely felt by your brother – and he could not be much disturbed, without the evil coming more or less home to you all at Brookroyd.

... ...

I trust and believe your brother John is right in his opinion of your own ailment. On no account let it alarm you – for I imagine that comparatively few people are wholly free from some such inconvenience as you describe. An over-sedentary life producing a confined state of the bowels – I suppose is at the root of it. Remembering the effect that iodine produced on you long since – I cannot help being glad that you have given up that remedy. It seems to me that those reducing drugs must be hazardous where the constitution is not robust. It is strange I have never heard of you as looking ill; but I have no doubt it was owing to the low state to which the pills &c had brought you – that that cold you caught in the winter took such hold on your system. So far I have been so favoured as to escape <u>severe</u> colds – but my headaches &c. still at times harass me and keep me thin. I am truly glad to hear that your Mother, Mr. Clapham and Mercy are well and that your Sister Ann is better. Mr. Teale will really do a good deed if he succeeds in curing her. Papa still continues well. Believe me my dear Ellen

Yours affectionately
C Brontë

My dear Ellen

I put off writing yesterday because I had a headache – I have it again to-day –not severe but depressing – however I will write a few lines – and if they are inefficient you will know the reason.

Miss Wooler kindly asked me likewise to go and see her at Hornsea –but I had a prior engagement this month – which, however, it now seems very doubt-ful whether I shall keep – it would have given me true pleasure to have joined Miss Wooler – had not my previous promise stood in the way.

... ...

Mrs. Richard Nussey's convalescence was good news also – I trust she will now steadily improve – and many years may elapse before she has any return.

... ...

Be sure and look after yourself dear Ellen –take exercise – Keep your spirits up – mind cold and the night-air. Tell me if you are in pretty good spirits when you write again

Yours affectionately C Brontë

How does your Sister Ann go on – and what treatment is prescribed by Mr. Teale?

Haworth, 28 March 1854, Tuesday Morn-g

My dear Ellen

The enclosure in yours of yesterday puzzled me at first – for I did not immediately recognize my own handwriting – when I did – the sensation was one of consternation and vexation as the letter <u>ought</u> by all means to have gone on Friday – it was intended to relieve him from great anxiety. However I trust he will get it to-day – and on the whole –when I think it over–I can only be thankful that the mistake was no worse and did not throw the letter into the hands of some indifferent and unscrupulous person. I wrote it after some days of indisposition and uneasiness and when I felt weak and unfit to write. While writing to <u>him</u>–I was at the same time intending to answer <u>your</u> note – which I suppose accounts for the confusion of ideas –Shewn in the mixed and blundering address.

I wish you <u>could</u> come about Easter rather than at another time – for this reason – Mr. Nicholls – if not prevented –proposes coming over then – I suppose he will stay at Mr. Grant's, as he has done two or three times before –but he will be frequently coming here–which would enliven your visit a little – perhaps too– he might take a walk with us occasionally – altogether it would be a little change for you such as– you know– I could not always offer.

If all be well– he will come under different circumstances to any that have attended his visits before– were it otherwise I should not ask you to meet him– for when aspects are gloomy and unpropitious– the fewer there are to suffer from the cloud– the better.

He was here in Jany. and was then received but not pleasantly. I trust it will be a little different now–

Papa has breakfasted in bed to-day and has not yet risen – his bronchitis is still troublesome– I had a bad week last week– but am greatly better now – for my mind is a little relieved though very sedate, and rising only to expectations the most moderate.

Some time – perhaps in May– I may be in your neighbourhood and shall then hope to come to Brookroyd– but as you will understand from what I have now stated –I could not come before.

Think it over, dear Ellen, and come to Haworth if you can.

Yours affectionately

C Brontë

Write as soon as you can decide.

Haworth, I April 1854, Saturday Morn—g

My dear Ellen

You certainly were right in your second interpretation of my note. I am too well aware of the dullness of Haworth for any visitor –not to be glad to avail myself of the chance of offering even a slight change. But this morning my little plans have been deranged by an intimation that Mr. Nicholls is coming on Monday–I thought to put him off – but have not succeeded–As Easter now consequently seems an unfavourable period both from your point of view and mine– we will adjourn it till a better opportunity offers. Meantime I thank you–dear Ellen, for your kind offer to come in case I wanted you.

Papa is still very far from well–his cough very troublesome, and a good deal of inflammatory action in the chest. To-day he seems somewhat better than yesterday– and I earnestly trust the improvement may continue. With kind regards to your Mother and all at Brookroyd – I am dear Ellen yours affectionately

C Brontë

Journal
Brookroyd, 3 April 1854

If I were my brother Henry, Clerk in Holy Orders, I would be now employed in the same circumstance as Arthur Bell Nicholls. However, whatever be my feelings for Charlotte or the possibility of her marriage, I would rather accept A.B.N. as her husband than again risk my health, my spirit, or indeed my mind.

I am a strong woman. My mind is made up. Had I not been strong, in ideas, imagination, laughter, spirit, would I have remained in the Quartette? So be it. Aunt Branwell, used to say, 'Ye pick yeself up, ye dust yeself down, ye soldier on, me 'andsome.'

Haworth, 11 April 1854

My dear Ellen

Thank you for the collar –It is very pretty, and I <u>will</u> wear it for the sake of her who made and gave it.

Mr Nicholls came on Monday 3rd. and was here all last week.

Matters have progressed thus since last July. He renewed his visit in September —but then matters so fell out that I saw little of him. He continued to write. The correspondence pressed on my mind. I grew very miserable in keeping it from Papa. At last sheer pain made me gather courage to break it –I told all. It was very hard and rough work at the time– but the issue after a few days was that I obtained leave to continue the communication. Mr. N. came in January   he was ten days in the neighbourhood. I saw much of him– I had stipulated with Papa for opportunity to become better acquainted– I had it and all I learnt inclined me to esteem and, if not love –at least affection – Still Papa was very – <u>very</u> hostile –bitterly unjust. I told Mr. Nicholls the great obstacles that lay in his way. He has persevered –The result of this his last visit is – that Papa's consent is gained – that his respect, I believe is won –for Mr. Nicholls has in all things proved himself disinterested and forbearing. He has shewn too that while his feelings are exquisitely keen –he can freely forgive. Certainly I must respect him– nor can I withhold from him more than mere cool respect. In fact, dear Ellen, I am engaged.

Mr. Nicholls in the course of a few months will return to the curacy of Haworth. I stipulated that I would not leave Papa –and to Papa himself I proposed a plan of residence –which should maintain his seclusion and convenience uninvaded and in a pecuniary sense bring him gain instead of loss. What seemed at one time – impossible –is now arranged–and Papa begins really to take a pleasure in the prospect.

For myself – dear Ellen–while thankful to One who seems to have guided me through much difficulty, much and deep distress and perplexity of mind – I am still very calm– <u>very</u>– inexpectant. What I taste of happiness is of the soberest order. I trust to love my husband–I am grateful for his tender love to me – I *believe him to be an affectionate – a conscientious – a high-principled man – and if with all this, I should yield to regrets– that fine talents, congenial tastes and thoughts are not added – it seems to me I should be most presumptuous and thankless.*

Providence offers me this destiny. Doubtless then it is the best for me –Nor do I shrink from wishing those dear to me one not less happy.

It is possible that our marriage may take place in the course of the Summer.   Mr. Nicholls wishes it to be in July. He spoke of you with great kindness and said he hoped you would be at our wedding. I said I thought of having no other bridesmaid. Did I say right?   I mean the marriage to be literally as quiet as possible.

Do not mention these things just yet. I mean to write to Miss Wooler shortly. Good-bye –There is a strange– half-sad feeling in making these announcements – The whole thing is something other than imagination paints it beforehand: cares –fears –come mixed inextricably with hopes. I trust yet to talk the matter over with you –Often last week I wished for your presence and said so to Mr. Nicholls –Arthur – as I now call him – but he said it was the only time and place when he could not have wished to see you.

Good bye
Yours affectionately
C Brontë

Brookroyd, 12 April 1854

My dearest Charlotte,

By the tone and contents of this letter I hope to convey to you that I am reconciled – fully –to marriage between you and Arthur Bell Nicholls. I pray for the successful conclusion of your decision and your plans. I trust you will hear from Mary Taylor – Surely she will be very angry with me for resisting your marriage. It is you, dear Charlotte, and only you, who is in a position to understand how this marriage affects me, my friendship with you, and my circumstances thereafter. In fear and dread of your marriage I came through one of my longest winters – my heart and soul travelled through dark and sombre days. Now it is again springtime, time for new growth, a time when your decision affects you for the rest of your life and me for the rest of mine.

My response and my decision are of the utmost importance for my future: I shall remain your friend, however difficult our changes & chances of our friendship shall be. I would rather continue as the friend of C.B. Nicholls than be cast aside, beyond redemption. Meanwhile for your duty and affection towards your papa, I am astounded at the depth, breadth, height of your filial sensibility. This is matched only by the genius of your authorial flight. You exceed Daedalos in both invention and courage. Long after we are all dust, girls and young women everywhere, shall read *Jane Eyre*, *Shirley* and *Villette* and shall take inspiration from a parson's daughter on a remote Yorkshire hillside. Whatever happens after you become Mrs. C.B. Nicholls, you shall know that I love Charlotte Brontë and Currer Bell in equal measure and shall remain always your true and faithful friend.

Yes, I will be bridesmaid.

This shall be my wedding gift to you.

E.N.

Haworth, 15 April 1854

My own dear Nell

I hope to see you somewhere about the 2nd week in May. ... ... I wrote immediately to Miss Wooler and received a truly kind letter from her this morning. If you think she would like to come to the marriage I will not fail to ask her.

... ... My hope is that in the end this arrangement will turn out more truly to Papa's advantage– than any other it was in my power to achieve. Mr. Nicholls only in his last letter – refers touchingly to his earnest desire to prove his gratitude to Papa by offering support and consolation to his declining age. This will not be mere talk *with him – he is no talker – no dealer in professions. Dear Nell – I will write no more at present. You can of course tell your Sister Ann & Mr. Clapham – the Healds too if you judge proper –indeed I now leave the communication to you – I know you will not obtrude it where no interest would be taken.*

Yours affectionately

C Brontë

Haworth, 28 April 1854

My dear Ellen

I have delayed writing till I could give you some clear notion of my movements. If all be well I go to Manchester on Monday 1st May, stay there till

Thursday – Thence to Hunsworth till Monday following – when (D.V) I come to
Brookroyd. I must be at home by the close of the week. Papa – thank God! contin-
ues to improve much. He preached twice on Sunday and again on Wednesday and
was not tired –his mind and mood are different to what they were –so much more
cheerful and quiet. I trust the illusions of Ambition are quite dissipated –and that
he really sees it is better to relieve a suffering and faithful heart –to secure in its
fidelity a solid good –than unfeelingly to abandon one who is truly attached to
<u>his</u> interests as well as mine – and pursue some vain empty Shadow–

Thank you– dear Ellen– for your kind invitation to Mr. Nicholls. He was
asked likewise to Manchester & Hunsworth. To Brookroyd & Hunsworth I would
not have opposed his coming—for a day—had there been no real obstacle to the
arrangement—certain little awkwardnesses of feeling I would have tried to get
over—for the sake of introducing him to old friends—but it so happens that he
cannot now leave on account of his Rector's absence. Mr. Cator will be in Town
with his family till June and he always stipulates that his Curate shall remain at
Kirk-Smeaton while he is away.

How did you get on at the Oratorio and what did Miss Wooler say to the
proposal of being at the wedding? I have many points to discuss when I see
you. I hope your Mother – Mr. & Mrs. Clapham – & Mercy are well. With kind
remembrances to all and true love to you I am dear Nell

faithfully yours
C Brontë.

Journal
Where the Waters Meet, 15 June 1854

Here I sit, in Charlotte's favourite valley, on stone slabs, which span the stream
where the waters meet. It is a beautiful sunny day, approaching midsummer.
My mare, Ginny, is tied to the hazel trees, resting – the sound of her breathing
harmonizes with splashing, tumbling water. A high lark is singing somewhere
but I cannot find her. She is beyond reach, like Charlotte, beyond touch, beyond
shared sleep. My future journey across this bridge takes me forward without her.
I sit here in uninvited solitude, in this place of sunlight & shadows where time
curves around corners, to bring the laughing voices of three sisters and myself,
when we were young & all four of us were alive.

My thoughts flow into this water. I tear leaves from a bright branch – I
bequeath them to the fast flowing current. Sweet air carries the sounds of

several blackbirds and a song thrush, their throats wide, their joy pouring forth.

I kneel by the stream, cupping water in my hands, pouring it over my hair like a baptism – as I have seen Emily so do, so many times. It splashes from me, back to the earth, while the air all around carries wild sounds, which I and the sisters love so well. Emily and Anne seem close by.

I know not whether Charlotte has begun already to love Arthur, though I suspect so. In her own words, if ever she must marry it must be *'for that full feeling which may bind together a man and a woman'*.

I take an old letter from my pocket.

10 July 1846 ... ... 'Who gravely asked you "whether Miss Brontë was not going to be married to her papa's Curate?" I scarcely need say that never was rumour more unfounded – it puzzles me to think how it could possibly have originated – A cold, far-away sort of civility are the only terms on which I have ever been with Mr Nicholls – I could by no means think of mentioning such a rumour to him even as a joke – it would make me the laughing-stock of himself and his fellow-curates for half a year to come –They regard me as an old maid, and I regard them, one and all, as highly uninteresting, narrow and unattractive specimens of the "coarser sex".'

From inside me there emerges a lapwing's cry splintering upwards through branches of hazels as it releases itself to the wild air, up, up above the valley. A scream? I don't know. I know only that – on whatever terms – to be Charlotte's friend is better than to endure between us any rift or unbridgeable chasm.

I kneel, like a peasant woman, letting forth a keening-cry that I never made in any air, in any place on earth, or under the sky, until this day. Thus is my soul fragmented – into sounds that split from me then join like wings in a fast wind-driven sky – meeting the far hills in full force, circling there like a flock of birds at sunset: 'Please God let him be a kind man.'

I uncurl from the earth, then lie back exhausted on the grassy bank, and look up at Heaven. As a child I asked Mama, 'Where does God live?' Dissatisfied with her answer, I decided that He lived in the sky. Now, as the bridesmaid of the woman I desire to share my life with, I lie flat under that very sky, praying to God above me, in His sunlit, cloud-scudded Heaven.

'Almighty Father, give me the strength to attend Charlotte's wedding a fortnight today.

'Our Father in Heaven, my Shepherd, witness my pleas to you today – A woman who loves another woman so much that she will follow her down the aisle, behind her.

'Give me courage to stand quietly, watching Miss Wooler give Charlotte away, if her papa cannot do so, when the time comes.

'Sustain me as I watch Arthur Bell Nicholls, but cannot see his fiancée's face – only the back of her wedding bonnet, as I witness him place his ring on her hand.

'Almighty God, give me the compassion which I know to be yours. Holy Father, be my Shepherd. Sustain me in the curve of your crook, that I may not tremble. Guide me to resilience and wisdom. Let me appear calm, resolute and gentle. Show not that I grieve, but rather, carry my spirit to *this lovely place*.

'Heavenly Father, I am a needle-woman – light and shade are mine, pattern and colour, texture and design. In skeins of silk and shining satin, across these clouds embroider my dreams. In feathered flights, with my compassion, stitch wide this sky. Above this earth, dissolve my screams, in the wild free air, in the lapwing's cry.'

Conway, 29 June 1854

Dear Ellen

I scribble one hasty line just to say that after a pleasant enough journey –we got safely to Conway   the evening is wet and wild – though the day was fair chiefly with some gleams of sunshine. However we are sheltered in a comfort-able inn. My cold is not worse. If you get this scrawl tomorrow and write by return – direct to me at the Post-Office. Bangor, and I may get it on Monday. Say how you and Miss Wooler got home. Give my kindest & most grateful love to Miss Wooler whenever you write – On Monday – I think we cross the channel no more at present

Yours faithfully and lovingly
C.B.N.

Journal
Haworth, 2 October 1854

A fire burns in my grate and I find a vase of autumn leaves & berries in my room. I retire early in order to read – again enjoying *Northanger Abbey* and shall read *David Copperfield* while I'm here. There is also a pile of 'Household Words' with the latest chapters of Mrs. G's *North and South*, which we talk about on our walks.

It's after eleven when, with a knock on my door, Charlotte enters with warm milk – two glasses on a tray – to bid me goodnight. She's in her nightshirt with a shawl around her shoulders. Surprised and pleased, I begin with:

'Charlie? You still awake? Are you unwell? Where's Arthur?'

'He is called away, Mrs. Schofield may not last the night.'

'Will he be gone many hours?'

'I know not but…'

'Come climb in here, keep warm.' So Charlotte snuggles in my wide bed, placing our milk by my bedside, as she looks around my cosy room. 'Are you comfortable, Nell, with both of us?'

'I'm comfortable, you gave me a fire – you need have no concern. I am all right. I am calm.'

'As to Arthur?'

'He is a kind husband. I observe that he loves you – he loves you very much, Charlie.'

'I'm so glad for this visit, Nell. Thank you. I'm looking plump, am I not?'

'You're…?' I shake my head. 'Not?… you're not, are you?'

'No, Nell. It's just the good food, companionship and, as far as Papa is concerned, I have now peace of mind.'

'Your papa has a cough. But he seems in High Spirits.'

'He is more than happy with our household arrangements. No one troubles him, and he has no intrusion.'

'Good. I'm reading the chapters of *North and South* – your magazines are there on the chest of drawers. You need them sooner?'

'No. I shall write to Mrs. G., this week. She tells me that the pressure to write for serialization is well nigh intolerable.'

'Oh, indeed, Charlie. I can well imagine. I should crumble under that schedule. Besides she is more than brave. A novel redolent with doubts and dissenters – Memory flies to the Red House – Mary, Martha, everyone, hammer and tongs!'

Charlotte laughs. 'Hot air and chilled expressions, eh Nell?' She pauses, her glance swiftly sweeping my room, 'I see your own journal there. I do not doubt you'll have more time for writing than shall I in the weeks to Christmas.'

'Too many tasks?' I shrug. 'For a parson's wife?'

'More than enough, Nell, but I undertake them gladly. I make my own decisions, you know. You see that I am travelling forwards more or less happily, do you not?'

'My anger is gone, Charlie, or I should not accept your invitations to Haworth.' I take hold of her left hand, which she doesn't pull away. With my fingers I trace the line of her ring. Our eyes meet, our hands part themselves as if they know and have their own lives, separate now. 'Besides I have my own teaching now with Mercy and I am myself busy and productive. It's our Virtue of Necessity, is it not?'

'Neither of us was ever lacking in courage, Nell. Nor compassion.'

'I pray to God that never shall I be – lacking in either. We *must succeed*, you and I.' Then I change tone, speaking very slowly, weighing my words like Emily weighing yeast. I continue: 'My desire, when I'm here, is that I attain belonging without longing.'

'You do belong here, Nell. Surely you know that? My sisters would… And Papa loves you, Nell. His face lights up when you arrive.'

'I welcome this hour because I have things to say, to you alone. I want to wake up *every day* looking forward to my hours ahead. William cannot do that, nor Joseph, nor Sarah. Nor your sisters…'

She looks at me with huge eyes. We feel Emily and Anne in the air around us. Neither of us speaks for a few moments.

Then I say, smiling, 'I imagine Sarah coming down from Heaven, shaking a finger at me, like this? "Nellie," she scolds me, "if you are down there miserable you can exchange with me. Be miserable here and I will be alive and laughing where you are now." So I'm beholden to "soldier on", am I not?'

'I hear Aunt Branwell, Nell.'

In unison we chant 'Ye pick yeself up, ye dust yeself down, ye soldier on, me 'andsomes.'

'Therefore, do you stay *busy*, Nell?'

'I endeavour to design my days like an engineer in Richard's and Robert's mills. I make lists and schedules – like them, for their mills to run efficiently. Or Aunt Branwell, like she did.'

'Lists were her singular pleasure! She excelled at them, which meant, as a rule, more work for all of us!'

'Yes I know. But imagine her arriving from Land's End. A total stranger. Did she not succeed? Did she not live gladly? Her image, I keep at the front of my mind. Likewise Miss Wooler – never does she suffer self-pity. She sends love into the world – she writes to her friends and visits them. She doesn't wait for life to begin. Nor shall we, eh, Charlie? We must *live* our lives, must we not?'

'That's my girl.'

Dear Nell

You would have been written to before now if I had not been very busy. Amelia, Joe, Tim & Anne came on Tuesday morning – Joe only stayed till the same evening –we had the others till yesterday. We got on with them better than I expected. Amelia seemed pleased and content and forgot her fancies for the time She looked– not at all pretty – but stronger and in better health. Tim behaved capitally on the whole. She amused Papa very much –chattering away to him very funnily – his white hair took her fancy –She announced a decided preference for it over Arthur's black hair –and coolly advised the latter to "go to the barber, and get his whiskers cut off". Papa says she speaks as I did when I was a child – says the same odd unexpected things. Neither Arthur nor Papa liked A's look at first –but she improved on them –I think.

Arthur will go to the Consecration of Heptonstall church –D.V. but I don't mean to accompany him – I hardly like coming in contact with all the Mrs. Parsons – if you were here I should go.

... ...

Arthur is impatient for his walk. –I am obliged to scrawl hurriedly.

When I go to Brookroyd if I hear Mr. C(lapham) or anybody else say anything to the disparagement of single women I shall go off like a bomb-shell –and as for <u>you</u> –but I won't prophesy,

Arthur has just been glancing over this note –He thinks I have written too freely about Amelia &c. Men don't seem to understand making letters a vehicle of communication –they always seem to think us incautious. I'm sure I don't think I have said anything rash –however you must <u>burn</u> it when read. Arthur says such letters as mine never ought to be kept – they are dangerous as lucifer matches – so be sure to follow a recommendation he has just given "fire them" –or "there will be no more." Such is his resolve. I can't help laughing – this seems to me so funny, Arthur however says he is quite serious and looks it, I assure you – he is bending over the desk with his eyes full of concern. I am now desired "to have done with it–" so with his kind regards and mine –Good-bye dear Ellen

Yours affectionately
CB: Nicholls

My dear Charlotte,

By an open window am I seated, to answer your letter of 20th, although it is very early in the morning. There is no chill in the air, which is very mild for the time of year, with barely a slight mist, now steaming off the lawn as the sun rises. It brings promise of a wondrous day, of deep burnished copper and gleaming gold. There are shimmering autumn leaves on silver birch trees – have I not always insisted these to be my favourite? I read all you say about Amelia and enjoy most thoroughly your description of her small daughter, Tim, and your frankness. It's quite like old times. How I would miss these letters full of information about the people and places we have known for so long. Very glad am I that Amelia and Joe came for a short visit and that it passed off without incident, even though Arthur doesn't like Amelia.

Forgive me – I must pause –I am interrupted – I will send this immediately [I enclose a letter from Mary Hewitt for your perusal] & continue with our news in my next – meanwhile I shall give serious consideration to the matter of setting fire to your letters to me.

Your faithful friend,

Ellen

Haworth, 31 October 1854

Dear Ellen

I wrote my last in a hurry, and as soon as I had sealed it – remembered that it contained no comment on what you had said about E. Cockhill's illness ... ... You will kindly remember to give me information respecting her when you write again.

The consecration of Heptonstall Church took place last Thursday—Arthur fully intended to go but a funeral kept him at home. I regretted this as the day happened to be very fine. Mr. Grant went. He said there was a good attendance of the laity –but very few clergy –this was owing to the fact of invitations not having been sent.

I return Mrs. Hewitt's letter –it bears that character of unassuming goodness and sense which mark all her letters – but I should fear her illness has perhaps been more serious than she allows. She is evidently not one to make much of her own ailments.

Dear Ellen – Arthur complains that you do not distinctly promise to burn my letters as you receive them. He says you must give him a plain pledge to that effect –or he will read every line I write and elect himself censor of our correspondence.

He says women are most rash in letter-writing – they think only of the trust-worthiness of their immediate friend – and do not look to contingencies – a letter may fall into any hand. You must give the promise – I believe– at least he says so, with his best regards – or else you will get such notes as he writes to Mr. Sowden –plain, brief statements of facts without the adornment of a single flourish – with no comment on the character or peculiarities of any human being – and if a phrase of sensibility or affection steals in – it seems to come on tiptoe – looking ashamed of itself – blushing "pea-green" as he says – and holding both its shy hands before its face.

Write him out his promise on a separate slip of paper, in a <u>legible</u> hand – and send it in your next. Papa I am glad to say continues pretty well – I hope your Mother prospers – and that Ann is better – with love to all – Mr. Clapham included– and Mercy if good –

I am yours faithfully
CB. Nicholls.

Brookroyd, 7 November 1854

My dear Charlotte,

Another lovely morning is promised, but is unfulfilled, not by the weather, which continues mild and sunny, but by the arrival of your note of 31ˢᵗ, upon reading of which I am given to much shaking, trembling – you will notice now by my hand that the lexicon forms less fluidly, with little confidence. I have indeed given much though to your first request – I have suspected from the beginning that A.B.N. desires our separation – and a cessation of the exchanges concerning the people & places we have both known & loved for many years. I am only too aware that he can – at any moment – threaten to burn my replies. Now he insists that all yours to me shall be burned. This is not un-anticipated. Cast your mind back, dearest Charlotte, to our dreadful, heated discourse, July '53. I am vindicated, am I not? This gives me no pleasure, no satisfaction. To be right *about this* bequeaths only deep disquiet.

Nevertheless, I shall comply with your second request – it being executed by you under Shadow of Demand. I have a clear picture of A.B.N., as he leans over your shoulder, to scrutinize your words to me, my replies to you. No doubt you shall observe a ripple of disquiet through his body when he reads this letter – even though he ought not so to do. It is my communication with you – whom I have known since I was a slip of a girl, merely thirteen years old.

I am hoping to live, like Mama, a very long time. I intend to spend the rest of my life writing letters – as I love to do and have always done. How could I bear such a thought – years passing without long newsy epistles from you? Do I cease to tell you about my life, and our mutual friends? I think not. Therefore do I enclose with this letter, which you shall burn, yeah watch its flames rise in Nebuchadnezzar's fiery furnace, a note which says that I comply with the request, on condition that there is no censorship of your hand, nor any composition therein by him. The note is for A. B. N., and is sealed. Sadly I sign my name,

Your loving and affectionate friend,
Ellen

Brookroyd, November 1854

My dear Mr Nicholls
As you seem to hold in great horror the ardentia verba of feminine epistles, I pledge myself to the destruction of Charlotte's epistles henceforth, if You, pledge yourself to no censorship in the matter communicated
Yours very truly
E.Nussey

Haworth, 19 January 1855

Dear Ellen
Since our return from Gawthorpe we have had a Mr. Bell –one of Arthur's cousins – staying with us—It was a great pleasure; I wish you could have seen him and made his acquaintance: a true gentleman by nature and cultivation is not after all an everyday thing. ... ...
I very much wish to come to Brookroyd—and I hoped to be able to write with certainty and fix Wednesday the 31ˢᵗ. Jany. as the day—but the fact is I am not sure whether I shall be well enough to leave home. At present I should be a

most tedious visitor. My health has been really very good ever since my return from Ireland till about ten days ago, when the stomach seemed quite suddenly to lose its tone—indigestion and continual faint sickness have been my portion ever since. Don't conjecture–dear Nell–for it is too soon yet–though I certainly never before felt as I have done lately. But keep the matter wholly to yourself— for I can come to no decided opinion at present. I am rather mortified to lose my good looks and grow thin as I am doing –just when I thought of going to Brookroyd.

Poor Joe Taylor! I still hope he will get better—but Amelia writes grievous though not always clear or consistent accounts.

Dear Ellen I want to see you and I hope I shall see you well.

My love to all Yours faithfully

C B Nicholls

Thank Mr. Clapham for his hospitable wish—but it would be quite out of Arthur's power to stay more than one night or two—at the most.

To Mary Hewitt née Gorham
Brookroyd, 3 February 1855

My dear Mary,

I am in receipt of your delightful letter with more news of baby Edward. How glad am I that your family fares so well this winter. I write to ask a favour, dear friend. I hear from A.B.N. – two letters in the space of only a few days – because Charlotte is so unwell that she cannot write & they cannot come to Brookroyd. From an earlier letter of Charlotte's in January, it seems that Charlotte *may* be pregnant and suffers her condition in similar manner as did yourself whilst carrying Edward. Now that you have a wonderful healthy child – the birth safely over and done with – it must be of some comfort to poor Charlotte to read that your sickness was 'symptomatic'. Would you please write me so I may [if appropriate, later] enclose with a letter to Charlotte your description that may bring her courage and hope? I am ever in your debt, Mary and I thank you in anticipation.

Your affectionate friend,

Ellen Nussey

My dear Charlotte,

Despite the miserable weather this month, today is a bright winter day – a brief respite in the chilly air – and I return from a wonderful visit over to Spen to see Amelia, Joe and little Tim.

Joe's illness is still a cause of anxiety for Amelia; and Tim is now just recovered from a winter cold, but our journey in the hired gig is smooth despite the snow – none of us takes chill. Spen being no distance at all from Brookroyd, we travel without hindrance in the hired gig, along snowy lanes between Cleckheaton and Gomersal, where Joshua Taylor owns his property. I believe that each winter he sets the village poor to clearing all around his lanes in return for fuel from his woodlands.

Surely you will take comfort from my seeing the whole family & I reassure you that Joe's illness is not considered terminal at present. Indeed you have long believed that the Taylor's health would improve away from the foul air around Hunsworth Mill. The woods are still in their winter garb – their leafless branches are etched like black lace, and some have a thin covering of snow against bright winter skies. We pass by Scotland Wood, where the Taylors have their graveyard – I have always enjoyed this place – an open air cathedral, its tall trees quietly awaiting the end of winter as the first lambs are bleating. Its great beech trees are bright in low sunshine with their curled russet dried leaves still attached– and some catch the recent snowflakes and hold them. I marvel each winter that they lose them not until the new ones come; and black tipped ash buds, flexible but stark, belie the soft green swaying fronds they will become.

On 21st it will be Ash Wednesday and so begins Lent – so, it is but a few weeks from now, approaching Easter, when this woodland will be in its youth again. Everything will re-awaken, but meantime here in the hedgerows are banks of snowdrops & magnificent drifts of them, eye-catching in white and green, piercing the snow, throughout Scotland Wood, as heralds of springtime. Thereby our travel to Spen and back is charming, in reflection of the company we find in Amelia and Joe's household. I enclose a picture of snowdrops drawn by little Tim for you. On my return Mercy had taken a turn for the worse – Her afflictions frighten Mama and we hope for an ease in her symptoms. I trust ere long I shall receive good news about your own health. My friends send love to you, your husband and your papa.

Your affectionate friend,

Ellen

A.B. N. to Ellen
Haworth, 14 February 1855

Dear Miss Nussey—

It is difficult to write to friends about my wife's illness, as its cause is yet uncertain – at present she is completely prostrated with weakness & sickness & frequent fever—All may turn out well in the end, & I hope it will; if you saw her you would perceive that she can maintain no correspondence at present—

She thinks of you & sympathises with you in your present affliction, & longed much to hear from you—

Believe me
Sincerely yrs.
A:B: Nicholls

Brookroyd, 18 February 1855

Dear Charlotte,

I write in a hurry, with our very good news. Mercy is much better – it seems that her turning point was two days past – the doctor told Mama to anticipate Mercy's steady improvement. Thanks be to God. To make my happiness complete I await likewise joyful news of your own return to health.

In haste,
Ellen

Haworth, 21 February 1855

My dear Ellen

I must write one line out of my weary bed. The news of Mercy's probable recovery came like a ray of joy to me. I am not going to talk about my sufferings it would be useless and painful– I want to give you an assurance which I know will comfort you—and that is that I find in my husband the tenderest nurse, the kindest support—the best earthly comfort that ever woman had. His patience never fails and it is tried by sad days and broken nights. Write & tell me about Mrs. Hewitt's case, how long she was ill and in what way.

Papa thank God! Is better –Our poor old Tabby is <u>dead</u> and <u>buried</u>. Give my truest love to Miss Wooler. May God comfort and help you.

C B Nicholls

Haworth, early March 1855

My dear Ellen

Thank you much for Mrs. Hewitt's sensible clear letter. Thank her too. In much her case was wonderfully like mine –but I am reduced to greater weakness—the skeleton emaciation is the same &c. &c. &c. I cannot talk –even to my dear patient constant Arthur I can say but few words at once.

These last two days I have been somewhat better—and have taken some beef-tea –spoonsful of wine & water –a mouthful of light pudding at different times—

Dear Ellen, I realise full well what you have gone through & will have to go through with poor Mercy—Oh may you continue to be supported and not sink! Sickness here has been terribly rife. Papa is well now. Kindest regards to Mr. & Mrs. Clapham your Mother, Mercy. Write when you can.

yours   C B Nicholls

To Mary Hewitt née Gorham
Brookroyd, 13 March 1855

My dear Mary,

Please forgive a very short note. I owe you a long letter. You will see from this stationery that we are in mourning – My dear brother-in-law, Robert Clapham, died very suddenly yesterday. We shall put a notice in the Leeds Intelligencer. He was ill for only two days. Ann is heavily sedated – the rest of us are busy with arrangements. Yours, sadly and in haste,

Your affect. friend
Ellen Nussey

The Revd Patrick Brontë to Ellen, 30 March 1855

My Dear Madam,

We are all in great trouble, and Mr. Nicholls so much so, that he is not so sufficiently strong, and composed as to be able to write—

I therefore devote a few moments, to tell you, that my Dear Daughter is very ill, and apparently on the verge of the grave—

If she could speak, she would no doubt dictate to us whilst answering your kind letter, but we are left to ourselves, to give what answer we can –The Doctors

have no hope of her case, and fondly as we a long time, cherished hope, that
hope is now gone, and we have only to look forward to the solemn event, with
prayer to God, that he will give us grace and Strength sufficient unto our day—

Will you be so kind as to write to Miss Wooler, and Mrs. Joe Taylor, and
inform them that we requested you to do so –telling them of our present
condition.—

Ever truly and
respectfully Yours,
P.Brontë

Haworth, Saturday 31 March 1855

My Dearest Charlotte,

Martha brings flowers and evergreens with which to adorn you. Vividly do I recall the room in Scarborough, you and I attending Anne's body. You lie here as if asleep. I have not seen you these past months – Now I have all the time I need with you – and you open not your eyes nor ever shall again.

Your papa's letter reaches me early this morning. I hurry here immediately, but you are already gone when I arrive, your skin no longer warm.

Your body is but thirty-eight years old – it's no age – this is no good time to die, to leave me here, ne'er so alone, so lost, so busy. Why, Charlotte? Why you, why now? I am reconciled to this marriage – and it avails you not. Tears stream as I place the flowers around you, in a silent parsonage, where the men closet their grief behind closed doors. It's said that you suffered excessive sickness due to pregnancy. But have you not struggled with chill soaking rain from your walks with your husband; no time for writing; no rest from the succession of visitors to this house? What of T.B.? They do not say, they give no information, even now to me, although they are kind & grateful that I am here to attend you.

What price must you pay, my beloved girl, for marriage and the safety of your papa's incumbency in this parish? What price, Charlotte?

To me, you have value above all else. Not your money, not your status in the world of publishing, just you, your warm arms, the sound of your voice, my hand reaching to yours in the night, your hair upon my pillow.

All the time I need with you. Treasure these moments, I must, I shall, for they are all that's left of intimacy. Nay, this is not true. I have your letters, more'n five hundred, if I count the tiny scraps of notes. All tied with ribbon. I take your hand, while my grief flows freely. A fine hand, delicate, clever and affectionate. If I'd been a man, my beloved girl, it would have been my ring on your wedding finger. Let my tears fall, they splash upon your flowers, like dew. Be forever at peace, darling girl. I shall pray with you, every night at ten o'clock, & cherish your life, my dear, departed.

Take with you this letter, beneath your pillow. Take with you my devotion, affection and gratitude. I love you, with loyalty & faithfulness.

Believe me, I am Yours.

Ellen

AIR

Ellen's Journal and Letters
June 1855 to November 1897

Brookroyd, 6 June 1855

Dear Mr Nicholls,

I have been much hurt and pained by the perusal of an article in Sharpe (for this month) entitled 'A few words about Jane Eyre'.

You will be certain to see the article and I am sure both you and Mr Brontë will feel acutely the misrepresentations and the malignant spirit which character-ises them. Shall you suffer the article to pass current without any refutation? The writer merits the severest contempt (even that of silence) but there will be readers and ignorant believers, shall such be left to imbibe a tissue of malign falsehoods or shall an attempt be made to do justice to one who so highly deserved justice (whose very NAME we speak, those who had known her, but with reverence and affection) and shall not her aged father be defended from the reproach the writer coarsely attempts to fix upon him ... I wish Mrs Gaskell who is in every way capa-ble would undertake a reply and give moral castigation to the writer. Her personal acquaintance with Haworth, the Parsonage and its inmates, fits her for the task and if on other subjects she lacks information I would gladly supply her with facts sufficient to set aside much that is asserted... Will you ask Mrs Gaskell to under-take this just and honourable defence ...

I hope you and Mr Brontë are well – My kind regards to both –
Believe me,
yours sincerely,
E. Nussey.

Journal
Brookroyd, 31 March 1856

My dearest One,

On the anniversary of your death you are so near to me – I feel certain of your knowledge of Mrs. Gaskell's biography, which now proceeds quickly. She has on loan many of your letters to me, it being in equal measure joy and pain when she reads. I miss you, dearest girl, everyday and every night. And so begins the interweaving – of my life now with our lives then. Between now and then are the letters.

I resist any pressure from your 'Dear Boy' to allow him personal possession of my epistles. Forgive me, but I do not trust him.

His threat to burn my letters to you may or may not have been carried out – sufficient to say that there appear none in the parsonage – and where else would they be if still intact?

Perhaps you sought to protect me – to safeguard us – and perhaps by your hand did my letters to you meet the flames. Did I not declare that if the contents were insignificant there would be no need *'to fire them'*? Any road, they exist not and I shall not give my drafts or copies – I have drafts or copies of all my letters to you – to Mrs. Gaskell because The Life is about you and only you.

In yours to me I make changes of names and cross out in dark ink the phrases too personal, tenderly I do. It is agony to me to thus inscribe upon the precious paper. Nevertheless I trust Mrs. Gaskell as the best author of our time to complete this task. She holds you in such high esteem. I trust she shall return my letters.

Thirty-nine shall I be in April – the age you were approaching when... – I still cannot believe the door to my room stays shut. I still wait for the knock, the turn of the knob, you smiling gaily, entering. You see, you see, I still wait. Sometimes I catch my breath, find a letter on the hall table for Ann, Mercy, or Mama. There is none in your hand.

I'm appreciative of life, of course I am, is it not a sin, else? But I pray for guidance – I ask, what is my life *for*? Thus do I re-design my purpose – my co-operation with Mrs. Gaskell – my facilitation of this biography, the very best we can do.

Be safe, dearest, in Heaven
Ellen

To Mary Hewitt née Gorham
Brookroyd, 2 December 1857

My dear Mary,

As you can see from this stationery we are now in mourning. Mama passed away this morning, peacefully. This was not unexpected. Our first consciousness was last spring when Mama became so very ill. Since then we have been in not a little anticipation. Ann, Mercy and I are harmonious in our arrangements for the funeral. Mama was eighty-six, cheerful and clear of mind until the very end. So loved was she in this area that Birstall church will be full, when Revd. Heald presides over her funeral. She will be buried with Papa in the family tomb in Birstall.

I will write more before Christmas.

My love to all the family,

Your affectionate friend,

Ellen Nussey

Brookroyd, 22 December 1857

My dear Mary,

Thank you for your kind condolences. My sisters ask me to send their thanks to you & all your family. This is indeed a queer season for the Nussey family – never have we felt less like celebrating Christmas but we are surrounded by so many friends & their kindness keeps our spirits from descending into gloom.

Dear Mary, forgive me if what I write appears to be inappropriate in haste or harsh in worldliness, but I must write of practicalities – Ann, Mercy and I have plans already – because Mama's death means that we must leave Brookroyd, which although built by Uncle Richard, is nevertheless leased from the estate of Batley.

God is kind to us, always he is my Lord Shepherd & always he cares for me as one of his flock. You may know already that the Cloth Hall in Gomersal, being no longer used for sale of goods, does now provide lodgings. Ann, who is always a good business woman and fine house-keeper, continues to be so. Her head for economies and domestic arrangements is always of the clearest, tidiest order. So we shall move to the Cloth Hall, Gomersal forthwith. Our intention is not that we remain there forever – but it is clean, comfortable, warm and with plenty of light – therefore as a temporary home it will suffice.

Despite our grief, Brookroyd is not by day a silent morgue – rather does it hum – its activity resembles a hive at summer's zenith as busy bees must sort their belongings. We ask one another: why do we so hoard goods & chattels? Our attic is stacked with trunks, boxes and household goods that ne'er do we use. Let this be a lesson to us!

So, dear Mary, we approach soon the end of 1857, a year of upheaval through-out every part of our lives at Brookroyd, not only with Mama's illness but also as consequence of unremitting publicity and controversy over the second and third editions of Mrs. Gaskell's biography. Could ever there be published an edition in which Charlotte's deep faith & love of God would be *happily* reflected?

At night, or rather, mid-evening, Brookroyd does fall quiet. Then loss builds upon loss – a veritable edifice of grief. Then to distract my mind, when Ann and Mercy retire to their rooms, consolation comes with my books and magazines. I set aside more and more time for reading. It helps me although I had not anticipated by how much I needed such comfort. Do you still purchase 'Household Words'? What do you think of Mr. Dickens this time? I believe my favourite still to be *David Copperfield* – but what's yours? Also I have turned again to the great Bard. I am currently re-reading *Pericles* and *A Winter's Tale*. Oh how his language lifts me. Bye the Bye, he sets Bohemia by the sea – is that not a neat trick? – for of course it is inland & is that not from whence came the first Moravian brothers?

Your friendship is of the utmost comfort, Polly, a warm shawl around my shoulders these long, dark, freezing winter nights.

My love to you, Swinton and all the family.

Your affect. friend

Ellen Nussey

To Amelia Taylor, née Ringrose
The Old Cloth Hall, Gomersal, 25 August 1858

My dear Milly,

One hardly knows how to express condolences, because to lose a child is the worse nightmare of any parent. We all know that dysentery is prevalent in the area this summer, but this is so sudden, so everyone here is reeling from shock. We loved her very much. C.B. called Tim her little 'grandchild'. Everything about Tim brought joy to all around her – her laughter, her singing, her little jokes, her mannerisms, her brightness. She has a beautiful soul, whose owner should be running through the door of her mama's & her aunties' homes. Of course we shall include her in all our prayers.

For you, my dear Milly, barely a year after your loss of Joe, it is utter devastation, and is incomprehensible.

Thank you very much for requesting my presence & my help. I'm honoured to be so asked & will send this by messenger. I will arrive first thing tomorrow morning.

My sisters both offer assistance – in any manner whatsoever – you must not hesitate to ask them. They also invite you to return here – for an extended stay – after the funeral, if you so wish. We realise that John Taylor is very kind – but he is no substitute for a woman friend. Mary, of course, will be home from New Zealand, perhaps before the year is out. My sisters send their kindest love and deepest sympathy. I send my warmest love to you, Milly, until I see you tomorrow.

Your affect. friend,

Ellen Nussey

To Mary Hewitt née Gorham
Laneside, Gomersal, 21 June 1861

My dear Mary,

I write on midsummer's day when all our marigolds are open in the sun. Fortunate are we to have found this large stone house, where we may anticipate harmonious years. Never would I imagine growing old with two sisters – Ann calls us the witches of Macbeth, but was it not Mercy whose rages would mimic *Lady Macbeth*? By comparison, Mercy is mellow now! Satisfied am I with this cauldron and my two sisters to stir the brew! I enjoy their company & we weather like old oak trees, withstanding winter's gales and summer's showers. Mercy likes to play cribbage – among our goods and chattels here we find our missing walnut cribbage board, which was from my Aunt Ann Nussey of Brookroyd, who died in 1834!

Aunt Ann Nussey was my Uncle Richard Nussey's sister. Uncle Richard owned two houses – Brookroyd which he built and Rydings which he bought from his cousin, Mrs. Mary Walker, in 1826, the year after she was widowed. When Papa died, sadly also in 1826, Uncle Richard invited us to live at Rydings. In 1835, when Uncle Richard died, he left his houses to his favourite two nephews – my brother John inherited the right to buy Rydings back for the Walkers [his in-laws] – my brother Richard inherited the lease of Brookroyd, to which he invited us. Generously, he put his roof over our heads. You see I have had so much kindness, Polly, and the two houses – Brookroyd and Rydings – have a spiral history, whose stories inter-weave as the Walker-Nusseys come and go. A small cribbage board illustrates our convoluted heritage. Between Rydings and Brookroyd our people have gone round and round like the pegs on the board.

Here at Laneside I have again a beautiful garden. Bye the bye, I have my sweet pea seedlings planted. They are strong & vibrant, wobbling not a little, as they prepare to twine around. Some don't know what to do – I tie them so they may learn. We plan to refurbish our somewhat neglected kitchen garden– please advise me about varieties. I think perhaps we should choose raspberries, Falstaff; an outdoors vine, Royal Muscadine; and strawberries, maybe Sir Harry Oscar.

Now then, I'm sorry to impart sad news. Within the past fortnight, I have attended the funeral of Revd. Patrick Brontë, a clergyman so well respected & loved. We had a fondness, he and I, you may say a mutuality – I found always kindness and generosity in his home. Rumour tells that A.B.N. shall return to Ireland.

Oh, Polly, I *do* try to move forward. But this funeral creates madness in my mind. If I wake before dawn my world is naught but emptiness. Time is emptiness. Future is emptiness. My bed is empty. My room is silent.

Air swirls cold, dim, empty. Nothing exists but all is disturbance.

My body trembles. Wide awake, fragmented am I with endeavour – I desire the sound of Charlotte's even breath in calm, peaceful sleep. Nothing. The very *Air* mocks me in its emptiness.

Then my mind betrays me – my own voice stealthily slides and slithers like silent mist in Haworth churchyard, until, above my bed, questions hover in the air, like creatures with wings & their own heartbeats. What if? What if? What if?

Just think Polly, with Mama & Mr. Brontë departed…?

What if C.B. were alive and unmarried?

This is nonsense. You do right to shake me till my teeth rattle. I shall not give in, Polly. I light a lamp & turn to my books. I *shall* move forward, Polly. I determine this, even in my most fragile hours.

Write to me soon, dear friend.

My kindest love to Swinton and the family,

Your affec. friend,

Ellen Nussey

To Miss Margaret Wooler,
West House, Dewsbury
Laneside, Gomersal, 30 June 1867

Dear Miss Margaret,

I am very pleased indeed to receive your welcome letter, wherein I discover that you're again a resident of our West Riding. What a happy circumstance for myself and my sisters. We write to welcome you back and ask you to visit us at Laneside.

I shall hasten to escort you around our kitchen garden which gives me constant delight through all seasons. We have now planted yellow, red and green gooseberries, two dozen strawberry plants and two new plum trees, one early, one late, which are exceedingly pretty in flower. Although we have already an outdoor vine, this year am I a scientist in experimentation with an indoor vine – its roots are outside a brick base but its stem runs indoors so that its branches grow under glass. I have a soft paint brush with which I am 'tickling the flowers' as per a book on loan from Lady Armytage of Kirklees. You will appreciate no doubt that at The Hall there are rather splendid glass houses. Mine is in miniature but the pleasure is nonetheless in great bucketsful. I trust that 'bucketsful' puts you in mind of Charlotte? Surely you will recall her spoonsful? I send kind greetings from Mary Taylor, who anticipates also with delight your visit to us. Her new house in Spen Lane is but a short distance, so our arrangements may easily be dovetailed. I await eagerly your reply with suggested dates. Please give my kindest regards to your family.

I am dear Miss Wooler,
yours sincerely,
Ellen Nussey

To Mrs. Mary Hewitt née Gorham
Laneside, Gomersal, 20 May 1869

Dear Mary,

Thank you so much for your recent letter and for your enquiries about my health. Thankfully, it is much improved now that summer approaches – resplendent are our gardens with bright tulips – how I love this time of year. Abundant orchards hereabouts are in blossom, bees are humming, the sun rises higher daily, and my heart feels lighter than it did when last I wrote to you.

Thank you also for your kindly interest in the matter of the letters. I deeply appreciate that I can write openly to you about them.

I have now completed the last of my current correspondence with Charlotte's publisher, George Smith, although I'm no further forwards, which circumstance I find most frustrating. George Smith suggests that I should be careful about any edition of extracts of Charlotte's letters – I can write for Cornhills magazine about Charlotte's life but I may not make any reference to Mr. Nicholls. George

Smith indicates that a legal problem would arise were I to make public any extracts from my copies.

I had considerable communication with him last year, for the additional purpose that Mary Taylor had asked me to recommend her for translation work – also to endeavour to secure publication of several of her own poems – sadly to no avail. Always my correspondent is polite and gracious, but nothing comes of it, so now the matters are closed, at least for the present.

It is my great joy that, when Mary Taylor returned from N. Z., just before this new decade began, she chose to settle in Gomersal & build her lovely house High Royd on Spen Lane. To be reunited with her, one of Miss Wooler's 'young lions', gives me comfort and companionship – though of course, Mary being Mary, she is still truly adventurous & leads groups of women on holidays all over Europe! But as I share my daily life with both my sisters, I'm never short of company and for that I give thanks to God.

Meanwhile – in the matter of 'The Letters' – it is a relief to have this temporary respite. I shall return, in due course, to the question of further publication – I'm not getting any younger, Polly, & sometimes I reflect upon my demise & the concomitant matter of the letters' future provenance. My heartfelt desire is that they remain in one complete collection – perhaps at the British Museum – but a permanent solution isn't yet procured.

Nevertheless I wonder whether I should pursue some American enquiries, because I'm keen to raise money for a memorial window in Birstall church. I shall take advice as to whether American interests might be successful commercially in this regard. But as yet I have no one from whom to seek such wisdom!

For myself, I've no personal ambitions, but on behalf of my church in Birstall I ask George Smith about contributions to the bazaar – for the church I'm a 'cheeky monkey' and would ask anyone! I receive a response in the negative. Publishers and church bazaars may not, it seems, inhabit the same world of commerce. One should but try?

Goodbye my dear Polly. I look forward to your lovely letters and to hearing from you very soon, my faithful friend.

Please give love from me and both my sisters, to Swinton and all your family.

Your affect. friend,

Ellen Nussey

Dearest Charlotte,

I have birthday news for you on your sixtieth – I want to speak about the editor of the Leeds Mercury, who has become a trusted friend. We met about three years ago – Thomas Wemyss Reid, whom I am assisting to weave some of your letters into a sketch of your life. I'm hopeful that he will include letters from yourself to Margaret Wooler & I believe that this man will acknowledge in a formal and financial way the help which Miss Wooler & I shall give with this forthcoming publication. It's still my intention to create a memorial in Haworth Church, to which purpose I shall bestow any rewards which accrue.

I try to be honest – I talk harshly to myself – that I must act only with an honourable intent, to remedy the shortcomings of Mrs. Gaskell's work, for it's my sincere belief that your religiosity, sense of duty and patient resignation were all underrated in her book – were she still alive I should of course attempt through her to modify that publication – but she is gone these ten years – time enough for me to set to work.

I will be writing to T. Wemyss Reid in the near future – I think it possible to enlarge the sketch into a Memoir – certainly I'm of the opinion that an alternative to *The Life* would be well received. To date, we have the proposal that preliminary 'sketches' will appear between August and October this year in Macmillan's magazine – could they not subsequently form the basic structure for a Monograph in volume form? I'm optimistic my dearest one, and this work makes me full of love & life – there is again excitement through the vocabulary of the printing & publishing world.

I hope you will appreciate the joy and trepidation with which I undertake such ventures – for myself, they make me feel alive, where I was dead. They bring you close to me, for I read and read again your precious words, all I have left, nay, that's untrue – I lie – I have so much more left that mere words. I have moonbeams and thunderstorms. I have lavender lightning, which sears open the night sky, like pink and violet ribbons slashed across indigo velvet, making their way to earth. I have trees bent over on the moors, their buds pruned by the cutting edge of the wind, bending indeed like old women under burden baskets. I have the sound of sheep bleating in the fields in spring, the tramp of wooden clogs on the cobbles by the mills, the creak of a mill wheel, the return of the swallows. In these and every moment of the world around me, when the earth is greening & clouds gather on the horizon,

I feel your presence, I recognise your literature and I know again the sound of your voice.

Now then, I have also a small anecdote – from my volumes of Greek Myth. So, my dearest, let me paint you a picture, from the poet, Virgil.

When Gaia, mother of Earth, meets Uranus, father of sky, their union begets three sons: Brontë [thunder], Sterope [lightning bolt] and Piracmon [burning anvils]. These giants have but one eye in their foreheads. Fearsome forgers in Fire are they beneath mighty Mount Etna, beside which flows a wide and beautiful river. One day, while at the river, they observe three nymphs, Scibilia, Salicia and Rivolia. Thus, there follows a joyful celebration, with music and feasting at a triple wedding. Their descendants – exceptional people, full of talent – create the town of Brontë, in that exact location, beside the volcano.

Astonished am I that ne'er did I read this till now, nor indeed heard not I this legend from you. How came not I by this tale when at Roe Head? Always have I known your name was Thunder, from the Greek language. But the name Brontë we associate always with the Duke of Brontë, our famous Lord Nelson. Never mind; it exists in its own time. Shall I, in forthcoming thunder storms, reside in the town of Brontë, redolent with myths and memories? Fifty nine years old I may be, my darling, but what of that? In my heart I am again thirteen, with my girl whose name means Thunder. Who dare say how old am I in heart and soul? Your letters signify what we were & how we were. At Laneside, I treasure their physicality, the visibility of your written script upon their leaves. I pray to the Lord, my Shepherd about them as I endeavour to listen to his wisdom. I ask whether it *be* God's will, that I should be guardian & keeper thereof. I ask him for guidance that I may obtain safe haven, where neither thunder nor lightning may strike, nor any human volcano may fire them. Thus do I pledge my labours – in these my last years – to preserve your words for posterity.

Therefore is it deeply gratifying to me to meet a good man like Thomas Wemyss Reid, whose attitude to your words validates the importance I attach to the life of Charlotte Brontë, and the authorship of Currer Bell.

Always remember, that I love you both,

And I am yourn,

Nell

My dear Mary,

Thank you for yours of 30th April with your kind condolences on the death of Ann. Her funeral was gentle and peaceful, as was the end of her life. April and May are beautiful months in the West Riding; and many friends hereabouts paid kind respects as Ann was laid to rest in the family tomb in Birstall churchyard.

Mercy and I talk kindly to one another. She is herself frail & she wishes to move to York, nearer to our dear George, because they both derive much comfort from her sisterly visits – indeed this gives me peace of mind.

However, Laneside is a large property, which is impractical for one tenant, so I shall accept an invitation to take temporary lodgings, possibly Ingwell House, North Terrace, Birstall, with my friend Annie Bradbury, until somewhere smaller shall be available. Fortunate am I that Joshua and Richard left provision in their wills. This makes me not a wealthy woman but one who can afford to inhabit a comfortable home until her own decease.

Now our re-designed kitchen garden will be the delight of new tenants. I shall transport my many jars and bottles from our harvests – never have I forgotten Mama's tuition in 'bottling and preserving'. Thus do I re-locate myself, my goods and chattels *again* & not for the last time!

Now I must mention the letters, about which you so kindly enquire. The Revd. Adolphus Wilkes informs me that he has fourteen notebooks full of a manuscript on the Brontë family. I know not the quality of his work, only the volume of it! There is also an author named J. Horsfall Turner whose book is entitled *Haworth: past and present*. I have not yet met the man himself, nor have I yet read his publication. I continue to have welcome correspondence with my friend Thomas Wemyss Reid, with whose Monograph I remain satisfied in most regards. Certainly he sets right those errors of interpretation, especially about C.B.'s brother, in *The Life*.

I will write with more news next time. My kindest love to Swinton and the family; & much for yourself, dear Polly,

Your affect. friend,

Ellen Nussey

My Dear Charlotte,

The swallows are flown – and so am I from my temporary lodgings – the months are flown, the summer is flown. Ann sleeps safely in Heaven – Mercy being in frail health these days, resides in York, and my life begins again here – alone – in this mid-terrace, where I hope to reside peacefully for many a long year. I am high on a windy hill, above the Gomersal dwellings – therefore reminded of my love of the parsonage at Haworth for its elevated position above the village.

The swallows swooping in silhouette against our September sunsets are so beautiful they are almost indescribable. Come with me – I am standing again with you, outside the parsonage, looking at the western sky, some September in our youth. The sunset is shimmering pink, which ne'er did I see in Oundle or Chiselhurst when staying with my brothers – only here in the heights of our West Riding does our pink autumn sunset really gladden my heart. The very air shimmers and pulses with pink. Deeper pink even than sugar mice at Christmas, deeper even than the pink of lightning or cottage roses, or sweet-peas, pink with a splash of orange, but still pink for all that. I go outside each night to breathe this colour. Is it not deeply healing to stand and stare? I imbibe long drawn breaths, filling my body; as if drinking the light. I wax poetic, do I not? I can hear you laughing – you and your sisters are dancing, claiming the edge on poetry – I am too shy to speak.

My good friend Sydney Biddell, with whom I'm now regularly in correspondence, wishes to erect a memorial to you three sisters – is that not wonderful? Apparently, he tries his charming approach with Smith, Elder and Co., but as usual they refuse to engage in charitable ventures. Sydney is disappointed. There will be no fund-raising from that source, more's the pity. It is unfortunate but no more than I have come to expect. Meanwhile the Revd. Alpheus Wilkes does not complete the manuscript about which he waxed enthusiastic – just after my sister Ann died, whilst I resided at Ingwell House – it's my uncomfortable belief that he will *eventually* publish some garbled sort of thing. I do try to encourage & help these men who purport to honour your work & your memory – but this individual seems incapable of fulfilling the standards required. It does not surprise me – for *yours* is literary genius & *he's* not up to scratch.

I love this little terraced house and I'm lucky to have found it at a reasonable rent. My only fear is that the very delight of its location will be also its demise

– hilly and chilly, perhaps. I am a tough old lady – and I'm not easily to be put off – but neither shall I take chances with my health. There is monumental work ahead – both with the manuscripts and with the poor hereabouts. I have continued with my pledge of one-tenth-my-income for the poor of our neighbourhood, because I'm so blessed to be provided for, through Richard's will – although I detest the executor of the same, my half-cousin, William Carr. He takes no account whatsoever of my wishes or feelings in the investments which my brother pursued & although I am a benefactor, my legal position is non-existent. I don't have one. The executor need take no heed of me. Besides, he thinks women are inferior beings, with no intelligence. My sadness – nay, in truth it is *anger* – lies in his having bad-mouthed me to the relatives in Chiselhurst. I did not anticipate such treatment by William Carr.

It is late. The skies deepen to indigo, dark blue velvet, upon which the stars arrive, cluster by cluster. My fire is stoked for the night, so the room should be warm for breakfast – I'm tired so shall away to sleep. Wherever you are, my dearest, be assured that I will do my utmost to preserve your treasured works, your memory & your precious letters. When I sleep, I feel your warm arms again around me. They're my comfort, every night.

Goodnight.

Ellen

Journal
Fieldhead, Gomersal, 21 April 1883

Dearest C.B.,

It's your birthday – almost thirty six years since the summer of 1847 when we stand – you, me, Emily, Anne – in blazing noontide upon Haworth Moor, as we witness in God's heaven, a magnificent parhelion phenomenon of the sun. To this recollection am I returned by a small biography of Emily, from the pen of Miss A. Mary F. Robinson, with whom I and my friend, Thomas Wemyss Reid, have been – over this year past – in not a little communication. Long hours have I spent with this lady, who steadfastly fulfils her promise to cherish my letters – all are safely returned by her own hand.

Miss R. desires to honour Emily's life and work, especially Wuthering Heights, the latter being described at some considerable length. I do believe that her intentions are honourable but, Charlotte, is she not still a *journalist?* Do not they – some of them – endeavour to draw us in – to sordid details, embellished sin, exaggerated human foibles? I hasten to assure you, my dearest, that not through me (or my letters) did Miss R. uncover unsavoury details of Branwell's behaviour & most assuredly not through me might she surmise that your papa's personality could take a violent turn. The latter is a *lie* but Miss R. herself is not of ill intent – I surmise that she struggles to comprehend the origins of W.H. Thus does she create myths which are controversial *and* derogatory. Of Branwell's gentleness to animals and his dying pleas for forgiveness, absolution & redemption, we hear but nought from Miss R. In this book I remain disappointed, overall; in her interpretations do I find errors of judgement; & I cannot recognise the Emily I knew and loved.

Help me, Charlotte – in whom shall I place my trust?

So much is there still to learn.

Ever your own, Nell

To Mary Hewitt née Gorham,
Fieldhead, Gomersal, 31 December 1885

My dear Mary,

Thank you so much for your Christmas letter, your package, and your good wishes for my health from all your family. The table doilies are a delight; I shall enjoy using them very much indeed. I'm glad you like my box of gifts – I was at that time in no mood for writing *long* letters but on receiving yours, I seek to remedy the same before the year is out.

Nevertheless this has been a queer, difficult year and I'm glad to see the back of it. Where shall I begin?

Familiar as I am with bereavement, I'm very deeply affected by the loss of my last remaining brother, George – my childhood friend, my riding companion, my confidant through my young years, always my loyal brother even when he became ill. He has been well cared-for in Dr Belstone's establishment in York & has taken great delight in visits from Mercy since she has lived nearby. He was only seventy-one – I shall miss him most terribly. But I do know how to withstand the immediate effects of grief – I have had plenty of practice. My former teacher, mentor and guide – and reliable correspondent – Miss Margaret Wooler also died, on June 3rd as I wrote you briefly at the time. Taking the two deaths so close together has made this indeed a sad year.

However I am strengthened and comforted by my burgeoning friendship with Sydney Biddell, bless the man. So enthusiastic is he that I should write a book about Charlotte – which never has been my intention. An author I'm not, definitely not, even though I would describe myself as a woman of letters, such is my pleasure in this endeavour.

Did you read Cross's *Life of George Eliot* – if so, you will have noted therein the treatment of George Eliot's letters – Sydney suggested back in the spring that I might try a similar utilisation of C.B.'s letters – but this is a task I would neither enjoy nor feel was appropriate. It would set me in the limelight – a place I should dread and shun. Meanwhile, I'm now acquainted with a local Moravian follower and, dare I say, 'Brontë enthusiast'. Should I shun that phrase, also? – maybe, but I cannot avoid it for it is entering current usage hereabouts. The person in question is named William Scruton, very likeable, the author of an attractive little book on Charlotte's birthplace. Our friendship now develops in a mutual liking & I lent him some epistles of C.B.'s. He pointed out to me a publication by the barrister Augustine Birrell – yes my dear, you will be confused by all these names, indeed as am I. I digress here to point out the friendship I already have with Sydney 'double 'd' Biddell' – so you won't confuse him with this barrister, who inhabits prestigious circles. During the year he – the barrister – has published *The Life of Charlotte Brontë*, in which is made particular mention of her papa and his former love, before he met Maria Branwell, all of which is treated with delicacy, in a manner befitting modesty and courtesy – it's an interesting and enjoyable text.

Not so the awful *Brontë Family with special reference to Patrick Branwell Brontë* by Francis Leyland. I detest the man, a reaction surpassed only by my disgust at this publication. You may recall that in the Athenaeum magazine, two years ago, he claimed that it was *my* information made public, which created a negative representation of Branwell's life and attitudes. I was broken in pieces when that came to my attention – it has never been my wish that any of the family should be traduced. If it occurred through my intervention, it would constitute a desecration of all I hold dear. Moreover Branwell is gone – unable to defend himself – and although Charlotte was indeed hurt by his so called 'illness', which damaged the entire household, it was *not* from my information that such was released. This dreadful man reminds me of village people with night soil buckets following the milk round – to fill with horse droppings for their vegetable plots. All that has gone into Leyland's book fertilises a growing industry around the Brontës as village scapegoats – I imagine the family in the stocks on the village green with folk aiming rubbish and kitchen waste. I wake in the night in a shiver & lather– terrible dreams – when I contemplate such publications. To suffer blame makes it worse. Blame and shame. I hear Charlotte's voice trying to soothe me, speaking of injustice – I do not deserve the attack from men like Francis Leyland.

269

On a much happier note, I am introduced to a good friend of William Scruton, (Scruton being my Moravian friend). The man is question is revered in the whole area as the antiquarian, J. Horsfall Turner, who published a title back in 1879: *Haworth – Past and Present*. So you see Polly, he is already a respected author, who wishes to create a new collection of Charlotte's letters – is this not most fortunate at this time? After reading a few letters on loan already to him, he tells me, confidentially, they change his whole perspective on Charlotte's second novel, *Shirley*. He jokingly refers to this area as 'The Shirley Country' – is that not both witty and appealing? It seems that J. Horsfall Turner's love of history endears Charlotte's work to him. However, I stipulate that a new collection is not published until after my death. My letters are on loan with that condition. You see Mary, under the law of copyright, I have their provenance but they cannot be published in this country without copyright permission from A.B. Nicholls, such as given to Mrs. Gaskell. I cannot bear the thought of personal communication with A. B. Nicholls.

Belatedly must I face the truth – A female author must relinquish her copyright as a consequence of marriage. It is a hard pill to swallow, I assure you.

Meanwhile, in respect of posterity, a conundrum continuously taxes my mind and forfeits my peaceful sleep – how best may I safeguard C.B.'s letters for posterity. Thomas Wemyss Reid has spoken to Lord Houghton, one of the trustees of the British Museum. Unfortunately, the outcome is that the B.M. will not actually *buy* C.B.'s letters. Therefore must I provide security by some other means. Perhaps it would be prudent to leave C.B.'s letters in my will to T. Wemyss Reid – a truly good man of great integrity – if he would on his death leave them to the British Museum. The riddle is yet to be solved. It is a comfort to me to share this information with you, my cherished friend. However, I must now finish – or this epistle will be book length.

My love and friendship as always,
Ellen Nussey.

Journal
The Vicarage, Leysters, Herefordshire, 21 April 1886

My dearest Charlotte,

I wonder what colour is your hair, at seventy? Still the same bright brown, thick and glossy? Is that not the trick of time, the riddle of bereavement? In my mind you appear always thirty-eight, approaching thirty-nine, the age when last

I saw you. In my heart, my darling, you are but twenty, writing to me of our cottage and a competency of our own.

I am very fortunate to have these two faithful, steady friends – I am invited here to spend my birthday, and yours, with Mary Hewitt and her husband, Swinton, in their beautiful part of England where three counties join: Shropshire, Herefordshire and Worcestershire. Their vicarage in Leysters is set in rolling countryside, so softly wooded, and with acres of farmland laid to hops & cider apples, whose buds are deep cerise, yet to open, but already exceedingly pretty. Here is none of the dry stone walling that marks out our West Riding, nor valleys with mills, nor steep-sided hill villages with crowded houses & folks living in dark cellars. Nevertheless there is poverty hereabouts and, as indeed everywhere, rural folk are leaving the land & moving to towns & cities in vast numbers. The country is now criss-crossed with railways, canals, roads & everywhere I journey, I witness desperate families on the move.

Leysters is just inside Herefordshire, Charlie, thus can we, easily, take the carriage over the border into Worcestershire – which boasts the sweetest, crunchiest autumn apples in the land! Here, this morning, we take a beautiful walk along the river Teme in Tenbury Wells - Queen Victoria's favourite "Little Town in the Orchard" & fascinated am I by the Pump Room, built in 1862, as consequence of mineral water discovered in the 40s. Ever optimistic are these Tenbury folk, who desire prosperity, and thus add "Wells" to the ancient name! At home again we take our repose in the garden, where columbines and sweet williams are not yet in blossom, but growing steadily, reaching for the spring sunshine. Both Mary and Swinton appreciate most deeply their secluded garden, and I never met a man more interested in the world of nature all around him than Mary's green-fingered gentle giant. He likes to take root cuttings, leaf and stem cuttings, and is extremely skilful at all forms of plant propagation. He has become my dear friend also, through these many years. He says but little about my friendship with the famous Currer Bell – it is sufficient that he knows this day would have been your seventieth – and that you and I could have been living together, with our own garden, for these many years.

Mary calls, we are out to tea. Her daughter is here keeping company with Swinton, as he isn't well at present. But we are hoping it's just a cold.

Bye the bye, I have white hair, now, at sixty nine. Do you know that? Can you see me? Can you hear me reading this letter aloud to you?

I am ever your loving and faithful friend,

Foreveralways,

Ellen.

To Mary Hewitt née Gorham
Fieldhead, Gomersal, 22 September 1886

My dear Mary,

As Autumn approaches, my dear friend, I must write again, following my earlier condolences, for this has been such a sad summer for you. I continue to pray for you in your widowhood every night, asking that you shall find the strength to bear this loss.

Swinton was a dear friend to me as well as your beloved husband. I have such wonderful memories of his sermons, while I visited your beautiful church: his voice, the music in your home; and your vicarage garden always gay with flowers.

This month I have been busy with geraniums – I cannot take my geraniums into the house for a frost-free respite without thinking of him. His picture comes immediately to mind. It is so rare to find a man with his liking for flowers – perhaps the only one I know other than Swinton is Sir George Armytage but even then, his true expertise is the melon house at Kirklees, which you so enjoy on your visits here. The Armytages send their kindest regards to you.

The first months after bereavement are always so very difficult, especially since your daily life in the vicarage has revolved Swinton – around Sundays, Services, and the festivals of the Christian calendar. I am so glad your daughters are with you. We are blessed indeed with our younger generation, are we not? They are such fine folk, Mary. You & Swinton have been wonderful parents. I enclose a note with this for Kitty. Please tell her I could not wish for a better God-daughter.

I also enclose two long letters from my friend Madame Cortazzo. [It is indeed a thrill to receive her enthusiastic epistles. She so admires C. B.'s novels, which she circulates to her American friends & family.] There's no hurry to return them – I have already replied to both letters.

My kindest love to you. Year upon year, dearest Polly, you place around my shoulders a warmly-woven shawl. 'Measure for Measure' shall I weave a shawl for you now.

Your affect. friend,

Ellen Nussey

My dear Mary,

Thank you for *your* letter of condolence! I remain in York to arrange the headstone for Mercy, who is now buried beside our dear George. The mason must add Mary Mercy Nussey, because Mercy was her chosen name from residence at Fairfield, nr. Manchester, till she returned home from the Moravian settlement there. The Lord is her Shepherd. She rests in peace. This is my final visit to a stone mason on behalf of my brothers and sisters. I trust to attend to it with love and generosity of heart but I struggle to understand God's will – Mercy's dates run before and after George. His are 1814-1885, hers 1801-1886.

As I have kind friends to visit known to both George and Mercy, I intend maybe another week here. My health is very good – you need have no concerns. I shall be home soon.

My love to you & your nearest and dearest.

Your affect. friend,

Ellen Nussey

Journal
Fieldhead, Gomersal, 20 April 1887

My dear Charlotte,

Today the daffodils are abundant in the garden and I anticipate with pleasure swathes of spring flowers & blossom in the grounds of Kirklees Hall, to which I am invited for my birthday party. The Armytages are so kind – they shall send their carriage and prepare for me a sumptuous lunch – I'm looking forward to it with happiness and delight, like a girl of ten might so do in 1827, with a party at Rydings and her brothers and sisters dancing attendance! I recall my new riding boots in shining brown leather.

Today for my seventieth my friends will allow me neither to be dull nor on my own. Be happy for me my dear.

I love you, foreveralways,

Your loving and affectionate friend,

Ten-years-old-again-Nellie

This is for you, Charlotte

It is two in the morning, the Saviour is born. I have the fire burning brightly, the lamps are alight. I am very well indeed, shining with hope & the joy of this season. The midnight mass is sung, completed. I am home again, and my visitors have departed for their own home. Sir George and Lady Morrison do me the honour tonight of attending Birstall Church for the mass, whence I am brought into my home, carefully in their comfortable carriage.

Never could any person come close in my heart to the place where you abide but this dear lady, Sophia, who lives happily with her husband, is a lady we could both love, in the ways we understand.

No one shall take your place. Indeed she is married. I remain alone here. But whereas, my beloved C.B., I can speak to you only on paper, Sophia, Lady Morrison, is alive & well, warm & affectionate. We spend hours talking most naturally, intimately, and you are the first to know how I feel about her.

You need not be a jealous ghost. I shall not expect rattling at the window pane, nor the advent of thunder storms, no crashing of chimney pots, or lethal branches from trees strewn across the lane. Histrionics are unnecessary, but I ask that you be joyful for me – there is again in my everyday life a representative of the kind of love of which we are capable. I desire that you respect this truth, in this letter, for where-else may I reveal such knowledge?

Often do I turn to my natural form of expression – writing letters – when I need to communicate with you. Was it not January 1831 when first I wrote to you? Years later did you read, laughing gently, with comprehension of my passionate nature? This January will be 1888 – fifty seven years of my love for you. Is that not long enough for you to trust me now?

I need not explain to Lady Sophia Anne Morrison herself. It is best that this remains unsaid. Sophia means wisdom, you know. She is kind, beautiful and wise. We hold one another, as if we are merely friends – for that is all I can offer to someone who is already married & at this my great age. But my heart isn't this age – tonight my heart is nineteen – reading a letter from a woman who desires to '*live and love on till <u>Death</u> without being dependent on any third person for happiness.*' As indeed is right and true. I have no regrets for any of the kinds of loving we have shared, you and me. Only that you are dead and I am alive & this is a long time for this kind of longing. The feelings are reciprocated between Lady Sophia and me. We do not need to say so. It is in our eyes, shining like children faced with Christmas candles, the joy of recognition.

I had not sought this, nor expected this. Why is it that when we are not looking, this love may enter our door? We can search down moonbeams; nay slide down rainbows, and not find this – then it arrives, disguised as daytime dialogue and ordinary intercourse, with bright intelligent friends. Here it is. Here and now, making me glad, in my last remaining years on earth. She signs herself, Sophie. Sometimes, Annie. Myself, I like to call her Sophia. It makes her laugh. Be glad for me.

I remain, your dearest Nell.

To Mary Hewitt née Gorham
Ingwell House, Birstall, 6 July 1892

My dear Mary,

I have returned to that same house, which comprised my temporary lodgings after my sister Ann died. I cannot face another winter at Laneside, although I shall miss the wonderful open views from there. I needed a warmer hearth – I shall not miss the wind upon the hill – this house is very comfortable, and has the advantage of familiarity, so I am well pleased. I anticipate with great pleasure your visit this autumn – are any of your daughters to accompany you?

I have some shocking news, simultaneously exhilarating. The burning of the J. Horsfall Turner pages has begun. Thoughts, words, feelings, all rising in smoke. Through the Air, the Ether. Smoke like angels, ascending. Whilst I witness this activity, all I can think of is, 'The Air, the very Air is filled with her, her words, her joys, her sorrows, her laughter, her voice'. I am listening – I can hear her, her words being read aloud. Smoke, words, flames: Air, Air, Air, Air. Eyre. I see the burning of the attic in Rochester's mansion. Eyre & Air. C.B.'s letters, printed, typeset, floating away in fragments, in little charcoal scraps, upon the air. Do you know how long it takes for paper to burn? My dear Revd. Ridley names it 'the martyrdom' – I stand there, thinking, 'How quaint an expression that is, how poignant'. I thought I shouldn't bear to watch but anyhow I am in attendance at one of the pyres and suddenly, I am jubilant. I cannot explain, not fully. Perhaps I feel hoaxed by J. Horsfall Turner? Of course, not to begin with, but, yes, as time goes on. Mocked, maybe? Betrayed, certainly. My feelings are that this man must never get his hands on C.B.'s letters, although by now I am reconciled to a publication in book form – sometime in the future – after I am gone.

I tell myself I shall be more wary of men in the future – men who want to make an industry out of Charlotte. I shall be on the look out, like a light-house beam – through the Air, vigilant. Forewarned is forearmed, is it not?

I have something else to tell you. I regret this – it's a confession. Don't lose patience with me will you? Slow am I, sometimes, slow to uncover the real human being, beneath a façade. I regret to have to tell you that it's happened again, Mary. Men of the cloth, or whose involvement in Christian ethics is public and honourable, sometimes parade in disguise like chameleons. Maybe still naïve am I, even at this age. Charlotte could always see through men of the cloth, if there was something foolish, or hypocritical to see. Did she not lose the affection of the Atkinsons, her God-parents, for satire upon the clergy in *Shirley*? Is she not famous for her depiction of Revd. Carus Wilson at Lowood, by revealing his hypocrisy?

So permit me, please dear Polly, to return to 1890 and paint you a picture.

This time it's one William Wright, from the British and Foreign Bible Society. His interest lies particularly in the Brontës in Ireland, and he indicates to me that justice hasn't been done, by A. B. Nicholls, in regard of Patrick's relatives, and I fall for it like a little bird's egg pushed from its nest by a great fat cuckoo. I fall down through the air, in slow motion, almost floating down, so slowly, but the ground is still hard, upon landing. At this time – 1890 – when first Wright appears on the scene, I'm recovering from the J. Horsfall Turner escapade & I discuss with my dear Sophia the possibility of publishing in America, for she has contacts with Scribners, for whom I wrote my Reminiscences, back in '71. Her dear George is to be the editor – lovely, lovely man – and there is [till 1891] no copyright problem for foreign authors, across the water. I am, in truth, all of a dither. In my journal I explore the rights and wrongs of my actions – I pray – my sleep evades me and I become exhausted. The sin of greed – I want both ends of the seaside rock. I desire to be invisible, to have C.B.'s letters focussed upon only her, her genius, her pure nature, her religious convictions: but my sinful pride intrudes – I desire also to be acknowledged, the recipient of her epistles, the significant friend. Thus, trapped in my own ambivalence, I begin to dither and, over the proposed American edition, I prevaricate, with the effect that Lady Sophia and Sir George don't know whether they're coming or going. I listen most carefully to this William Wright, as if he were Right not Wright. He offers to be joint editor, with me, which sends me into a tizzy, and distracts me from all the American negotiations. I hadn't chosen an editorial position, never wanted such. Sir George is a wonderful choice for he is sound as a bell, which rings a respectful Brontë tune. Onto the scene arrives another newcomer, Clement

276

Shorter, who offers to assist Sir George Morrison with the American edition, as joint editor, at which time we feel it isn't necessary. Mr. Wright then proposes to secure C.B.'s letters in a strong room in the Bible House – that is appealing – but I realise with a shock that he isn't referring to copies – there are twelve printed sets still extant – but Wright wants the originals.

What does it take for a silly old mare like me to see sense? I do repent – I am guilty as charged. I have made a thorough mess of things, Polly. Thankfully, Wright then goes too far – he says something that rings *dozens* of bells. All cathedrals in the land do surely jangle. Even I can hear them! Suddenly I have a mental image of hundreds of peals, but the only editor holding a true bell with a clear tone, joyful and steady, is Sir George Morrison himself. What Wright says is that the originals can be put in a national repository after 'our' deaths. *Ours*.

Now then, please shake me till my teeth rattle, Mary. You may call this my 'Saul' moment. [Did ever I show you C.B.'s drawings of Saul cowering on the road to Damascus, shielding his eyes form the one true light?] This time do I truly see the light! I decide this Wright has a presuming interference and tell him so, in no uncertain terms. I enjoy that. He is gone.

Meanwhile I am assured, by Augustine Birrell, that the letters can be published without delay in America & without a copyright problem. Their laws on foreign authors are different. Nevertheless, the morality continues to leave me worried and confused. Believe me, the egg which lands in one piece, without cracking, proceeds to hatch into the proverbial chicken with two heads. This way, that way. Somebody should wring my neck, have me for Christmas dinner and, as they say in the mills, be done wi' it.

In truth, my friend, I really do not seek publicity. Nevertheless, it would come, upon any publication, assuredly. So, now we are back in 1892, by which time I have foregone an American edition, although I remain in my heart unconvinced of the correctness of my decision.

In the midst of this turmoil, helps seems to be finally on my horizon. Now I am being really careful this time. I am lending a few of C.B.'s letters to the 'newcomer' – the journalist name of Clement Shorter, whose career in journalism continues to accelerate ever upwards – I understand he is the newly promoted editor – or about to be, I'm unsure of the precise date – of the Illustrated London News, which affirms his authenticity, surely?

My reasoning goes as follows: my friend Thomas Wemyss Reid is not intending to enlarge his Monograph and is, anyway, extremely busy now as manager of Cassell's publishing house, therefore he is unavailable for work on a new *Life of Charlotte Brontë* – and the Gaskell *Life* is very old by now. Therefore, have I the good fortune in this experienced journalist, Clement Shorter, to have found a replacement for Mrs. Gaskell – someone who can take a new Biography to a satisfactory conclusion? I sincerely hope so.

No doubt while you are with me I shall be communicating with Mr. Clement Shorter – I shall so enjoy confessing upon your shoulder, when you're here. I am a very fortunate lady – Not only do I have the Morrisons to help me, but also my dear friends, the Armytages to confide in, and their advice is always most heartening; I take comfort day by day from my friendship with Lady Sophia: I continue to receive warm letters from Sydney (dear, 'double d') Biddell; and Mme Cortazzo from America, whose travels with her daughter are a source of inspiration and delight, so vividly does she describe the places she visits, the people she meets.

You're one of my oldest, longest friends, aren't you, by now? God is kind, the Lord is good – He gives me friends like you.

My fondest love to all the family,

Ellen Nussey

To Mary Hewitt née Gorham
Ingwell House, Birstall, 1 March 1893

My dear Mary,

Forgive the very short note. I am the only remaining member of a group of schoolgirls known as Miss Wooler's Young Lions.

Mary Taylor has died.

I shall go to Scotland Wood tomorrow, to say my own prayers, very quietly, alone. It's the private burial wood for all the Taylor family. Wish me a beautiful day.

Your affect. friend,

Ellen Nussey

To Mary Hewitt née Gorham
Ingwell House, Birstall, 6 July 1893

My dear Mary,

By the date above, I observe that by chance not design, today is exactly one year after my long confession!

Unfortunately this is –almost – possibly – a repeat circumstance. So I will keep it short and to the point. News arrives via my American friends that there are for sale in America, signatures of letters I gave on loan to Clement Shorter & his friend, another newcomer, Thomas James Wise. Wise is a thoroughly charming man and seems to have connections to the British Museum, [you will recall my desire to have C.B.'s letters deposited there for safe-keeping] so although I cannot get a straight answer to a straight question, the letters for sale, or rather the parts thereof, can have come *only* from Shorter or from Wise. So far there is only one hint, just one, that something of this nature is taking place. Very many of my letters from C.B. are in the hands of those two friends. I am so tired.

My American contacts shall endeavour to ascertain the provenance of these signatures or hand-written fragments. Indeed they may not be C.B.'s as there are some excellent forgers in the New World, who of course learned their art in Europe!

I look forward to your forthcoming visit, so very much.

My love to you, your nearest and dearest.

As always, your friend, Ellen Nussey

Journal
Moor Lane House, Gomersal, 23 September 1895

My dearest Charlotte,

On this beautiful golden day, I wait for you. I walk slowly through the autumn roses, towards my sturdy wooden bench. From this position the soft, low-angled light shows my solid, stone house in Moor Lane to fine advantage. My new home – I have a wonderful garden again. Now, seated thankfully in the sunshine, with my stick within reach, I wrap the folds of my cloak against any hint of breeze and take cognisance of my new home here. My garden's golden in the slow shifts of sunlight and shadows, for it is late afternoon.

I feel old today, tired in my bones, aware of both of endings and beginnings. It is now forty years since you passed away – and I am ready, almost ready, for my next journey. I hope to be re-united with you before long.

It's almost the end of the nineteenth century – I am sure that it will soon be the end of my own life though only God in his wisdom knows how much time is left to me, and I have still so much to do.

I am deeply troubled by some recent correspondence – this trouble of which I speak is not about missing you. I am used to the dull ache of grief, the loss of my loved one. I still pray for you every night at ten o'clock. As years become decades, life continues, even though my beloved is gone. There are ways of moving forward & I have tried them all. It is more than that, and beyond the individual.

My grief and loss are held no longer in that cherished private space where grief is intense and every minute is lonely, even when the room is full of family & friends. This new beginning is something which is birthed into the public domain and my personal role in its gestation has become my continuous nightmare, which does not depart at day break.

Charlotte, can you hear me? I am deeply distressed that I have, without forethought, acted as catalyst for the germination of a small industry, here in this tiny corner of Yorkshire where once there was an ageing Irish parson mourning his beautiful, talented children.

Five years from now, a new century begins and with it a new era of trade and industry. My fears and dreads are focussed upon the unwelcome growth of a disrespectful commercialism, which seems now certain to flourish around the lives and legends of you and your sisters. A new phrase enters the English language: The Brontës of Haworth. This tiny collection of four words takes on huge significance. With the new century approaching it's obvious to me that the speed of change will increase dramatically, which will of course include publishing houses.

My unhappiness and guilt arise from my part in the dispersal of your letters, written to me. My peace of mind vanishes. I understand now that I have been instrumental in allowing things to get out of control. Never shall I regain control – a fact which belatedly I begin to accept. The ironic truth of this situation is that – as a woman who has never borne children – I am a midwife for the future, part of the whole complicated nightmare of cause and effect. This troubles me now by day and night.

Please, come, come take my hand, put again your loving arms around me, and relieve me of this burden.

Sometimes, I see the future as clearly as one of those new-fangled mediums, who make themselves small fortunes in the Spiritualist Church. They're far beyond the reach of our Church of England. Now, using only my own intelligence, which you always remark upon with affection, I recognise that as the forthcoming decades unfold, the fascination of the reading public with 'The Brontës of Haworth' will not cease. Nay, it will escalate, until none may sort myth from reality not fiction from fact.

I inform myself bitterly, nay regale myself nightly, with the wisdom of hindsight. There will arrive more and more visitors to the church and parsonage where you lived, where you died, where you are buried.

As I wait for you I hear myself speaking aloud like a mad woman:

'Oh Charlotte, Charlie, what have I done? How will you have peace now where you are laid, sleeping your eternal sleep? My dearest love, what have I done?'

This garden is full of very small sounds, today, sounds that will become familiar to me. No longer do I sit out-of-doors sewing – but how I shall enjoy being able to sit outside to write to you. The very grass makes a sound as it grows, and I listen this afternoon & I'm comforted. The rustle of foliage in a distant border indicates the silent passing of my neighbour's cat. My own is curled up indoors by the fire. A leaf floats noiselessly down from a silver birch, whose trunk shines with peeling silver. The leaf hovers momentarily in a sunbeam, where motes and fine seeds pirouette. A ripe pod splits open scattering its contents. I think of the Biblical farmer broadcasting from his basket, sewing seeds as he strides along. A late marigold opens its petals and reaches upwards.

I'm glad that I have now moved to this lovely house after the betrayals by both Clement Shorter and his friend, Thomas James Wise. I could not bear the memories in my previous place and besides, I have yearned again for a garden. It's worth the upheaval, at my age, just to be here, where the red berries of intertwined honeysuckle remind me of another time, a different bower. We are young again, you and I, & I'm in Brookroyd's bower reading one of your most passionate letters. My mind and heart skip most easily back through time, like a bonnie Yorkshire lass skips on a far off lawn. You are still alive, both of us are sure of one-another, confident of what we want. My long term memory appears to gain in clarity, although I daily forget things in the here and now. Each and every moment of my years with you is as bright as this day's sunlight, illuminating your words from the past. Light from your words shines and shimmers in the air in this garden. It slants along the slim trunks of trees, like embellished capitals. You, yourself, are tracing them, intricately, in leather bound books. You have slim hands, very small, neat, meticulous artistic hands.

Across time and the green lawn I become aware of the distant sound of a tram in Gomersal. The stone houses & steep ginnels are known to me. From the direction of the Church I hear the clock chime four – the house and tea are beckoning. I rise with some difficulty, proceeding with great care as to the exact placement of the ferrule of my walking stick as I take each well measured, chosen step.

The house is too large for me really – I can barely afford one servant to maintain it, let alone fill it with the bustle & scurry of human activity. Nevertheless I appreciate its peacefulness which is some compensation for my present state of mind.

Yesterday another old friend from the parish came to visit me. This may amuse you – let me paint you a picture.

Indoors, as the exterior sunshine fades to twilight, a golden afternoon is replaced with a warm interior glow from fire light & my soft oil lamps with engraved glass globes. At the back of my parlour, in a darker corner, over one of my upright chairs, lies my friend's cloak, outdoor bonnet and gloves, but the foreground consists of two matching fireside chairs placed purposely either side of the hearth, so that we aged occupants may talk easily, across a delicately laid tea trolley, with bone-china tea cups & lace-edged doilies.

Dressed are we both in garments of dark silk, which almost match in design and colour. We laugh heartily at our recognition – for it is indeed unintended. So symmetrical is the oil-painting we make, there in the firelight, that I fancy it folded in half down the middle, when we each may be mistaken for the other. Each old woman has designed the hand-embroidered collar of her dress & on each head of white hair is a small neat cap of lace & silk, which catches the light as our heads move this way and that whilst talking.

My hearth contributes to the tableau, being framed by a polished wooden mantle shelf with solid burnished uprights around a tiled fireplace, whose tiles are patterned in green and gold on a beige background. The windows of my elegant room are framed by gold and cream damask drapes & our scene is completed by light beige walls down to the dado rail and wooden panelling. She stays but an hour for tea and muffins – after which I am extremely tired.

Now, today, I pause reflecting on the oil-painting, here outside with the ferrule of my stick placed carefully as I stand, gathering up my strength for the return indoors.

I'm conscious that you're laughing – your head's thrown back in the sunshine at the sight of me, a static icon. You laugh gaily and not unkindly, noticing the slow movement of my aged limbs that once were young and free. You're imagining us on the moors holding hands and running – the only time one could ever observe you running. Generally you do not run, and no one at Roe Head even knows that you can or do or might or would. But I know. Only the moors conjure up such activity from you – like a magician's box. I suppose my deepest sadness is that in the portrayals of you in all these new tomes, in all these stolen extracts of letters which did I only lend, all these letters which I exchanged for cash for safe keeping, to be guarded after my death in a museum – that the public distortions have not the sound of your laughter in them. To me this seems the worst betrayal, to which I myself have contributed: the appropriation of your Laughter. I feel it in my bosom as a physical hurt. Forgive me. The myth that

282

you cannot laugh, that you do not laugh, is the saddest most heart-rending mis-understanding of all. This is what I remember most: the sound of your laughter. You, Emily and Anne. The four of us – our treasured Quartette – our laughter on the high moor-land – through sunlight & the summer air.

Now this is the autumn of my life, and for the sunshine, this beautiful September, I am most truly thankful – and for this garden.

For the dispersal of your treasured words, please forgive me,

Forgive me, I beg you – my intentions were honourable.

Your loving and affectionate friend,

Nell.

To: Mary Hewitt née Gorham
Moor Lane House, Gomersal, 20 April 1896

My dear Mary,

Thank you so much for your beautiful letter, today, for my 80th birthday. After a lovely spring day – lunch with Lady Sophia and Sir George Morrison – I am now at home, resting, as I imbibe the soft apricot colours of sunset. Your birthday letter, with its questions, is timely, appropriate and generous, because you and I know that I have almost completed my lifetime here.

Thus, to your first question, 'What do you want to happen to your memoirs?' I have this to say: Everything I have spoken to you, written for you, is my most cherished possession – my memories, the loving and living of my life. I know that you don't hold it against me.

As to your other question: 'What of the immediate future?' I have one of my pictures to paint, because into my mind comes the Sleeping Beauty story. So, with some wry amusement I shall reply:

For one hundred years, let perhaps my story sleep. Let it not be disturbed. Place it safely, in good hands. Let it be a whisper in quiet grasses, in a mature woodland, which grows around it. It is a story of Fire, Water, Earth and Air. Let my story sleep, with all its meanings and interpretations of test and testament. So be it.

My wish is that, more than a hundred years from now, there will arrive a younger woman, to whom my words will have meaning, to whom they will give peace, hope and strength. Perhaps she may be a woman who has lived and loved in Yorkshire, as I have done. She must, of necessity, understand the ways of the church. I hope for someone who can step into the heart of this woodland, a gardener maybe, a tree planter, someone who knows why a thicket of protective thorns may have to be grown around an old and beautiful life-story; someone who has creative hands, for planting, growing, sewing; someone who can re-work the fabric; someone who understands that my words are threads connecting centuries.

Undeterred by thorns and brambles, she will clear a route through the undergrowth, find a path through the woodland, to the centre of the circle.

She will take my story in her open arms, recognise it, wake it with tenderness, treat it with compassion, make it out.

I'm so tired, Mary. I will write soon with proper news. My love to you and your family, and my sincere thanks for those questions.

Your affectionate friend,

Ellen Nussey

To Lady Sophia Anne Morrison,
Stanleigh, Headingley, Leeds
Moor Lane House, Gomersal, May 25 1897

My dear Sophia,

It would be my great joy if you would come to a small ceremony, which we shall have here in Gomersal, when I shall present to each of our local employees of the Tramway a Testament in celebration of the Jubilee of Queen Victoria next month. There will be dancing and merriment in this vicinity – is this not a splendid opportunity for a party?

I hear music from the large room above my empty coach house – in which the children are practising their dancing. What a joy and delight they bring to me. How glad am I to provide this simple, essential resource.

I wonder which days would be convenient for you in the week of Jubilee celebrations, and whether you would like to come to the presentations.

Your affect, friend

Ellen Nussey

P.S. These plans take my mind off my utter distress at Clement Shorter's publication, which continues to cause embarrassment to those who are implicated in anecdotes about which he assured me of complete confidentiality. The Thomas James Wise sale of C.B.'s [stolen] letters continues. I long for respite, but you know the story – Enough of that.

Dearest Charlotte,

The Jubilee was wonderful. Now the sound of children dancing in the upper room above the coach house fills my heart with gladness. Above the rhythm of the dancing feet, beyond this window, I can hear the wildness of the East wind. I am recovered from this latest bout of pleurisy – I can sit here and write today. Mary's daughter, Kitty, is here and Mary Hewitt herself comes this weekend.

Such lovely kind friends. I am very blessed.

I hear your voice. I am coming. Truly I am. You are so close to me, this month. I pray to God, throughout this autumn – thinking and reflecting – upon my garden here, upon life, death, nature. All my life I have experienced love and beauty, friendship, and faith in God. But our world has changed since Victoria came to the throne. You, me, Emily, Anne, Mary and Martha – were we not the young pre-Victorians – carefree with our young friends, innocent and natural? Not so now, my darling. People have begun to scrutinise such friendships.

I hear you calling me – as your voice does through all your letters. But I have made serious errors of judgement concerning their dispersal. You know that already, my darling. I experience deep remorse. I feel that I was wrong, but not all of my motives were sinful. Every morning, on waking, I long to discover that the dispersal is NOT taking place – that it has all been a dreadful nightmare – and in the clear light of dawn it is NOT happening. But in this matter, I shall remain unresolved. So I pray to the Lord my Shepherd, that He – and you – will understand, forgive, and bring me to your place of peace, beauty and restfulness. I am so very tired.

Charlotte Brontë, I believe in you and me.

For in my life I have two loves.

Along the wings of the wind, I can hear you.

When the trees bend, shaking their leaves away, I hear you.

When the embankment lights flicker as the rail-workers' bonfires gleam in the dark, I hear you.

When the clank of the branch-lines being laid comes echoing across the valley, I hear you.

When the echoes of the wind, carry your voice, I hear you.

I have two loves: And one is God and the other is Charlotte Brontë.

You are calling. I am coming.

Good night

E.N.

Acknowledgements

My partner, Cynth Morris, came to a reading of *The Hide and Seek Files*, in January 1989, to tell me how much my first novel, *Three Ply Yarn 1986*, had meant to her. We have been friends since that time, partners since 1999, and civil partners since 2007. Thanks to her for all those years of love, support and interest in my work.

I cannot write any acknowledgements without re-affirming the part played by the publication of vols 1, 2, 3 of *The Letters of Charlotte Brontë* by Margaret Smith for The Clarendon Press, Oxford University. I began my research long before the first volume became available but during the subsequent years, I have owed an immense debt of gratitude for her amazing scholarship.

Thank you also to Barbara Whitehead for talking with me about my novel and my ideas about the role of Ellen and Charlotte in each other's lives. I have turned many times to *Charlotte Brontë and her Dearest Nell,* during the course of the construction of *Letters to Charlotte*.

Thank you to all the women who worked so hard at The Women's Press, my publishers in the twentieth century, who offered me the initial contract for *Letters to Charlotte*. The demise of The Women's Press was an early indicator of what frequently happens to Feminist Publishers in impending recession. It was with both intuition and deep regret about the economic situation that I decided not to take up the contract at that time.

Thank you to four women friends who read the first draft of *Letters to Charlotte*. Their enthusiasm for this project and their interest in the hidden history of Ellen and Charlotte's relationship helped to sustain me through many hours of reading, research, writing and re-writing. The four women are Helen Hutchinson from Gloucester; Margaretta Jolly from Sussex; Avril Laycock from Thornton, near Bradford; and Cas Nolder from London. Without their support and feedback in those early years, I might have lost momentum and Ellen's story might remain untold. Special thanks are due to Avril Laycock for accompanying me on our research to Scarborough, Filey and the East Coast and for introducing me to Barbara Whitehead.

Thanks to friends in the north for visits to many Brontë locations, such as the Red House, Cowan Bridge, Wycoller, Hathersage, Bolton Abbey, Rydings and Brookroyd.

I am indebted to The Brontë Society for days out to Scarborough, and for creating links with Leeds University for study courses in the late 1990s.

Thank you to Sallyann Sheridan for my introduction to my publishers; to the Indepenpress for all their enthusiasm and interest; to Linda Lloyd, Editor, Kathryn Harrison, Production Manager, for their patience and skill with the manuscript; and to Jacqueline Abromeit, Art Director, for a beautiful cover design.

My two sons and daughters-in-law are always supportive of my life as a writer – and they have helped to boost my morale and provided help when faced with computer glitches. For family life with them and fun with my grandchildren, I am deeply grateful.

Many libraries have provided kind, generous support and interest.

Thank you to Ann Dinsdale, Collections Manager, and Sarah Laycock, Collections and Information Officer, at the Brontë Parsonage Museum. The library is a lovely place to study and I am indebted to the staff for provision of facilities and resources there. I am grateful to all the staff, past and present, for their own writings and publications with photographs. Thank you also to the staff of the Museum shop, where I have found so many useful and enjoyable local books and research pamphlets, as well as tapes, cards, maps and pictures.

Thank you to the staff of Leeds University Library, which houses the Brotherton Collection. Thank you to the staff in Halifax Central Library – where I researched news-cuttings and collections on Kirklees Hall, and many biographies, for example those by Winifred Gérin and Mary Robinson. Access to the Ancestors web site, which is funded in the library, gave me the children of Mary Hewitt, via the 1871 census, and the death certificate for Thomas Swinton Hewitt, whose name was difficult to research being wrongly spelled – as Thomas Saintort. The eldest daughter was spelled Warysara – surely an error by the same registrar.

Thank you to Miss Lorraine Parsons, Archivist for the Library of the Moravian Church in London. During my telephone research we discussed the philosophy and origins of the Moravian Church and its contemporary place in the world. Not only was this invaluable for confirming Ellen's attitudes to Calvinism, but also the Moravian Church website shows how the facility of the internet is so relevant to historical research.

Thank you to Sally Matthews, library manager for Tenbury Wells, Worcestershire, who helped me to clarify the county borders and locations for Leysters and Tenbury Wells. Her enthusiasm for the significant Brontë link, via Mary Hewitt, was delightful.

When I began this book, the technology was completely different, and it is awesome to consider that Charlotte, Emily and Anne Brontë all created their plots, characters, locations and time-scales, without memory sticks, editing or copying facilities.

The novels, poems and letters of Charlotte, Emily and Anne remain my most important – and thrilling – acknowledgement. Grateful thanks are due from all Brontë scholars and Brontë enthusiasts, across the centuries, to Ellen herself, for *not* burning her Letters from Charlotte.